Is Asperger syndrome a syn_____ ___ ___ _ form of autism? Sufferers from the syndrome are like _ _____ they show the same kind of impairments from early childhood; ___ _____ke them in being far more verbally articulate and socially adapted. They can be highly intelligent and reminiscent of eccentrics with their unusual interests, special skills and unworldliness

In this volume several ___ the major experts in the field discuss ___ criteria of the syndrome, named after Hans Asperger who ___ condition in the 1940s, and illustrate their views with case studies ___ ___ __ clinical practice. These clinical studies are complemented by personal ____ and placed in a new theoretical framework. Significantly, Uta Frith provides the first English translation of Asperger's paper: his work has long been neglected, but his insights reflect a very modern awareness of the broad continuum of autistic disorders. They also provide surprisingly practical suggestions on the education and management of autistic children.

Current opinion on Asperger syndrome and its relationship to autism is fraught with disagreement and hampered by ignorance. This book gives the first coherent account of Asperger syndrome as a distinct variant of autism and will undoubtedly arouse a good deal of debate.

Autism and Asperger syndrome

Hans Asperger. From the collection of Dr Maria Asperger-Felder

Autism and Asperger syndrome

Edited by Uta Frith

MRC Cognitive Development Unit,
London

CAMBRIDGE
UNIVERSITY PRESS

PUBLISHED BY THE PRESS SYNDICATE OF THE UNIVERSITY OF CAMBRIDGE
The Pitt Building, Trumpington Street, Cambridge, United Kingdom

CAMBRIDGE UNIVERSITY PRESS
The Edinburgh Building, Cambridge CB2 2RU, UK
40 West 20th Street, New York, NY 10011–4211, USA
477 Williamstown Road, Port Melbourne, VIC 3207, Australia
Ruiz de Alarcón 13, 28014 Madrid, Spain
Dock House, The Waterfront, Cape Town 8001, South Africa

http://www.cambridge.org

First published 1991
Fourteenth printing 2002

Printed in the United Kingdom at the University Press, Cambridge

Typeset in Linotype Sabon 10/12 pt [GE]

A catalogue record for this book is available from the British Library

ISBN 0 521 38448 6 hardback
ISBN 0 521 38608 X paperback

Contents

Illustrations

Acknowledgements

I would like to thank the contributors to this volume for the enthusiasm and forbearance they have shown towards this project. I am particularly indebted to Lorna Wing for allowing me to use and quote her own case reports, and for tutoring me on the many varieties of the developmental progress of autistic individuals. She was the instigator of the translation of Asperger's 1944 paper, recognising its importance and topicality long before anyone else. Christopher Gillberg and Digby Tantam who themselves have done much to increase awareness and knowledge of Asperger Syndrome have also been instrumental in the origin of this book. To Francesca Happé I am much indebted for stimulating discussions of the theoretical issues and for her vital help in clarifying thoughts and words. My writing has benefited immeasurably from Margaret Dewey's magic touch. Dr Maria Asperger-Felder graciously provided materials pertaining to her father as well as vivid biographical information. I am thankful also to Judith Ayling for her careful reading of the translation and expert help in keeping the text faithful to the original yet readable in English. Jacqueline Harvey's meticulous copy editing has prevented innumerable infelicities and inconsistencies. John Morton, who has been a constant provider of intellectual and material support, is owed an enormous debt of gratitude. My deepest thanks go to Chris Frith who read every line of innumerable drafts and persuaded me that this volume – preliminary as it is in the future history of Asperger syndrome – must now meet the critical eye of its readers.

Chapter 2, '"Autistic psychopathy" in childhood' by Hans Asperger, was first published as 'Die autistischen Psychopathen im Kindesalter' in 1944 in the journal *Archiv für Psychiatrie und Nervenkrankenheiten*, 117, 76–136. It was reprinted in *Heilpädagogik* (Springer-Verlag, Vienna, 1952, latest edition 1968). We acknowledge the permission of Springer-Verlag, to print this translation of Asperger's article.

I

Asperger and his syndrome

UTA FRITH

Asperger's pioneering paper published in 1944 is part of the classic literature of child psychiatry, and a landmark in the development of the concept of autism. So far it has been accessible only to the German reader. While Kanner's original paper on autism, published in 1943, has become extremely well known, Asperger's has been strangely ignored. The neglect in turn has led people to believe that Asperger did not merit their attention. Nevertheless, the terms *Asperger syndrome* and *Asperger's syndrome*[1] are fast becoming used to describe certain patients who have never been easy to classify but who seem to constitute a recognisable type of autistic individual.

In the last ten years there has been an increasing interest in Hans Asperger and his syndrome.[2] This volume makes a start in answering some of the questions that are now being asked. It contains a translation of Asperger's 1944 paper, and in addition, presents reviews of current concepts of autism. These reviews suggest that the time has come to differentiate various forms of autism. As the contributors to this volume contend, one of these forms is justifiably called *Asperger's syndrome*. Supporting the argument are a number of case histories. At this stage it is largely through detailed case studies that we can begin to understand the syndrome. Just as one comes to recognize a Mondrian painting by looking at other Mondrians, one can learn to recognise a patient with Asperger syndrome by looking at cases described by Asperger and other clinicians.

[1] Both terms are widely used. There seems to me no virtue in being dogmatic about the letter *s*, and for this reason Asperger syndrome and Asperger's syndrome appear in this volume.
[2] Wing's (1981) paper was instrumental in kindling interest in Asperger syndrome; Tantam (1988), Gillberg (1990) and Green (1990) provided annotations; diagnostic manuals (World Health Organization, 1990) and textbooks (for example, Rutter and Hersov, 1985) began to define the category, and systematic studies are now appearing (for example, Schopler and Mesibov, in press).

Should autism and Asperger syndrome be seen as distinct and mutually exclusive diagnostic categories, or should Asperger syndrome be seen as a subcategory of autism? This question cannot yet be answered definitively from existing scientific data. In this volume the subcategory view has been adopted which, in the absence of compelling evidence to the contrary, presents the parsimonious option. The terms autism and Asperger syndrome are therefore not treated as mutually exclusive. We propose that the Asperger individual suffers from a particular form of autism. This form does not seem to be particularly rare.[3]

The developmental diversity of autism

To understand why and in what sense Asperger syndrome can be claimed to be a type of autism, it is useful to start with a general picture of autism as it unfolds in development.[4] This is not the place for detailed evidence. Instead, a number of simplified statements must suffice to summarise the prevailing clinical and scientific opinion. Autism is due to a specific brain abnormality. The origin of the abnormality can be any one of three general causes: genetic fault, brain insult or brain disease. Autism is a developmental disorder, and therefore its behavioural manifestations vary with age and ability. Its core features, present in different forms, at all stages of development and at all levels of ability, are impairments in socialisation, communication and imagination.

The first year of life of the autistic child is still shrouded in mystery.[5] It is as yet unknown if at this early stage behavioural abnormalities can be picked up that are truly specific to autism. This is not to say that no abnormalities whatever can be observed or will not be found in the future. The problem is to know whether they are specific or non-specific. General developmental delay is often associated with autism but is also present in mentally handicapped children who are not autistic. One of the first signs that is specific to autism is a lack of pointing and looking to share interest and attention with another person. If a child is very delayed in all respects, however, then absence of such behaviour would not be a *specific* sign. In non-autistic children with developmental delay the phenomenon of shared attention would also be expected to make a delayed appearance. It is therefore very difficult to make a secure diagnosis of autism before the age of two or three years.

The pre-school years, often stormy in normal development, frequently

[3] Gillberg and Gillberg (1989) estimate the prevalence of Asperger syndrome in the population of Swedish schoolchildren as between 10 and 26 per 10,000. If confirmed, this proportion is twice as high as for more classic types of autism (4 to 10 in 10,000).

[4] This brief sketch is based on the more detailed account in Frith (1989a).

[5] A recent study (Lösche, 1990), based on home movies, suggests that the timing and sequence of developmental gains differs between normal and autistic children only from the second year of life.

mark the phase of most troublesome difficulties for autistic children and their families. At this stage autism produces a highly recognisable pattern of behaviours, even though there is an enormous amount of individual variation. All sorts of behaviour problems can worry parents at this time. In almost all cases language learning is delayed, and in some cases language is never acquired at all. Most young autistic children do not seem to comprehend what others are saying to them or, indeed, what is going on around them. Deafness is often suspected but ruled out. Social interaction is severely limited. Imaginative pretend play is noticeably absent. The children are often fixated on simple activities, and may inadvertently tyrannise their family by intolerance of any change in routine. It has often been stated that young autistic children behave as if other people did not exist. Again there are degrees, but, taken with a grain of salt, this description sums up their behaviour quite well.

Developmental changes which are rightly experienced as improvements are often a marked feature between the ages of five and ten. From here the paths begin to diverge to such an extent that the idea of subtypes cannot be ignored.[6] Progress will be very different for the autistic child who speaks fluently and the child who has little or no language. Progress will also be different for the child who shows evidence of ability in some areas and the child who suffers from such pervasive brain damage that all his or her intellectual abilities are impaired.[7] Language and general intellectual ability tend to go hand in hand, but there are exceptions. These exceptions are not addressed in this volume, but deserve to be studied in their own right.

How should we tackle the question of subgroups? It may not be through a distinctive pattern of signs and symptoms at a particular moment in time, but rather through differences in developmental progress that we will be able to discern variants of autism. In this volume we focus on those autistic children who make good progress and are not crippled by multiple and severe learning disabilities. How do they diverge from other autistic children? Perhaps the main feature of children for whom we propose the label Asperger syndrome is that they tend to speak fluently by the time they are five, even if their language development was slow to begin with, and even if their language is noticeably odd in its use for communication. Some of these children show dramatic improvements despite having had severe autistic symptoms as toddlers.[8] As they grow older they often become quite interested in other people and thus belie the stereotype of the aloof and withdrawn autistic child. Nevertheless, they remain socially inept in their

---

[6] Problems in diagnostic classification when the whole range of ability and course of development are taken into account are discussed by Cohen, Paul and Volkmar (1987).

[7] Rees and Taylor (1975), as well as Bartak and Rutter (1976), drew attention to differences in developmental progress in autistic children with and without additional mental retardation.

[8] Rapid improvement in bright autistic children's social and communicative behaviour just before the age of five was found in a questionnaire-based study by Shah (1988).

approaches and interactions. By adolescence many will vaguely realise that they are different from their peers and that there is a whole sphere of personal relationships from which they are excluded.[9] They may learn many facts about the world, but their knowledge seems to remain curiously fragmented. They somehow fail to put their experience and knowledge together to derive useful meaning from these often unconnected bits of information.[10] Like other autistic individuals, they tend to show a highly typical pattern of performance on IQ tests, but unlike them, they usually score in the average range of intelligence.[11] It is a frequent complaint of parents, however, that their children, despite sometimes high academic abilities, lack common sense.

As adults Asperger syndrome individuals can become, superficially at least, well adapted and some are exceptionally successful. On the whole they tend to remain supremely egocentric and isolated.[12] They do not seem to possess the knack of entering and maintaining intimate two-way personal relationships, whereas routine social interactions are well within their grasp. Because of their idiosyncrasies, their egocentric bluntness and fragility, they find it difficult to live and work with others and may require psychiatric help. This is despite the fact that they may be intellectually able and often have special skills and talents. In line with these skills they tend to be preoccupied with some fanatically pursued interest, and in favourable circumstances they can achieve satisfaction and success. Adults with Asperger syndrome bear no physical resemblance to each other, but often appear gauche in the way they move and almost always sound odd in the way they speak. They seldom enter the natural flow of small-talk, and their use of language and gesture is often stilted. Even those individuals who are

[9] This observation was made by Kanner (1971) in his follow-up study of the eleven children he had described in 1943.

[10] Frith (1989a) attempted to sketch out the preliminary theory that one deep underlying cognitive deficit in autism has to do with a lack of coherence. In other words, autistic people lack the drive to pull information together into overall meaning. This theory addresses itself to the peculiarly fragmented pattern of abilities, the fragmented sensory experiences and the stereotypic repetition of fragments of behaviour. All these phenomena are associated with autistic spectrum disorders, and are particularly conspicuous in Asperger syndrome.

[11] Elisabeth Wurst (1976), a member of Asperger's team in Vienna, studied the performance on Wechsler IQ tests of fifteen seven- to eight-year-old children with Asperger syndrome diagnosed by Asperger himself. She found peaks on information and block design subtests, but troughs on comprehension and picture arrangement. This pattern of abilities is very similar to that shown in other studies with able autistic children (for example, Rutter and Lockyer, 1969; Lockyer and Rutter, 1970; Rumsey and Hamburger, 1988). The IQ level of the Asperger syndrome sample was average or above, while a comparison sample of what in this study were termed Kanner autists scored in the range of moderate to mild mental retardation.

[12] Volkmar (1987) reviews research on the social development of autistic individuals in general, and Sparrow et al. (1986) report on the social adaptive functioning of a very able group. It is possible that there are many undiagnosed individuals who would be recognised as having Asperger syndrome but who are doing so well that they never come to the attention of clinicians. How to distinguish such people from the normally shy is, of course, a very difficult question.

very able intellectually and have coped well with their handicap will strike one as strange. This strangeness may be perceived as anything from chilling cold-bloodedness to endearingly old-fashioned pedantry.[13]

Within this very brief and general outline of typical Asperger syndrome individuals there is much variation. Some show extreme behaviour difficulties, others are gentle and easy to manage. Some suffer from specific learning disabilities and do badly at school, others do very well academically and have university degrees. Some may find a niche in society and lead a reasonably contented life, but others become outcasts or remain misfits. For all their strangeness, people with Asperger syndrome seldom find the help and sympathy they deserve and need. As we shall see, theirs is a devastating handicap.

So far, Asperger syndrome is the first plausible variant to crystallise from the autism spectrum.[14] No doubt other variants will follow. In this volume we address the question of how best to characterise the syndrome from our present state of knowledge. A good starting point is to find out more about Asperger and to see how his ideas differed from those of Kanner.

Names and labels

Hans Asperger and Leo Kanner were both born in Austria and trained in Vienna, but they never met each other.[15] Kanner, born in 1896, emigrated to the United States in 1924 where he became head of the Johns Hopkins clinic at Baltimore. With his textbook on child psychiatry he became the founder of a new discipline, but his greatest fame came from his discovery of autism. In 1943 Kanner introduced the label *early infantile autism* for a type of disorder hitherto unrecognised as a clinical entity, although it is possible to find earlier case descriptions. These early descriptions had failed to leave their mark because nobody pointed out their significance or gave them a name. After Kanner, every major clinic immediately found cases which fitted the category of early infantile autism.

Asperger, ten years younger than Kanner, pursued a career in general medicine with a view to specialising in paediatrics. He was attracted by the approach of remedial pedagogy, which had been practised with difficult children from about 1918 at the University Paediatric Clinic in Vienna, and

---

[13] This brief generalised description roughly distils Asperger's clinical description of the syndrome in its mature form. It also corresponds to descriptions of adults given by many other authors (for example, Wing, 1989). It also fits in with descriptions of less well-adapted cases as, for instance, in Tantam's (1986) study of a sample of adult psychiatric patients, subsequently diagnosed as suffering from Asperger syndrome, whose main characteristics were unusual interests, impaired non-verbal communication and clumsiness. This study is discussed by Tantam in chapter 5.

[14] Different forms of autism, seen as part of a spectrum of autistic disorders, have been described by Wing and Attwood (1987).

[15] A sympathetic appraisal of both men has been provided by Lutz (1981).

joined the staff of this clinic, where he worked on his Habilitation, that is, his second doctoral thesis. The topic of his thesis was what he called *autistic psychopathy* and what we would call autism. He submitted his thesis in 1943 and it was published in 1944. It is this paper which appears in translation in chapter 2.

By a remarkable coincidence, Asperger and Kanner independently described exactly the same type of disturbed child to whom nobody had paid much attention before and both used the label autistic.[16] They were pioneers in recognising that autism is a major developmental disorder and not merely a rare and interesting childhood affliction. From the start Asperger had an idea of what these children would be like as adults. He was interested in the subtle, and possibly milder, manifestations of autism in more able children. Nevertheless, he also emphasised that autism could be seen throughout the whole range of ability and that it produced a particularly striking picture when accompanied by mental retardation.

At the time of Asperger's and Kanner's pioneering studies a concern with subgroups would have seemed remote. Both men were intent on one aim, to convince colleagues that there was a previously unidentified entity, a highly recognisable disorder, which was present from early childhood and per-sisted for many years. It is only now, after autism has become almost a household term, that refinement into subgroups begins to make sense. Just where the category boundaries for such subgroups should be drawn is a difficult question, and readjustments from time to time are to be expected. The present volume is a first step in this process.

I wish to express the hope that the translation of Asperger's paper will not be used as a means for a false othodoxy. It contains some startling insights which are still new to many. It also reveals some misconceptions that have crept into secondary sources. Nevertheless, we cannot extract from this paper a definitive view of Asperger syndrome, or of autism for that matter. In the first description of a few cases of a puzzling clinical entity of unknown aetiology it cannot be presumed that *all* the essential features and *only* the essential features will at once be identified. After all, such a description hinges on the happenstance of individual cases that come to the clinic. The task of identifying the core symptoms of autism has taken many decades, and a definitive answer will be reached only when we have full knowledge of the biological origins and their effects on brain development. It will undoubtedly be some years before Asperger syndrome is fully defined and recognised. We shall now take a closer look at Asperger and his back-ground, and then briefly compare Kanner's and Asperger's first thoughts on autism.

[16] This label, first used by Eugen Bleuler to describe the schizophrenic patient's loss of contact with the world around him, was chosen presumably because detachment from the social world strongly characterised the special children Kanner and Asperger were studying. An English translation of Bleuler's textbook of psychiatry (1916) appeared in 1951.

The man behind the syndrome

To understand Hans Asperger (1906–80) it is necessary to understand the idea of *Heilpädagogik* or remedial pedagogy. This approach to the treatment of disturbed children must not be confused with that form of remedial education which is entirely anchored within education and outside medicine. Instead, it is a seemingly intuitive synthesis of medical and educational practice applied by inspired doctors, nurses, teachers and therapists in a team effort. The children who in Asperger's view most urgently needed such treatment and could most benefit from it were children who suffered from what he called autistic psychopathy. Asperger believed that these children suffered from an inherited personality disorder which made them troublesome but also fascinating. He set out to prove that they constituted a real type – a recognisable clinical entity – with specific and persistent handicaps. He was sure that despite their difficulties the children were capable of adaptation – provided there was appropriate educational guidance.[17]

Asperger clearly cared about these children, who in most people's eyes were simply obnoxious brats. They were very unchildlike children. They did not fit in anywhere and were troublesome because they lacked any respect for authority. They made their parents' lives miserable and drove their teachers to despair. So unappealing were these strange boys that other children and adults were drawn to ridicule them. That a young doctor was captivated by these difficult children was a small miracle. Asperger appreciated their many surprising positive features while fully recognising their negative ones. He admired their independent thinking and capacity for special achievements, but also candidly documented their learning problems and seemingly spiteful and malicious behaviour.

Why did Asperger become the champion of these misfits and how did he approach the task of explaining their problems? Indirectly, we may find an answer through a lecture he gave to commemorate his predecessor as head and founder (in 1918) of the University Paediatric Clinic, Erwin Lazar.[18] Asperger spelt out three pairs of paradoxical virtues that he admired in Lazar: first, there was the mixture of tolerant humanity and deep scepticism that, he claimed, marks the genuine Viennese; secondly, there was the mixture of scientific thinking and love of the arts; and thirdly, there was the combination of razor-sharp scientific formulation and popular expression. Each of these virtues seems to apply to Asperger himself. Equally apposite seems Asperger's characterisation of Lazar's 'unsentimental, apparently cool, but in reality deeply empathic contributions'. Lazar, moved by the

---

[17] Examples of practical hints for the education of individuals with Asperger syndrome can be found in chapter 6. These hints are very similar to techniques advocated by remedial pedagogy. Examples are also given in Asperger's original paper (chapter 2) and in his textbook *Heilpädagogik* (1952).

[18] This lecture was published in 1962.

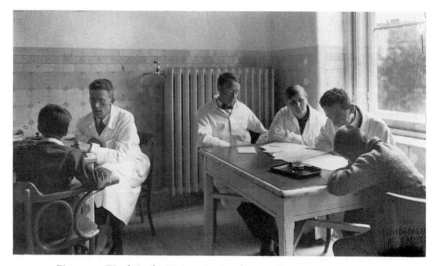

Fig. 1.1   Work in the University Paediatric Clinic, Vienna: Hans Asperger and his team testing children. Asperger is second from left. From the collection of Dr Maria Asperger-Felder

plight of neglected and deprived children following the First World War, was involved in voluntary organisations that ran homes and day centres in Vienna and provided help with forensic problems for children and adolescents. His compassion and commitment to this work were no doubt an inspiration to all who worked at the clinic.

Asperger frequently acknowledged his debt to the work of his predecessors and colleagues at the university clinic. The special and novel feature of the remediation practised at this clinic was its biological basis. This meant that the design of any programme began with the identification of organically caused limitations or deficits of individual children. After the handicap was identified, the children would be treated sympathetically. Education and therapy were the same thing. It is fascinating to read of the development of this work. To begin with, the remedial ward was like any other clinical ward. As in the hospital's other wards, the children lay in neat little rows of beds, and twice daily there was a ward-round. They were treated as sick children who needed to be made well again. As the team's experience grew, their ethos changed. Soon the children were out of bed during the day and played and worked in a busy round of activities. Now the aim was to give handicapped (rather than sick) children as positive an education as possible. In 1926 the ward moved to the beautiful purpose-built Widerhofer Pavilion, with its airy rooms, architect-designed furniture and artistic wall friezes.

The daily programme of play and lessons was led by a remarkable woman, Sister Viktorine Zak. Asperger called her a genius. Her intuitive diagnostic skills and therapeutic effects as a teacher were legendary. One of

Asperger's formative experiences, he reports, was witnessing Sister Viktorine calm a panic-stricken toddler in the midst of a destructive tantrum. Sister Viktorine's programme started daily with a PE lesson, using rhythm and music. There were organised dramatic enactments of events or of songs. There were also proper school lessons and speech therapy. The pervading ethos was that the clinic's work should be governed by the wish to understand and help children. Tragically, Sister Viktorine was killed when the ward was destroyed by bombs in 1944.

The team were keen to use psychological tests, but the qualitative assessment of performance was considered more important than the quantitative. Early on, Lazar had experimented with psychoanalysis and employed one of the first child analysts. However, he finally rejected the methods as unsuitable for children. With psychoanalysis flourishing in Vienna at the time, it is surprising to find little sign of the influence of the ideas of Freud or other analysts on Asperger's ideas on autism. At most, one can find an acerbic remark about possible psychodynamic factors; for instance, Asperger's paper mentions Adler's ideas on severe psychological problems that arise from being an only child in the family, but dismisses them as a possible cause of autism. This was not because he did not think that autistic children often were only children, in fact, he mistakenly believed that this was frequently the case. Turning the psychodynamic proposition on its head, he thought that it was the parents' own autistic pathology that made them produce only one child. He was convinced that autism ran in families and never wavered from the assumption that organic or constitutional factors were the causal roots of autistic children's problems. It is no coincidence that the remedial ward was situated within paediatric medicine and not psychiatry. For this reason he also tended to be sympathetic to the parents who, as he said, often understood their autistic child very well and did their best to bring him up.

Lazar died suddenly in 1932. His successor, Hamburger, who was interested in the unconscious affective life of children, carried on the tradition of remedial pedagogy at a time when Asperger was preparing for his Habilitation. The idea of a deep affective disturbance at a biological level of drives and instincts strongly influenced Asperger's conception of autism. It is interesting to note that the core team of doctors, nurses and teachers met at each other's homes for dinner once a week to talk about their cases informally. More than likely, the characteristic features of autistic children were debated on these occasions. Thus, the roots of the concept of autistic psychopathy originated in the vision and work of an extraordinary group of people during one of the darkest times in European history.

Asperger's private life was uneventful. He was married with four children. He was a quiet, reticent man, steeped in the humanist tradition, with an extensive knowledge of classics, history, art and literature. He enjoyed giving tutorials in all school subjects to the children on the ward, and regularly accompanied groups of them on summer camps. Such camps were important to him because of his own schoolboy experiences of youth groups and camps run by enthusiasts of the *Jugendbewegung*.[19] The romantic ideology of such groups was comparable to that of the Boy Scouts, and the freedom of outdoor life represented a vivid contrast to the then stern discipline of school. Asperger spoke of these early influences as decisive, citing them to explain what had first interested him in the children who could never join in with the gang and would panic when forced to participate in a group. Far from despising the misfits, he devoted himself to their cause – and this at a time when allegiance to misfits was nothing less than dangerous.

After the war, Asperger was appointed to the Chair of Paediatrics at the University of Vienna which he held for twenty years. Large crowds of students always attended lectures, and his influence on many generations of them was significant. He received national and international recognition and obtained major academic distinctions. He died suddenly in 1980 while still actively engaged in clinical work.

Asperger versus Kanner

There is a great deal of overlap between Asperger's and Kanner's views of autism (see chapter 3 for Wing's discussion of the similarities and differences). Both recognised as prominent features in autism the poverty of social interaction and the failure of communication; highlighted stereotypic behaviour, isolated special interests, outstanding skills and resistance to change; insisted on a clear separation from childhood schizophrenia; and observed the attractive appearance (although Asperger emphasised odd aspects of appearance as well) and similarities in children's and parents' behaviour. On all the major features of autism Kanner and Asperger are in agreement.

In their original papers some important observations were made by one but not the other. Kanner first described language peculiarities, such as echolalia, pronoun reversal and difficulties in generalising word meanings. The children Asperger first described, apparently, did not show these features, but had clever-sounding language, invented words and generally spoke more like grown-ups than children; these comments suggest that there was something not quite right in the way they used language. Asperger, on the other hand, was the first to report oddities of non-verbal communication: eye gaze, gestures, posture, voice quality, prosody and word choice. He highlighted lack of humour and pedantry. Influenced by

[19] Asperger provided this information in a talk given in 1977 at Fribourg, Switzerland and translated into English in 1979. This publication has long been the only primary source accessible to English speakers. Unfortunately, his reference to the *Jugendbewegung* has occasionally been wrongly interpreted as an allegiance to Nazi ideology.

Ludwig Klages' (1936) then popular science of expression, he considered these phenomena to be of fundamental importance in the clinical picture of autism.[20]

In his original paper Asperger reported examples of obsessive collecting of meaningless sets of objects which has since become recognised as a prototypical feature of autism. He also claimed that there could be severe homesickness and strong attachment to selected people, observations which have not always been endorsed by others. Asperger was keen to stress the possibility of social adaptation and academic achievement in those of his cases whom he presented as highly original thinkers. Like Kanner he may have been inclined to overestimate their intellectual abilities. Nevertheless, he also believed that there were some serious attention deficits and specific learning disabilities even in children with good intellectual skills.

The slight differences in the first two accounts of autism point to the possibility that the prototype Kanner had in mind was younger – with delayed and markedly deviant language acquisition – was, in short, a child with a more blatant and severe communication disorder. There remain, however, some contradictions which have so far hardly been formulated let alone investigated. Kanner believed that only the relation to people was disturbed and that the relation to objects was, if anything, superior to that found in normal development. Consequently he commented on the dexterity with which autistic children manipulated objects. Asperger, on the other hand, believed that there was a disturbed relation not only to people but also to objects. This for him explained the notable impracticality and clumsiness of the autistic person as well as the social ineptness. These two conjectures are interestingly different and amenable to being tackled by experimental techniques.

Asperger's paper is relevant to the understanding of autism in all its variants but may not serve as the ultimate yardstick for what will be called Asperger syndrome in the future. As more clinical and epidemiological studies are completed, different investigators will offer their own interpretations. Such studies are reported by Lorna Wing in chapter 3, Christopher Gillberg in chapter 4 and Digby Tantam in chapter 5.

Kanner's cases are so well known that they will always remain prototypes for new similar cases. Children who do not talk or who parrot speech and use strange idiosyncratic phrases, who line up toys in long rows, who are oblivious to other people, who remember meaningless facts – these will rightly conjure up Leo Kanner's memory. Children and adults who are

---

[20] Asperger reported having met Klages when he was studying at Leipzig in 1934 and being much helped by his ideas. The history of a science of expression goes back a long way and includes Charles Bell's (1774–1842) *Anatomy and philosophy of expression* (1806) and Charles Darwin's work on the origin of the emotions (1872). Impairments in emotion recognition and expression in autistic individuals have been investigated only relatively recently (Hobson, 1986a, 1986b). Their relevance to Asperger syndrome is highlighted by Tantam in chapter 5.

socially inept but often socially interested, who are articulate yet strangely ineloquent, who are gauche and impractical, who are specialists in unusual fields – these will always evoke Hans Asperger's name.

Diagnostic categories and diagnostic signs

Our knowledge of Asperger syndrome is still patchy, but a consistent picture is beginning to emerge. The developmental course of able, as well as less able, autistic individuals from childhood to adulthood has been traced.[21] Excellent progress is observable in at least some cases, whether these have been labelled high-functioning autism or Asperger syndrome.[22] We are also beginning to arrive at an understanding of problems that arise even for very able autistic individuals in certain situations, and of aspects of their behaviour that those around them find difficult to understand. This knowledge should have benefits for management. On the other hand, because the diagnostic classification is still in a fluid state, communication between different centres is, unfortunately, much hampered. This volume will have served its purpose if it provides a basis for discussion for future developments of diagnostic procedures.

There is unanimity among the contributors to this volume. All agree on the assumption that Asperger individuals belong to the autistic spectrum. All believe that Asperger syndrome has in common with autism in general a special type of communication failure and social ineptness. Nevertheless they see Asperger syndrome individuals as distinct from other autistic individuals, as better at communicating by virtue of their better language, and as more likely to achieve successful adaptation. The differences that have already been noticed and those that may yet come to light may suggest that Asperger syndrome is a separate clinical entity, not merely a subgroup of autism. Even within the subgroup view, there is disagreement; for instance, some have argued that it is unnecessary and confusing to use the label Asperger syndrome and that *high-functioning autism* or *mild autism* would be preferable, while others suggest that both categories might be useful. However, it is not yet clear where, and on what basis, the line

---

[21] Bartak and Rutter (1976) compared progress in retarded and normally intelligent autistic children, showing considerable differences between these groups. Newson, Dawson and Everard (1982) conducted a questionnaire-based study in Britain on a sample of over ninety very able people, most of them between sixteen and twenty-six years old. Discussions of practical issues in the life-span development of autistic individuals of very different capacities for adaptation can be found in Cohen, Donnellan and Paul (1987) and in the series edited by Schopler and Mesibov (1983 onwards).

[22] Szatmari *et al.* (1989), in a follow-up study of high-functioning autistic children, reported some excellent and near-normal adaptation (four out of sixteen). On the other hand, Rumsey, Rapoport and Sceery (1985) documented rather poor outcomes in able autistic adults. Other cases of excellent adaptation have been described by Kanner, Rodriguez and Ashenden (1972) and Brown (1978).

between high-functioning autistic and Asperger syndrome individuals should be drawn, if at all.[23]

There are also disputes on the drawing of boundaries between Asperger syndrome and *semantic–pragmatic disorder*[24] and other types of learning disability.[25] Others have argued that the concept of *schizoid* or *schizotypal personality* would fit the clinical picture of Asperger syndrome.[26] Relationships to other developmental disorders, such as attention deficit disorder, have also been pointed out. All these questions are addressed and discussed from different points of view in the chapters by Wing, Gillberg and Tantam on the basis of their own extensive clinical experience of autism and related disorders. The authors, who have published key papers elsewhere, draw up helpful guidelines and spell out their own diagnostic criteria. As Wing points out in chapter 3, there are in fact great similarities between the sets of criteria used by a wide range of clinicians.

In defining clinical categories two kinds of error are common: the categories aimed at are too small and leave the majority of patients unaccounted for, or they are too large and do not differentiate patients who, in most clinicians' opinions, present different types of problems. In autistic spectrum disorders the twin dangers are omnipresent, accounting for pendulum swings between over-inclusion and ultra-specificity.

Diagnostic differentiation will eventually also have to take account of certain similarities between Asperger syndrome and schizophrenia. It is worth noting that the so-called negative signs of schizophrenia (poverty of speech, poverty of ideas and flattening of affect) bear a striking resemblance to the prevailing features of some types of autism in adulthood.[27] Progress in diagnostic classification depends on a better understanding of diagnostic

[23] Examples of the first studies tackling the question of how to differentiate high-functioning autism from Asperger syndrome can be found, for instance, in Gillberg (1989a); Szatmari, Bartolucci and Bremner (1989); Szatmari *et al.* (1990); Kerbeshian, Burd and Fisher (1990); and Ozonoff, Rogers and Pennington (in press). It has to be said, however, that these studies suffer from the current lack of consensus concerning the diagnostic characteristics of the groups compared. No study so far has avoided the danger of contrasting what may, in fact, be overlapping groups. This may be why no useful unanimous conclusions have as yet emerged.

[24] Bishop (1989) discusses possible differences between semantic-pragmatic language disorder, autism and Asperger syndrome.

[25] A number of neuropsychological investigations, recently reviewed by Semrud-Clikeman and Hynd (1990), have all identified a pattern of impairments in children which is suggestive of right hemisphere involvement. These impairments prominently include social ineptness, and the group so identified may well belong to the autistic spectrum.

[26] The schizoid or schizotypal individual (or schizothymic in Kretschmer's (1925) terminology) is usually described as unsociable, over-sensitive, cold (lacking in affectionate resonance), stubborn and pedantic. Wolff and Barlow (1979) and Wolff and Chick (1980) used the labels schizoid personality and Asperger syndrome interchangeably. Nagy and Szatmari (1986) came to the conclusion that patients with schizotypal personality disorder could also be diagnosed as suffering from mild autism. Many clinicians, however, prefer not to collapse the categories (Tantam, 1988b, 1988c).

[27] Frith and Frith (in press) discuss the relationship between autism and schizophrenia and suggest that there is a hidden similarity in the underlying cognitive deficit.

signs. One behavioural sign especially in need of clarification concerns the much reported clumsiness of Asperger people. It is tantalising not to know whether their gaucheness is in fact a motor co-ordination problem, or will turn out to be a problem not so much with movements as with the *use* of movements. It is also not yet clear if clumsiness can act as an important discriminating diagnostic sign of Asperger syndrome as opposed to other variants of autism.

Stereotypic behaviour remains a puzzle. In times of stress, able autistic individuals are just as likely to show stereotypic movements as less able ones. Those who have more social awareness, however, learn to suppress stereotypic movements more successfully.[28]

The odd interests of Asperger people are a largely unexplored feature. Their special interest is often their sole topic of conversation. Asperger individuals seem to love talking about their interest, regardless of whether one has heard it all before. Autistic repetitions and obsessions appear to be different from compulsions as the autistic person does not try to resist them, but apparently greatly enjoys enacting them. Attempts at deflection will be met with extreme annoyance.[29] The interest may appear excessive, abstruse and sterile to others, but not to the Asperger person. The special interests of Asperger individuals are so striking that they offer themselves as *aide-mémoire* labels for individual cases, for example, the case of the little frog expert in chapter 4. Fortunately, the ability to sustain strong interest in a particular area and to be absorbed and even enraptured by its pursuit can lead to outstanding achievements.

One mysterious feature that is not currently given much importance may hold further clues. Some Asperger individuals give first-hand accounts of sharply uncomfortable sensory and strong emotional experiences, often including sudden panic. From autobiographical accounts we learn that again and again the Asperger individual's interpretation of perceptions by ear, eye or touch, tends to be either extremely faint or overwhelmingly strong.[30] There can be hyper- as well as hyposensitivity. Feeling scratchy clothes, for example, is not merely uncomfortable, but agonising. On the other hand, pain may be tolerated to a phenomenal degree. Both the interpretation of the sensation and the subsequent emotional reaction, or lack of it, seem to be out of the ordinary. The same may also be true for

[28] Rumsey, Rapoport and Sceery (1985) provide results which support this claim. However, Szatmari, Bartolucci and Bremner (1989) found that stereotypic movements were observed much less frequently in their Asperger group than in their high-functioning autistic sample.

[29] Rumsey, Andreasen and Rapoport (1986) highlighted the finding that able autistic adults who showed considerable similarities to schizophrenic patients with negative features, such as poverty of speech, poverty of ideas and flattening of affect, were, nevertheless, much more likely than schizophrenics to exhibit perseveration on a given topic and single-mindedness in its pursuit.

[30] Grandin (1978), for example, describes extremes of sensitivity to certain types of sensory stimulation.

other types of autistic individuals but, unlike the Asperger syndrome person, they cannot tell us about their sensations. Unfortunately, we are far from a clear understanding of the mechanisms by which human beings normally interpret sensations and react to them.

These poorly understood features do not mean that Asperger syndrome is impossible to identify. Asperger himself maintained that the persistent, if sometimes subtle, impairments typical of the individuals he described are very obvious once one has come to recognise them.

The biological basis

Asperger was convinced that the syndrome he described was of constitutional origin and genetically transmitted. In the less favourable cases, however, where additional physical and neurological abnormalities were present, he assumed a different type of biological cause, for instance, encephalitis. He speculated on whether the preponderance of males pointed to a sex-linked form of transmission. In Asperger syndrome this preponderance is particularly marked. Today these ideas are still topical as more information on putative brain abnormalities becomes available.

Gillberg, in chapter 4, presents results of pedigree-tracing and neurobiological investigations and discusses their implications. The evidence for a biological basis seems as strong for Asperger syndrome as it is for other variants of autism. As Gillberg's studies show, the difference is simply in the severity of the biological signs (Gillberg, 1989a). Asperger individuals tend to show less severe and fewer signs. The evidence for a genetic contribution to autism in general is impressive, while studies on Asperger syndrome are as yet rare.[31] What emerges in Gillberg's family genetic studies is that Asperger syndrome and autism frequently occur in the same family, for instance, a man with very mild Asperger syndrome may have a totally mute and autistic nephew. This finding suggests that the two conditions may indeed be different expressions of the same basic defect. Results of neuropsychological tests of able autistic people have been highly consistent. They are strongly suggestive of frontal lobe dysfunction.[32] These results do not necessarily mean that the frontal lobes are damaged. Since autism is a developmental disorder with very early onset, brain abnormalities would be likely to occur even before the frontal lobes are functioning. The kind of damage we are looking for may occur at a particular point in brain

[31] For recent reviews of genetic and neurobiological factors in autism in general see Rutter *et al.* (1990) and Gillberg (1989b, 1990).

[32] Rumsey (1985) investigated verbally able autistic people and found marked deficits on the Wisconsin Card sorting test which is sensitive to frontal lobe dysfunction. Rumsey and Hamburger (1988) showed a clear profile of performance impairments on so-called frontal tests, but not on temporal or parietal tests. Ozonoff, Pennington and Rogers (in press) also used frontal tests and found severe impairments in Asperger Syndrome individuals, and indeed in high-functioning autistic people in general.

development where a critical pathway is being prepared. This pathway may well project to the frontal lobes, possibly, from some much older part of the brain.

It is likely that the investigation of the biological basis of autism will advance faster by studying those autistic people for whom we propose the label Asperger syndrome. Only when complicating brain abnormalities can be ruled out, when there are no additional mental handicaps, can one begin to make links between specific patterns of impairments and results from brain scans or autopsies. The unravelling of the biological origins may therefore be expected sooner for Asperger syndrome than for any other variant of autism.

The cognitive explanation

If Asperger syndrome is a type of autism, we must seek to understand its nature and origin in terms of explanations that apply to the whole spectrum of autistic disorders. The cognitive explanation of autism provides the most complete understanding of the cause of this disorder so far and it is useful to have a brief summary. Alternatives to cognitive theories in the explanation of autism are psychodynamic theories and behaviourism. Neither of these has succeeded, partly because they focus on only *some* aspects of autism and partly because they ignore biological factors. By the 1960s, facts had accumulated that made it no longer tenable to believe that a pathological relationship between mother and infant might be the cause of autism. Behaviourism induced researchers to look at the behaviour of autistic children in its own right. Social and communication impairment were seen as patterns of wrongly learnt behaviour which new learning might put to rights. It turned out, however, that behaviour modification – the practical application of behaviourist principles – involved heroic effort, and often the effort did not justify the limited results. Specific learning did not lead to the hoped-for generalisation. There were always new situations in everyday life where previously learnt behaviours were not appropriate and where new behaviour had to be generated. Nevertheless, behaviour modification remains an exceedingly useful tool in dealing with specific problem behaviours.[33]

The cognitive view, to put it simply, maintains that between behaviour and the brain there is a legitimate level of description: the *mind*. As a cognitive psychologist I do not take the behaviour of autistic children merely at its surface value, nor do I see it as symbolic of remote psychodynamic conflicts. Instead, the cognitive approach attempts to explain behaviour by a set of mental processes and mechanisms. These mechanisms need to be specified eventually in computational form, so that

[33] For a comprehensive review and a discussion of the principles and applications of behaviour modification see Schreibman (1989).

they can be mapped on to brain processes. The mind is neither an irrelevant black box nor a seething sea of unconscious primeval drives. The image I prefer is that of a wondrously complex machine. There are some simple but helpful hypotheses about the working of the mental machinery. For a start, we assume that the mind is made up of components which are innately programmed to process information, to produce knowledge and abilities, thoughts and feelings. Secondly, we know that great changes take place during development. If one of the innate components is faulty the whole course of development will be affected.

What particular advantage does the cognitive view offer? Above all, it provides a framework which may eventually allow us to bridge the vast gulf between brain abnormality and behavioural manifestations. It has already helped us to distinguish behaviour that is truly a manifestation of autism from behaviour due either to additional factors or to a secondary reaction to the primary problems. We can attempt this analysis because of a remarkable convergence of clinical, epidemiological and psychological studies.[34] The clinical studies told us which symptoms always occur together. The cognitive theory of autism tries to explain why they occur together.

The classical image of the autistic child – the child in the glass shell – was shattered by these studies. First, it was found that autistic children, especially when they are older, often show active social approaches. Their active social behaviour, however, suggests impairment just as much as their aloofness.[35] Secondly, a most prominent feature, often the major reason for referral of the child in the first place, namely, problems in language and general intellectual development, has had to be reinterpreted. It was not that poor language or poor intelligence caused poor communication and socialisation, rather, it was the other way round.[36] Thirdly, the autistic adult has come into focus. All these changes opened the way for reclassifying children and adults who did not previously fit into a more narrow concept of autism but whose oddness and vulnerability had long been recognised.

The most important theoretical change in the concept of autism centred around a deceptively minor feature, the lack of creative play, which was found to be as unique and universal a feature in young autistic children as was communication and socialisation failure.[37] This finding led to the critical question that enabled a breakthrough in our understanding of autism. What did pretence have to do with social and communication problems? Conversely, why did mentally handicapped non-autistic children, despite limited language and social interaction, show an appropriate level of pretence?

[34] See Frith (1989a).
[35] See Wing and Attwood (1987) for descriptions of different types of social impairment.
[36] See Frith (1989c).
[37] Wing and Gould (1979) contributed these important findings on the basis of a large epidemiological study.

An answer was provided by a new theory of cognitive development. In this theory Alan Leslie[38] distinguished first-order and second-order representations. He highlighted pretence as a major developmental milestone. The ability to pretend presupposes the capacity to form and process internal memory representations of mental states, and keep them separate from internal memory representations of physical states. The child can represent, for instance, the thought 'Mummy pretends that the banana is a telephone' without getting mixed up about what one does with real bananas and real telephones. This same capacity that underlies pretence is also fundamental to the child's ability to conceive of somebody else having a different belief. Here again, an internal memory representation of a mental state (that is, a belief) has to be created and kept separate from that of a physical state (that is, the real world situations that the belief is about). The processing capacity involved here is taking a propositional attitude, that is, pretending or believing something while temporarily suspending the normally active processes that check the truth and falsehood of states of affairs. You can pretend something that is not actually the case and, likewise, you can believe something that is not true.

There was a moment of 'Aha!' in this convergence of different perspectives. A strong prediction was made that if autistic children lack pretend play then they would also lack the ability to understand what beliefs are.[39] This ability was tested, for example, by the following test: Sally has a basket, Anne has a box. Sally puts a marble into her basket. Sally goes out for a walk. While Sally is out of the room, Anne (naughty Anne!) takes the marble from the basket and puts it into her own box. Now it is time for Sally to come back. Sally wants to play with her marble. Where will Sally think her marble is? Where will she look? The correct answer is: in the basket where she has put the marble and where she must believe her marble still is. This answer presupposes an understanding of belief. The results of the experiment suggested that autistic children did not understand the concept of belief. They expected Sally to *know* that the marble had been transferred even though she was absent at the time. They could not conceive of Sally looking anywhere but in the place where the marble was.

More findings have been systematically accumulating and they all support the hypothesis that autistic individuals have inordinate difficulty in conceiving of mental states such as belief, knowledge and ignorance.[40] They have

---

[38] Leslie (1987) has set out in detail the requirements for the achievement of pretence and has specified a mechanism which can explain pretence as well as the ability to form and use a so-called theory of mind. For updates of the theory see Leslie and Frith (1989) and Leslie and Thaiss (in press).

[39] This prediction was first tested and confirmed by Baron-Cohen, Leslie and Frith (1985). Frith (1989b) discusses the origins of the theory of mind hypothesis and the relevance of such studies as, for example, Leslie and Frith (1988) and Perner et al. (1989) to explaining the core symptoms of autism.

[40] A recent review of the field is provided by Baron-Cohen (1990).

no problems in understanding what it means to see and not to see something, but they cannot reliably relate seeing and knowing. They can tell what a scene looks like for different people at different places, but they cannot understand somebody else's point of view if by this we mean somebody else's attitude or belief. The cognitive fault we hypothesise is subtle, but has far-reaching implications for social interaction. One consequence is that the concept of an inner world of thought would be immensely difficult for the autistic person. On the other hand, their understanding of the physical world should not be severely affected.[41] One particularly striking consequence of the deficit is that their understanding of emotions in themselves and in others would be very limited.[42]

Encouraged by our empirical results, we work with the assumption that the normal child comes equipped with a mechanism for manipulating representations of mental states, and that, given normal developments, this mechanism causes us to understand mental states such as pretence and belief. We hypothesise that autism results if this particular component of the mind is faulty. Above all, the fault would impede development and learning of social imagination and communicative skills.[43]

How does this theory apply to Asperger syndrome? The theory addresses itself to the core symptoms that apply to the whole of the autistic spectrum, namely the triad of socialisation, imagination and communication impairments. Asperger individuals appear to be less severely impaired in these core symptoms than other autistic people. Furthermore, given a relatively high age and ability, they tend to solve simple theory of mind tasks such as the Sally–Anne test.[44] Do they, then, possess a normally working theory of mind? Not necessarily. Bearing in mind that the tasks are normally passed by the age of four, and that autistic children who can solve false belief tasks do so at a much later age than normal, they may well solve them by a different strategy which is not theory-based.[45] Those who manage to perform simple tasks such as the Sally–Anne test still tend to fail more complex theory of mind tasks which normal seven- to eight-year-olds solve easily.[46] Thus, by using theory of mind tests of varying complexity, we can

---

[41] Evidence for this prediction has been obtained, for instance, in studies by Baron-Cohen, Leslie and Frith (1986) and Baron-Cohen (1989a).

[42] Hobson found evidence for a specific impairment of emotion recognition in able autistic individuals. He proposes that this impairment is a primary deficit, not a consequence of lacking a theory of mind. For discussions of this issue see Hobson (1989) and Leslie and Frith (1989).

[43] Possibilities and problems in the causal connection between the basic cognitive dysfunction and the core symptoms of autism are discussed by Morton (1989).

[44] This result was obtained recently by Ozonoff, Rogers and Pennington (in press).

[45] In a study carried out at the MRC Cognitive Development Unit, we found that out of fifty able autistic children (minimum verbal mental age of 3:6y) no child passed theory of mind tasks with a chronological age of under eleven and a mental age of under five years. Furthermore, the majority of those beyond these levels failed still.

[46] Baron-Cohen (1989b) documented that a group of ten able autistic individuals, selected for passing a simple false belief test, failed a higher order belief test.

objectively distinguish several degrees of competence. It remains to be seen if these distinctions map on to diagnostically valid categories. If so, the diagnosis of Asperger syndrome and other variants of autism would be greatly facilitated. For instance, one criterion for the diagnosis of Asperger syndrome as opposed to, say, high-functioning autism, may be success on belief attribution tasks. This success may be no more and no less than a further sign of the superior adaptation of Asperger individuals.

Clearly, there are theoretical advances to be made in order to understand what enables some individuals to gain a measure of success on theory of mind tasks and what this success implies for their social and communicative abilities. One such advance has been the application of Relevance theory. In Dan Sperber and Deirdre Wilson's (1986) theory of Relevance the essential element in successful communication is the ability to infer the speaker's intentions. According to this theory, if this inference cannot be made automatically, then communicating with each other becomes arduous. Genuine interactive communication (as in understanding irony and reading between the lines) becomes impossible. Specific predictions can be made as to which aspects of communication will be learnable and which will not. For instance, understanding of factual information can be developed to a high degree. Understanding of intended implicit information will not be as good as understanding of literal information. The theory is suited *par excellence* to guide research into the problems of Asperger syndrome individuals. Their fluent, yet literal use of language is elegantly explained in this new framework. Francesca Happé, in chapter 7, discusses Sperber and Wilson's theory of Relevance and applies it to the autobiographical writings of some very articulate individuals with Asperger syndrome. Their writings seem to test the very limit of communication that can be achieved with impaired cognitive ability for inferring intentions and computing relevance.

If we take seriously the notion of Asperger syndrome as a subspecies of autism, we must attempt to apply the hypothesis that the underlying cognitive deficit in Asperger syndrome is the same as in autism in general. If the underlying cognitive deficit were shown to be different – and it may be different – then a more complex model of autism and its variants would have to be worked out. In the absence of such evidence, however, we must try to conceptualise how a single cognitive abnormality can result in severe autism in one case and mild Asperger-type autism in the other. Could it be that the underlying cognitive deficit can be more or less severe? A less severe underlying deficit would have less severe repercussions. The mechanism we propose to be faulty can be faulty in a mild sort of way. One could think of partial, intermittent or slow functioning, or of more or less extreme developmental delay. All these possibilities deserve to be explored.

We can also consider another, perhaps stronger, hypothesis: the underlying cognitive fault does not come in degrees, but at one end of the spectrum of autistic disorders there are aggravating factors, such as additional handicaps, and at the other end, where Asperger syndrome is situated, there are mitigating factors which cushion the effect of the deficit. The problem is to specify what such mitigating factors are. Here then is a chance for speculating and producing testable ideas. To start with, could it be that one such factor is the presence of a sociable disposition? Asperger syndrome individuals seem to be distinguished from other autistic individuals by a desire to communicate and be part of the social world.[47] Their desire to communicate is often demonstrated in their tendency to talk incessantly about their pet interest. Their desire to be part of the social world is often seen in their expressed frustration and sorrow at not finding friends or spouses. Could it be that a sociable disposition drives the acquisition of very detailed social learning, which can be applied to great effect in routine situations, as well as in the Sally–Anne test? One test of this hypothesis would be to see whether meaningful subgroups of autistic children can be identified at very young ages in terms of their basic sociability. Measures of sociability would have to be independent of the ability to conceptualise mental states.

Those Asperger-type individuals who have found effective ways of coping in social and communicative interactions and still retain their autistic oddness present a great challenge for theory and practice. In the next section I shall tentatively explore the hypothesis that we are looking at compensatory learning in the presence of a severe deficit rather than at a very mild form of deficit. In line with this hypothesis I propose that well-adapted Asperger syndrome individuals may have all the trappings of socially adapted behaviour, may have learnt to solve belief attribution problems, but yet may not have a normally functioning theory of mind. The hypothesis allows us to describe behaviour as *resembling* the normal pattern but arising from quite abnormally functioning processes.

How far can they go?[48]

An exceptionally well-adapted and able autistic person resembles that imaginary creature, the mermaid, of Hans Christian Andersen's fairy-tale. The mermaid, who was in love with a human prince, desired to take on human form, but could do so only at considerable cost. She had to sacrifice her voice to gain legs but when she moved it was like walking on knives. As she was unable to communicate, those around her did not understand her

---

[47] Case studies show that not all Asperger individuals are talkative and show a desire to be sociable. Indeed, some are distinctly reticent and keep themselves to themselves (Wing, 1989). As a coping strategy this may be highly effective. Perhaps it is this type of person who occasionally appears in family histories as a relative who was recognised as eccentric but never needed specialist attention.

[48] This title echoes that chosen by Kanner, Rodriguez and Ashenden (1972) in their follow-up study.

true nature. This led to the prince marrying someone else, and to her own failure to gain a place in this world.

Superficial resemblance to normality is, as case histories in this volume show, within the reach of at least some Asperger individuals. It may well be that this capacity to achieve near-normal behaviour is the single most distinctive feature of Asperger syndrome as opposed to other forms of autism.

It is possible for the Asperger person to learn social routines so well that he or she may strike others as merely eccentric. They would not consider that there was anything wrong with them. Of course, such hard-won adaptation is achieved only at a price. The Asperger person will have had to learn with great effort what others absorb quite naturally. He or she will have needed unstinting help and a high degree of motivation. Unfortunately, achievements bought at high cost are often fragile, and he or she will have to run where others stand still. The question arises whether such gains are worth the high price. One has to acknowledge too that not all Asperger syndrome individuals can achieve near-normal social integration for all their strenuous efforts.

Just how high is the cost, and how much effort is being spent in keeping up appearances? Often outsiders do not appreciate that there is a cost at all. Parents must find it irksome to be told by someone who has seen their Asperger son or daughter for a brief and pleasant interview that they are fussing about nothing. If the family members bring up anecdotal examples of difficulties, they will probably be told that these are normal problems that could happen to anybody. For instance, they may mention the embarrassing occasion of an autistic adult sitting in a crowded underground train and readjusting his or her underwear. 'So what?' comes the well-meaning but naive reply, 'Anybody in extreme discomfort might do this!' As for the charmingly humorous example of the autistic man who always forgets to take off his bicycle clips, the standard comment is 'Well, which bicyclist hasn't!'

Many examples of Aspergerish behaviour – to do with being oblivious of other people's reactions or with being over-concerned – can be cited, but there is always a retort handy that implies it is nothing out of the ordinary. Even the more outlandish examples, such as the young man who came down naked to a living room full of visitors asking where his pyjamas were, can be put down to a healthy disregard for stuffy conventions. In terms of behaviour the autistic person can be so well camouflaged that his or her occasional slips are generously discounted. Is it truly generous to overlook such problems? Or is it in fact a mistake not to acknowledge that there has been a cover-up of much more serious problems?

Sometimes the incompatibility of interest groups – the person with Asperger syndrome, the family, the community and the specialists – has to be kept in mind. Imagine a child with Asperger syndrome who is up for adoption. If his or her difficulties are ignored or dismissed as within the normal range by a well-meaning care-professional, this would be a great disservice to the child and the family. Would the family be able to cope without being warned about the problem and without some guidance? Probably not. Would they become demoralised when the hoped-for normal relationships with the adopted child fail to develop? Probably so. On the other hand, if properly prepared, the adoptive parents may be willing to enter into the challenging but rewarding process of guiding such a child, to use Asperger's own words.

One can, of course, look at the struggle for adaptation in another way. What, after all, is normality? Given that there is an enormous range of social behaviour with many degrees of adaptation and success or failure in the normal population, where does normality end and abnormality begin? Does it make sense to talk about deficits and exclusive categories? Should one instead talk about normal and abnormal behaviour shading into each other? To put it another way, should one look at Asperger syndrome as a normal personality variant?

A word to the person with Asperger syndrome

What would follow if the autistic individual saw himself or herself as just like everyone else and were treated as such? When routines have been long established and when things are going well, this attitude may be justified. It can convey a well-earned feeling of triumph and success. But what if things do not go well? And what if nobody, including the autistic person, is aware of the deeper underlying problems? To what extent can Asperger people themselves be aware of their difficulties? The uninformed employer might request something that for a normal person would be a trifling effort – unwittingly demanding a major effort from the Asperger individual. Sudden panic could result. For example, an autistic person who retains an extreme dislike of breaks in routine may be asked to accept a change that seems reasonable to the employer but which will throw him or her into despair. Presumed normality does not make allowance for sudden gaps in the carefully woven fabric of compensatory learning. A catastrophic reaction like screaming can cost a job, then.

The person with Asperger syndrome may well ask, 'What is so good about being normal anyway? So what if I am different?' The single-minded pursuit of a special interest or an outstanding artistic or musical talent is worthy of admiration and can lead to great social success. Those who care for an autistic individual may be captivated by his or her beauty and egocentric dependence. There is a fascination about eccentricity which is missing in conformity. Much that is obnoxious can be forgiven. Many people find autistic innocence appealing. 'Autistic is beautiful' could be a slogan which helps to increase confidence and happiness.[49] Asperger went out of his way to emphasise how valuable to society the autistic person can be. The autobiographical writings of Asperger individuals discussed in chapter 7 represent concrete examples of outstanding achievement, a coming to terms with the handicap.

However, only a few Asperger syndrome individuals adapt so successfully as to pass even fleetingly for normal. As yet we have little idea what makes the vital difference. Common sense suggests that high general ability, determination, a controllable temperament and a favourable environment all play a positive role. Chapter 6 presents the examples of Jack and Anne, two people who have adapted admirably. They have accepted the problems created by their handicap in a realistic fashion and even suggest ways of coping that might be helpful to others in a similar situation. The recognition of a handicapping condition leads to greater general tolerance, but not everyone can be informed. Ultimately, it may fall on handicapped people to explain themselves and request patience. Asperger individuals need to strive to be tolerant of those in their social environment who lack understanding and who can cause them anguish. It is not easy, but in controlling themselves they are dealing with the one person over whom they rightly have power.

Malice and the law-abiding citizen

Perhaps Asperger's most provocative speculation is his characterisation of spiteful and mischievous behaviour in the children he describes. What are we to make of this? Some readers of Asperger's paper in the past have been antagonised by these uncompromising statements. Nobody else has described autistic children as malicious. Margaret Dewey, in chapter 6, makes a convincing case for considering the examples Asperger gives as motivated by a simple desire for physical ends, not psychological effects. This is the case, for instance, when Fritz V., Asperger's most prototypical case, made his teacher angry simply because he enjoyed seeing a display of anger. Fritz readily admitted to this, just as another similar boy admitted that he enjoyed seeing blood spurting out after a knife wound. Malice does not come into it, but Asperger failed to distinguish between a deliberately malicious act and a merely unpleasant one.

Acknowledgement that some autistic children can be guilty of peculiarly repulsive acts has been rare.[50] Yet it is vital to acknowledge this problem of

[49] Mesibov and Stephens (1990) reported on high-functioning autistic individuals' perception of popularity among peers and found that they valued humour, attractiveness, intelligence and athletic ability though they did not necessarily agree with other people's perceptions of these attributes.

[50] Examples of socially unacceptable behaviour in the children described by Asperger include running away, shouting, violent attacks, self-injury, inappropriate sexual behaviour, temper tantrums and eating and sleeping disturbances.

which practitioners have long been aware. It helps us to understand repugnant behaviour if we realise that the autistic person does not calculate the effect his or her behaviour has on other people's states of mind. Likewise, violent and dangerous acts can be committed by an individual who does not automatically take account of his or her own and other people's mental states.[51] Autistic people are not intent on hurting other people's feelings. Hurting another person's feelings is a behaviour that presupposes an active theory of mind, something which autistic people conspicuously lack. If care-givers are upset by an autistic child's apparent enjoyment of the distress that he or she provokes, they need to remember that without an understanding of the underlying mental states, delight and fury give rise to equally fascinating facial and vocal displays. In this way an innocent detached curiosity can be the cause of socially harmful behaviour.

Autistic people, and particularly those of the Asperger type, have been involved in some difficult forensic cases. Sometimes their offences are part of their single-minded pursuit of a special interest, sometimes the result of a defensive panic-induced action and sometimes the consequence of a complete lack of common sense. Police officers and magistrates profess to the strong but subjective feeling that the person before them cannot be held responsible for his or her action. Typically, the Asperger individual, when apprehended, does not seem to feel guilt, does not try to conceal nor excuse what he or she did, and may even describe details with shocking openness. Sometimes, however, law officers misunderstand and thus mistreat the unfortunate and unwitting culprit. This is especially likely in the case of the relatively well-adapted Asperger individual whose behaviour is superficially normal, whose appearance and demeanour do not elicit the help he or she needs.

It should also be said that many Asperger individuals, far from becoming delinquent, are excessively concerned with doing the right thing. They anxiously refrain from doing what they believe to be unlawful, and also expect others to behave lawfully. One very small and gentle 25-year-old carried with him for a time a set of police handcuffs so that he could make a citizen's arrest if he spotted unlawful behaviour. Examples of Asperger people as law-abiding individuals are shown in many case studies in this volume and elsewhere. One cannot make reliable generalisations regarding autism and antisocial behaviour because of the observed range of actual behaviour, from violence to saintliness.

One viewpoint assumes that essentially everything experienced by humans, however extreme, is within the range of normality. Only degrees of difference exist. At extremes one may talk, merely as a shorthand, of

---

[51] An example is given by Baron-Cohen (1988) who describes a case of a 21-year-old with Asperger syndrome who often violently beat his 71-year-old(!) girl-friend.

abnormality. Autistic features in particular show a whole range of mani-festations. Surely everyone is a little bit autistic on occasion?

From the point of view of the diagnostician there is much support for the idea of Asperger syndrome shading into normality. After all, the diagnosis is, so far, based on behaviour and not on tests that clearly identify underlying problems. If it is difficult to diagnose Asperger syndrome, one might argue that a case could be made for its being a normal personality variant rather than a brain abnormality. I am fortunate to be allowed to reproduce here an example of a professional report on a case which seems to fall into this borderland, a case which does not show all the classic features of Asperger syndrome. Let us refer to it as 'The case of the lonely cyclist'.

Dear Dr Robertson,

Re: James Jones. Aged 16 years

Thank you for asking my opinion concerning James's diagnosis, which presents an interesting problem. I saw his mother on 13 February 1987 and she gave an account of his developmental history. I saw James himself on 15 February with two colleagues.

Infancy

James was the first and only child of his parents. Labour was prolonged and delivery was by forceps, but his condition was said to be satisfactory at birth. As a baby he was very placid and noticeably less demanding than other babies of his mother's friends and relations. He was not cuddly and did not positively reach out for attention and affection, although he smiled when approached. He would lie in his pram and gurgle happily at the trees. He was easily toilet-trained and slept well from birth onwards.

Development of basic skills

He walked rather late, but was not slow enough to cause alarm. He was somewhat delayed in talking and when he did talk his speech was very unclear. For a long time his mother was the only person who could understand him. Dressing and self-feeding skills were also delayed.

Play and imagination

James was quite good with fitting shapes, but had no pretend play. He had many toy cars, which he would arrange in lines and push along. He did not use them imaginatively. Before going to school, he played with other children in the street but always followed what they did – he never initiated activities. He lacked curiosity and did not go through the usual childish stage of asking questions about everything.

Behaviour at school

When James was three years old a nursery schoolteacher informed Mrs Jones that he interfered with the other children, often knocking their toys down, and was very restless. However, he was allowed to stay at the nursery.

When he transferred to primary school, he was unco-operative, over-active and disturbing to the class. He was slow at learning and was found to be below average in intelligence. He was placed in a special school with a structured, organised programme, and there he got along well. This seems to have been the best placement of his childhood.

For his secondary education he was first placed in a school with a permissive regime. His behaviour became extremely disturbed, worse than anything before. Again, a move to a school with a more structured regime produced improvement.

Social interaction and communication

Now, at the age of sixteen, James seems fond of his mother, his grandmother and the family pets, but does not seem able to understand what upsets other people. When his family has visitors he goes to his own room. He desperately wants to have friends but his peers will not put up with him. He always wants his own way and does not seem able to develop a give-and-take relationship. His attempts to interact are clumsy and irritating to others. He makes remarks which upset his peers; he pushes people and takes their possessions. However, if others turn on him, he does not fight but runs away and cannot be caught.

He has never been able to converse, and cannot explain his own actions or motivation. He replies briefly to questions. This has been the case all his life.

He is just beginning to be interested in girls but does not have the social skills to make friends with a girl.

Motor skills

He can swim, horse-ride and cycle with a fair degree of skill. On the other hand, he is hopeless at team games of any kind. He appears unable to co-ordinate his actions with those of the rest of the team and ends by aggravating everyone. He is quite likely to kick the ball into his own goal.

Current interests

At home he still likes his toy cars, which he continues to push around in long lines.

He has no interest in his own appearance and his mother has to choose his clothes for him.

He also needs help with brushing his hair.

He likes watching television and has a remarkable memory for past programmes. He also remembers routes to places, even those visited only once. He memorises routes on the London Underground and likes looking at maps. He seems to have no interests apart from these and spends much time in his room when at home. He goes out alone for long rides on his bicycle. His parents worry about him going out alone but do not want to deprive him of one of the few things he enjoys.

Difficult behaviour

James has never been much trouble within his own home, where the main concern has been his passivity and isolation from social interaction. However, there has been a series of problems in other environments, beginning with his disturbed behaviour on starting school. He tends to make inappropriate comments to strangers in the street and will push past other people or barge into them as if they did not exist. He sometimes attempts to join in the street games of younger children and does odd things such as throwing bricks or running away with their footballs or cricket bats, to their bewilderment and fury. There have been several incidents of his taking money, apparently to try to buy friends. He has also been seriously assaulted by two of his age-peers, an incident which he recounted with little emotion.

Reasons for present referral

Recently, James went out alone on his bicycle and was away for longer than usual. It seems that he cycled into town, entered a supermarket, filled a basket with a random assortment of items for which he could not have had any use, then walked out without paying, in full view of the employees. He was apprehended, his parents were contacted and, eventually, a referral for a psychiatric opinion was arranged. He could offer no explanation for his irrational act beyond suggesting that he 'wanted a bit of fun'.

He tends to elaborate some answers to questions to the point of fantasy. For example, he described a purely imaginary episode that, he claimed, occurred on a skiing holiday which ended with him hanging by his arms from a cable car. It is likely that these stories were copied from television commercials current at the time of referral.

He shows no guilt or concern for others. When asked to talk about and describe his mother he said she had blonde hair and 'looked American'. He expresses no affection for his parents nor worry about the effect of his behaviour upon them. His plans for the future are singularly unrealistic, comprising the intention to live with one of his earlier school-mates whose father, he claims, owns a travelling fair and is a millionaire!

On examination

James is small for his age and has a naive, immature appearance and manner. He was friendly and amenable and did not seem to be at all disconcerted by the situation. He answered questions fully and elaborated some of his answers. He was by no means monosyllabic in the interview. He made good eye contact, used appropriate gestures and intonation when speaking and was prepared to involve all three people present in the conversation. He had none of the mannerisms, odd intonation and lack of gesture typical of autism or Asperger syndrome.

James has an overall IQ of 67 on the WAIS with no marked discrepancies on subtests. He was given tests of his ability to understand sequences of events in picture stories and their consequences for the characters involved. These he completed at a level a little above that predicted from his WAIS IQ.

Formulation

James is in the mildly retarded range of intellectual ability, but this on its own does not account for his strange behaviour.

His developmental history, while showing elements of both conditions, is not typical of Kanner's early childhood autism or of Asperger's syndrome. His profile on the WAIS does not show the very marked discrepancies found in these conditions in the classic form. In particular, he has no special skill with block design, although he is quite good at object assembly and is reported to be adept at jigsaw puzzles. He is able to arrange pictures to tell a story which is unusual in typical autism and Asperger syndrome.

He lacks some other common features of the above syndromes, that is, the stereotypes, odd bodily movements, repetitive routines and idiosyncratic language of typical autism, and the long-winded repetitive speech on special topics found in Asperger's group. On the other hand, his language development was delayed and he failed to develop imaginative play. His mother says that he is capable of affection but his social interaction skills and empathy with others are limited and, in practice, disastrously inappropriate. His gross and fine motor development was delayed, and he is inept when attempting to join in team activities, although he can perform reasonably well in solitary physical activities. He conspicuously lacks common sense which, Asperger emphasised, was a cardinal feature of his syndrome. He appears to have little capacity to describe his feelings and motivations. His pattern of interests is markedly limited, and he has the unusual memory for routes, maps and television programmes typical of conditions in the autistic continuum. His 'fantasies' seem to be limited to scenes he has watched on television.

It can be argued that James has a developmental disorder affecting his capacity to plan his own life and fit into the social world. Classification as socially impaired and having a disorder within the autistic continuum would seem to be appropriate. The assignment of a precise diagnosis for his pattern of behaviour is of academic interest. From the practical point of view, it is important to realise that the prognosis is poor for young adults with similar histories and behaviour patterns. Because of their lack of inner resources of understanding or imagination, they are unable to benefit from programmes of re-education that are based on psychotherapy, group therapy or family therapy. They function best in a closed, structured, organised but sympathetic environment, with staff who understand their handicaps and a high staff-to-resident ratio. They need to be provided with a range of activities but should not be under any pressure to achieve beyond their level of ability. The fact that James did well at a school with this type of regime is evidence of his needs.

Ideally, such an environment should be provided on a long-term basis. Unfortunately, in most such cases, any improvement is specific to the situation. Once the programme ceases, relapse to the former difficult behaviour is only too likely to occur. People like James are, because of their developmental impairment, unable to build an organised inner world of ideas capable of regulating their own conduct. They need other people to provide structure for them over the course of many years, and perhaps for their whole lives.

Yours sincerely

X.Y.

The goalposts have shifted

This report was taken almost at random from a busy clinician's files. It makes clear just how much has changed from the days when everything outside classic autism, but nevertheless resembling autism, was a no man's land of diagnostic uncertainty. With a more precise clinical picture of Asperger syndrome, the no man's land has shrunk considerably, and now we can acknowledge that there are cases, like James Jones, who do not follow any textbook and would probably not have been recognised previously as belonging to the autistic spectrum at all. More recently, he might have been described as a mildly retarded person who has some autistic features – in the way that an unrecognised clinically depressed patient may be described as a dull person with some depressive features. Both autistic and depressive features can be shown by anybody occasionally. They are behavioural signs and need not necessarily be caused by autism or depression. Conversely, autism and depression can exist in unrecognised and/or camouflaged forms where clear behavioural signs may be suppressed. Therefore, the diagnostician needs to consider signs as clues and to evaluate them as positive or negative evidence for the hypothesis he or she holds about the condition, rather than the other way round. This is very much the procedure followed in the report. Behavioural symptoms are almost always attributable to many different causes. We cannot find the causes merely by going backwards from observation; we also need to go forwards, guided by hypotheses.

The category Asperger syndrome – even when it is seen as a subcategory belonging to the spectrum of autistic disorders – has itself associated with it a spectrum of more or less prototypical cases. Just as within the range of normality there are ordinary people and eccentrics, so within the Asperger syndrome there are typical and less typical cases. In clinical practice, of course, the less typical is the more frequent. This is because circumstances and efforts at compensation muddle even the purest case.

We can now ask the question that prompted the inclusion of this case: Is James Jones normal, only very odd? Is he, in fact, a case which belongs at one extreme of the distribution centred around the prototypical normal? If this is our conclusion, then we would have to consider that all his different oddities are there by coincidence. This may be so – we cannot be sure. If, on the other hand, we conclude that James Jones suffers from Asperger syndrome, all the oddities would fall into place. However, he would be a less typical case of Asperger syndrome. This is no idle speculation, since it is amenable to being tested. Using the cognitive theory, we would predict that James Jones has subtle communication problems and would not be able to understand irony, for instance.

There is no reason to suppose that behaviour shading into normality will ever cease to be a problem for diagnosis. The aim of compensatory learning is to produce behaviour that more and more shades into normality. As demonstrated by the report, one solution of diagnostic problems presented by cases where camouflage is achieved is to reconstruct a full childhood history. The history would reveal if there once were important signs (for example, lack of pretend play) and if difficulties were overcome by special efforts.

The categorical distinction of normal and abnormal functioning of mental processes at a deeper level can only be inferred and cannot be directly derived from the initial observation of behaviour. As far as the naive observer is concerned, anything can happen. Not so the expert, who asks specific questions guided by specific hypotheses. Differences in observed behaviour outweigh similarities to such an extent that one often hears the argument that there is no point in classification since every child is unique. This conclusion is inevitable if one restricts oneself to only observed behaviour, which is infinitely variable. It would be quite different if we aim to explain behaviour at a cognitive level – we would draw together superficial differences and bring out hidden similarities. This is no easy task, and in the case of Asperger syndrome it is only just beginning.

A dash of autism

Hans Asperger deserves to be recognised as a pioneer and champion of all Asperger children. His case studies of Fritz V. and Harro L. are enthralling to read. These extraordinary boys have, unbeknown to themselves, contributed greatly to the study of developmental disorders. Asperger pleaded for the recognition of such children, pointing out the potential that they had to offer society, and from the start he argued that they should be given very special education and guidance. He warned of them being teased and bullied at school, and of being misunderstood by teachers. He identified with them to the extent that he believed that to help autistic people one needs to have a dash of autism oneself. He also suggested parallels between autism, scientific originality and introversion. As a classicist he was undoubtedly influenced by Seneca's famous words that there is no genius without madness.[52] While this idea has been with us for centuries, it is only now that we are considering that the madness in question may point to autism.

Asperger's views on the positive value of autism as an important aspect of creative thought and intellectual style are still fresh and provocative, and perhaps just as controversial as his views on malicious behaviour. The cause of autistic originality was, for Asperger, not some mysteriously intact special ability but, rather, the result of an inability to learn by conventional means. There is no getting round the fact that autism is a handicap. Even the best-adjusted individual with Asperger syndrome has more than the usual share of problems. It would be tragic if romantic notions of genius and unworldliness were to deprive bright autistic people of the understanding and help they need. The case studies presented in this book serve to document the severity of the sometimes well-camouflaged handicap.

Like Asperger, I too would sometimes like to claim a dash of autism for myself. A dash of autism is not a bad way to characterise the apparent detachment and unworldiness of the scientist who is obsessed with one seemingly all-important problem and temporarily forgets the time of day, not to mention family and friends. True to the recursive pattern of thought it is possible to conclude that an appropriately never-ending subject for such a single-minded interest could be Asperger's syndrome.

References

Asperger, H. (1944). Die 'Autistischen Psychopathen' im Kindesalter. *Archiv für Psychiatrie und Nervenkrankheiten*, 117, 76–136.

Asperger, H. (1952). *Heilpädagogik*. Berlin: Springer.

Asperger, H. (1962). Erwin Lazar und seine Heilpädagogische Abteilung der Wiener Kinderklinik. *Heilpädagogik*, 32, 1–8.

Asperger, H. (1979). Problems of infantile autism. *Communication*, 13, 45–52. (Lecture given at Fribourg, Switzerland on 13 March 1977.)

Baron-Cohen, S. (1988). An assessment of violence in a young man with Asperger's syndrome. *Journal of Child Psychology and Psychiatry*, 29, 351–60.

[52] Seneca (c. 4BC – AD65), in *De tranquillitate animi*, formulates the statement 'nullum magnum ingenium sine mixtura dementiæ fuit', reflecting Aristotle's (384–322 BC) similar beliefs about the relationship of melancholia and creativity.

Baron-Cohen, S. (1989a). Are autistic children 'behaviourists'? An examination of their mental–physical and appearance–reality distinctions. *Journal of Autism and Developmental Disorders*, 19, 579–600.

Baron-Cohen, S. (1989b). The autistic child's theory of mind: a case of specific developmental delay. *Journal of Child Psychology and Psychiatry*, 30, 285–98.

Baron-Cohen, S. (1990). Autism: a specific cognitive disorder of 'mind-blindness'. *International Review of Psychiatry*, 2, 79–88.

Baron-Cohen, S., Leslie, A. M. & Frith, U. (1985). Does the autistic child have a 'theory of mind'? *Cognition*, 21, 37–46.

Baron-Cohen, S., Leslie, A. M. & Frith, U. (1986). Mechanical, behavioural and intentional understanding of picture stories in autistic children. *British Journal of Developmental Psychology*, 4, 113–25.

Bartak, L. & Rutter, M. (1976). Differences between mentally retarded and normally intelligent autistic children. *Journal of Autism and Childhood Schizophrenia*, 6, 109–20.

Bell, C. (1806). *Anatomy and philosophy of expression*. London: George Bell & Sons.

Bishop, D. V. M. (1989). Autism, Asperger's syndrome and semantic-pragmatic disorder: where are the boundaries? *British Journal of Disorders of Communication*, 24, 107–21.

Bleuler, E. (1916). *Lehrbuch der Psychiatrie*. Trans. A. A. Brill, (1951), *Textbook of psychiatry*. New York: Dover.

Brown, J. (1978). Long-term follow-up of 100 'atypical' children of normal intelligence. In M. Rutter & E. Schopler (eds.), *Autism: a reappraisal of concepts and treatment*. New York: Plenum.

Cohen, D. J., Donnellan, A. M. & Paul, R. (eds.) (1987). *Handbook of autism and pervasive developmental disorders*. New York: Wiley.

Cohen, D. J., Paul, R. & Volkmar, F. R. (1987). Issues in the classification of pervasive developmental disorders and associated conditions. In D. J. Cohen, A. M. Donnellan & R. Paul (eds.), *Handbook of autism and pervasive developmental disorders*. New York: Wiley.

Darwin, C. (1872). *The origin of emotions*. London: John Murray.

Frith, C. D. & Frith, U. (in press). Elective affinities in autism and schizophrenia. In P. Bebbington (ed.), *Social psychiatry: theory, methodology and practice*. New Brunswick, N.J.: Transaction.

Frith, U. (1989a). *Autism: explaining the enigma*. Oxford: Blackwell.

Frith, U. (1989b). Autism and theory of mind. In C. Gillberg (ed.), *Diagnosis and treatment of autism*. New York: Plenum.

Frith, U. (1989c). A new look at language and communication in autism. *British Journal of Disorders of Communication*, 24, 123–50.

Gillberg, C. (1989a). Asperger syndrome in 23 Swedish children. *Developmental Medicine and Child Neurology*, 31, 520–31.

Gillberg, C. (ed.) (1989b). *Diagnosis and treatment of autism*. New York: Plenum.

Gillberg, C. (1990). Autism and pervasive developmental disorders. *Journal of Child Psychology and Psychiatry*, 31, 99–119.

Gillberg, I. C. & Gillberg, C. (1989). Asperger syndrome – some epidemiological considerations: a research note. *Journal of Child Psychology and Psychiatry*, 30, 631–8.

Grandin, T. (1984). My experiences as an autistic child and review of selected literature. *Journal of Orthomolecular Psychiatry*, 13, 144–74.

Green, J. (1990). Annotation: is Asperger's a syndrome? *Developmental Medicine and Child Neurology*, 32, 743–7.

Hobson, R. P. (1986a). The autistic child's appraisal of expressions of emotion. *Journal of Child Psychology and Psychiatry*, 27, 321–42.

Hobson, R. P. (1986b). The autistic child's appraisal of expressions of emotion: a further study. *Journal of Child Psychology and Psychiatry*, 27, 671–80.

Hobson, R. P. (1989). On acquiring knowledge about people and the capacity to pretend: a response to Leslie (1987). *Psychological Review*, 97, 114–21.

Kanner, L. (1943). Autistic disturbances of affective contact. *Nervous Child*, 2, 217–50.

Kanner, L. (1971). Follow-up study of eleven autistic children originally reported in 1943. *Journal of Autism and Childhood Schizophrenia*, 1, 119–45.

Kanner, L., Rodriguez, A. & Ashenden, B. (1972). How far can autistic children go in matters of social adaptation? *Journal of Autism and Childhood Schizophrenia*, 2, 9–33.

Kerbeshian, J., Burd, L. & Fisher, W. (1990). Asperger's syndrome: to be or not to be? *British Journal of Psychiatry*, 156, 721–5.

Klages, L. (1936). *Grundlegung der Wissenschaft vom Ausdruck*. 5th ed. Leipzig: Barth.

Kretschmer, E. (1925). *Physique and character*. London: Kegan Paul, Trench & Trubner.

Leslie, A. M. (1987). Pretence and representation: the origins of a 'theory of mind'. *Psychological Review*, 94, 412–26.

Leslie, A. M. & Frith, U. (1988). Autistic children's understanding of seeing, knowing and believing. *British Journal of Developmental Psychology*, 6, 315–24.

Leslie, A. M. & Frith, U. (1989). Prospects for a neuropsychology of autism: Hobson's choice. *Psychological Review*, 97, 122–31.

Leslie, A. M. & Thaiss, L. (in press). Domain specificity in conceptual development: evidence from autism. *Cognition*.

Lockyer, L. & Rutter, M. (1970). A five to fifteen year follow-up study of infantile psychosis: IV. Patterns of cognitive ability. *British Journal of Social and Clinical Psychology*, 9, 156–63.

Lösche, G. (1990). Sensorimotor and action development in autistic children from infancy to early childhood. *Journal of Child Psychology and Psychiatry*, 31, 749–61.

Lutz, J. (1981). Hans Asperger und Leo Kanner zum Gedenken. *Acta Paedopsychiatrica*, 47, 179–83.

Mesibov, G. B. & Stephens, J. (1990). Perceptions of popularity among a group of high-functioning adults with autism. *Journal of Autism and Developmental Disorders*, 20, 33–43.

Morton, J. (1989). The origins of autism. *New Scientist*, 1694, (Dec. 1989) 44–7.

Nagy, J. & Szatmari, P. A. (1986). A chart review of schizotypal personality disorders in children. *Journal of Autism and Developmental Disorders*, 16, 351–67.

Newson, E., Dawson, M. & Everard, P. (1982). The natural history of able autistic people: their management and functioning in a social context. Unpublished report to the Department of Health and Social Security, London. Summary published in 4 parts in *Communication*, 19 – 22 (1984–5).

Ozonoff, S., Pennington, B. F. & Rogers, S. J. (in press). Executive function deficits in high-functioning autistic children: relationship to theory of mind. *Journal of Child Psychology and Psychiatry*.

Ozonoff, S., Rogers, S. J. & Pennington, B. F. (in press). Asperger's syndrome: evidence of an empirical distinction from high-functioning autism. *Journal of Child Psychology and Psychiatry*.

Perner, J., Frith, U., Leslie, A. M. & Leekam, S. R. (1989). Exploration of the autistic child's theory of mind: knowledge, belief and communication. *Child Development*, 60, 689–700.

Rees, S. C. & Taylor, A. (1975). Prognostic antecedents and outcome in a follow-up study of children with a diagnosis of childhood psychosis. *Journal of Autism and Childhood Schizophrenia*, 5, 309–22.

Rumsey, J. M. (1985). Conceptual problem-solving in highly verbal, non-retarded autistic men. *Journal of Autism and Developmental Disorders*, 15, 23–36.

Rumsey, J., Andreasen, N. & Rapoport, J. (1986). Thought, language, communication, and affective flattening in autistic adults. *Archives of General Psychiatry*, 43, 771–7.

Rumsey, J., & Hamburger, S. D. (1988). Neuropsychological findings in high-functioning men with infantile autism residual state. *Journal of Clinical and Experimental Neuropsychology*, 10, 201–21.

Rumsey, J., Rapoport, J. & Sceery, W. (1985). Autistic children as adults: psychiatric, social and behavioral outcomes. *Journal of the American Academy of Child Psychiatry*, 4, 465–73.

Rutter, M. & Hersov, L. (1985). *Child and adolescent psychiatry: modern approaches*. 2nd ed. Oxford: Blackwell Scientific.

Rutter, M. & Lockyer, L. (1969). A five to fifteen year follow-up study of infantile psychosis: III. Psychological aspects. *British Journal of Psychiatry*, 115, 865–82.

Rutter, M., Macdonald, H., Le Couteur, A., Harrington, R., Bolton, P. & Bailey, A. (1990). Genetic factors in child psychiatric disorders – II. Empirical findings. *Journal of Child Psychology and Psychiatry*, 31, 39–83.

Schopler, E. & Mesibov, G. B. (eds.) (1983 onwards). *Current issues in autism* (series). New York: Plenum.

Schopler, E. & Mesibov, G. B. (eds.) (in press). *High-functioning autism*. New York: Plenum.

Schreibman, L. (1989). *Autism*. Vol. XV of *Developmental clinical psychology and psychiatry*. London: Sage.

Semrud-Clikeman, M. & Hynd, G. W. (1990). Right hemisphere dysfunction in nonverbal learning disabilities: social, academic, and adaptive functioning in adults and children. *Psychological Bulletin*, 107, 196–209.

Shah, A. (1988). Visuo-spatial islets of abilities and intellectual functioning in autism. Unpublished Ph. D. thesis, University of London.

Sparrow, S., Rescorla, L. A., Provence, S., Condon, S., Goudreau, D. & Cicchetti, D. V. (1986). Follow-up of 'atypical' children – a brief report. *Journal of the American Academy of Child Psychiatry*, 25, 181–5.

Sperber, D. & Wilson, D. (1986). *Relevance: communication and cognition*. Oxford: Blackwell.

Szatmari, P., Bartolucci, G. & Bremner, R. (1989). Asperger's syndrome and autism: comparison of early history and outcome. *Developmental Medicine and Child Neurology*, 31, 709–20.

Szatmari, P., Bartolucci, G., Bremner, R., Bond, S. & Rich, S. (1989). A follow-up study of high-functioning autistic children. *Journal of Autism and Developmental Disorders*, 19, 213–25.

Szatmari, P., Tuff, L., Finlayson, A. J. & Bartolucci, G. (1990). Asperger's syndrome and autism: neuro-cognitive aspects. *Journal of the American Academy of Child and Adolescent Psychiatry*, 29, 130–6.

Tantam, D. (1986). Eccentricity and autism. Unpublished Ph. D. thesis, University of London.

Tantam, D. (1988a). Annotation: Asperger's syndrome. *Journal of Child Psychology and Psychiatry*, 29, 836–40.

Tantam, D. (1988b). Lifelong eccentricity and social isolation: I. Psychiatric, social and forensic aspects. *British Journal of Psychiatry*, 153, 777–82.

Tantam, D. (1988c). Lifelong eccentricity and social isolation: II. Asperger's syndrome or schizoid personality disorder? *British Journal of Psychiatry*, 153, 783–91.

Volkmar, F. R. (1987). Social development. In D. J. Cohen, A. M. Donnellan & R. Paul (eds.), *Handbook of autism and pervasive developmental disorders*. New York: Wiley.

Wing, L. (1981). Asperger's syndrome: a clinical account. *Psychological Medicine*, 11, 115–30.

Wing, L. (1989). Autistic adults. In C. Gillberg (ed.), *Diagnosis and treatment of autism*. New York: Plenum Press.

Wing, L. & Attwood, A. (1987). Syndromes of autism and atypical development. In D. J. Cohen, A. M. Donnellan & R. Paul (eds.), *Handbook of autism and pervasive developmental disorders*. New York: Wiley.

Wing, L. & Gould, J. (1979). Severe impairments of social interaction and associated abnormalities in children: epidemiology and classification. *Journal of Autism and Childhood Schizophrenia*, 9, 11–29.

Wolff, S. & Barlow, A. (1979). Schizoid personality in childhood: a comparative study of schizoid, autistic and normal children. *Journal of Child Psychology and Psychiatry*, 20, 29–46.

Wolff, S. & Chick, J. (1980). Schizoid personality in childhood: a controlled follow-up study. *Psychological Medicine*, 10, 85–100.

World Health Organization (1990). *International classification of diseases: tenth revision*. Chapter V. Mental and behavioural disorders (including disorders of psychological development). Diagnostic criteria for research (May 1990 draft for field trials). Geneva: WHO (unpublished).

Wurst, E. (1976). *Autismus*. Berne: Huber.

2

'Autistic psychopathy' in childhood

HANS ASPERGER
Translated and annotated by Uta Frith

In what follows, I will describe a particularly interesting and highly recognisable type of child.[1] The children I will present all have in common a fundamental disturbance which manifests itself in their physical appearance, expressive functions and, indeed, their whole behaviour. This disturbance results in severe and characteristic difficulties of social integration. In many cases the social problems are so profound that they overshadow everything else. In some cases, however, the problems are compensated by a high level of original thought and experience. This can often lead to exceptional achievements in later life. With the type of personality disorder presented here we can demonstrate the truth of the claim that exceptional human beings must be given exceptional educational treatment, treatment which takes account of their special difficulties. Further, we can show that despite abnormality human beings can fulfil their social role within the community, especially if they find understanding, love and guidance. There are many reasons for describing in detail this type of abnormally developing child. Not the least of them is that these children raise questions of central importance to psychology and education.

Name and Concept

I have chosen the label autism[2] in an effort to define the basic disorder that

[1] The first seven pages of general and somewhat discursive introduction, which Asperger himself omitted from a slightly revised reprint of the paper in his textbook *Heilpädagogik* (1952), are omitted in this translation. The omitted section consists of a discussion of various then current typologies, whose aim it was to categorise personalities in normal as well as pathological forms. It finishes with the suggestion that it is possible to overcome their limitations by using general descriptions as well as individual case studies.

[2] The title of Asperger's landmark paper has propagated the term autistic psychopathy. This term could have been translated as autistic personality disorder or else autism to bring it into line with current terminology.

generates the abnormal personality structure of the children we are concerned with here. The name derives from the concept of autism in schizophrenia. Autism in this sense refers to a fundamental disturbance of contact that is manifest in an extreme form in schizophrenic patients. The name 'autism', coined by Bleuler, is undoubtedly one of the great linguistic and conceptual creations in medical nomenclature.[3]

Human beings normally live in constant interaction with their environment, and react to it continually. However, 'autists' have severely disturbed and considerably limited interaction. The autist is only himself (cf. the Greek word *autos*) and is not an active member of a greater organism which he is influenced by and which he influences constantly. Bleuler's formulations of schizophrenic autism included the following:

> The schizophrenic patient loses contact with reality to varying degrees. He ceases to care about the real world. He shows a lack of initiative, aimlessness, neglect of reality, distractedness, but also impulsive and bizarre behaviour. Many of his actions, as well as his whole attitude to life, are insufficiently externally motivated. Both intensity and extent of attention are disordered. There is lack of persistence, but occasionally certain goals are held on to tenaciously. One often finds 'whimsical obstinacy', that is, the patient wants something and at the same time the opposite. One finds obsessional acts, automatic acts, automatic commands etc. Schizophrenic patients often live in an imaginary world of wish fulfilment and ideas of persecution.

Bleuler here describes a particular type of thinking which he calls 'autistic' or 'dereistic' thinking.[4] This thinking is not goal-directed but is guided by desires and affects. Apart from schizophrenia, where it is at its most bizarre, autistic or dereistic thinking can also be found in people who are not psychotic, and indeed in everyday life, for example, in superstition or pseudo-science. However, this type of thinking does not play a role in the children we are concerned with here. At most, there may be occasional hints at this particular type of thought disturbance.

All but the last mentioned feature of Bleuler's concept of autism can be

---

[3] The Swiss psychiatrist Eugen Bleuler, who wrote an influential textbook of psychiatry, coined not only the term autism but also the term schizophrenia. Bleuler differentiated autism and autistic thinking. In English translations of his writings these are usually translated as dereism and dereistic thinking, referring to a loss of contact with reality.

[4] For Bleuler autistic thinking meant thought associations driven by affects. He applied this concept not only to schizophrenic patients but also to normal people. 'Autistic thinking turns the boy playing soldiers into a general, the girl playing with her doll into a happy mother . . . it enables the dreamer to express his wishes and fears.' In 1919 Bleuler published *The autistic-undisciplined thinking in medicine and how to overcome it*, where he castigated then current medical practice. He gave examples of beliefs in medicine that are wishful rather than truthful, analogical rather than logical, fantasy rather than reality. It is clear from this bitter treatise that autistic thinking in Bleuler's sense has nothing to do with autism as we know it. This is also recognised by Asperger, who in his later revision for his textbook (1952), omits any reference to dereistic thinking.

found in the type of personality disorder to be described here. While the schizophrenic patient seems to show progressive loss of contact, the children we are discussing lack contact from the start. Autism is the paramount feature in both cases. It totally colours affect, intellect, will and action. Essential symptoms of schizophrenia and the symptoms of our children can thus be brought under a common denominator: the shutting-off of relations between self and the outside world. However, unlike schizophrenic patients, our children do not show a disintegration of personality. They are therefore not psychotic, instead they show a greater or lesser degree of psychopathy. The fundamental disorder that we have identified in our children affects all expressions of their personality and can explain their difficulties and deficits as well as their special achievements. Once one has learnt to pay attention to the characteristic manifestations of autism, one realises that they are not at all rare in children, especially in their milder forms. A few prototypical cases will be described below.

Fritz V.

We start with a highly unusual boy who shows a very severe impairment in social integration. This boy was born in June 1933 and came for observation to the Heilpädagogische Abteilung (Remedial Department) of the University Paediatric Clinic in Vienna in the autumn of 1939.[5] He was referred by his school as he was considered to be 'uneducable' by the end of his first day there.

Fritz was the first child of his parents. He had a brother two years younger who was also somewhat difficult but not nearly as deviant as Fritz. Birth was normal. Motor milestones were rather delayed. He learnt to walk at fourteen months, and for a long time was extremely clumsy and unable to do things for himself. He learnt the practical routines of daily life very late and with great difficulty.[6] This will be looked at in more detail later. In contrast, he learnt to talk very early and spoke his first words at ten months, well before he could walk. He quickly learnt to express himself in sentences and soon talked 'like an adult'.[7] Nothing was reported about unusual childhood illnesses and there was no indication of any brain disease.

From the earliest age Fritz never did what he was told. He did just what he wanted to, or the opposite of what he was told. He was always restless

[5] This famous clinic was founded in 1918 by Erwin Lazar and pioneered a combination of special education and paediatrics.

[6] Practical routines include self-help skills such as washing, dressing and, generally, keeping clothes and body clean, and probably also some typical social skills, such as eating properly at table, and sitting still and paying attention at school. Toilet training is never mentioned while it looms large as a problem in Kanner's cases.

[7] Donald, Kanner's first case, also appears to have had rather early and unusual development of speech. By the age of two, he was said to be able to name large numbers of pictures and to recite poetry and prose. Asperger's descriptive phrase 'talking like an adult' suggests oddness over and above precocity.

and fidgety, and tended to grab everything within reach. Prohibitions did not deter him. Since he had a pronounced destructive urge, anything that got into his hands was soon torn or broken.[8]

He was never able to become integrated into a group of playing children. He never got on with other children and, in fact, was not interested in them. They only 'wound him up'. He quickly became aggressive and lashed out with anything he could get hold of (once with a hammer), regardless of the danger to others. For this he was thrown out of kindergarten after only a few days. Similarly, because of his totally uninhibited behaviour, his schooling failed on the first day. He had attacked other children, walked nonchalantly about in class and tried to demolish the coat-racks.

He had no real love for anybody but occasionally had fits of affection. Then he would embrace various people, seemingly quite unmotivated. The effect, however, was not at all pleasant. This behaviour never felt like the expression of genuine affection, instead, it appeared to be as abrupt as a fit. One could not help thinking that Fritz might never be able to love anyone and would never do something solely to please somebody else. He did not care if people were sad or upset about him. He appeared almost to enjoy people being angry with him while they tried to teach him, as if this were a pleasurable sensation which he tried to provoke by negativism and disobedience.[9]

Fritz did not know the meaning of respect and was utterly indifferent to the authority of adults. He lacked distance and talked without shyness even to strangers. Although he acquired language very early, it was impossible to teach him the polite form of address ('Sie'). He called everybody 'Du'. Another strange phenomenon in this boy was the occurrence of certain stereotypic movements and habits.[10]

Family history

The mother stemmed from the family of one of the greatest Austrian poets. Her side of the family were mostly intellectuals and all were, according to her, in the mad-genius mould. Several wrote poetry 'quite beautifully'. A sister of the maternal grandfather, 'a brilliant pedagogue', lived as an eccentric recluse. The maternal grandfather and several of his relatives had been expelled from state schools and had to attend private school. Fritz strongly resembled this grandfather. He too was said to have been an exceptionally difficult child and now rather resembled the caricature of a

---

[8] While conduct problems are highly prominent symptoms in Asperger's cases, they are not in Kanner's sample although the problems mentioned there do include aggressive and destructive behaviour. This difference can perhaps be explained by the more child-centred attitudes prevalent in the United States at the time, while in Europe the instilling of respect and discipline had remained a major aspect of education.

[9] The social impairment described here closely resembles the picture of the 'odd' rather than the 'aloof' or 'passive' type, using Wing and Gould's (1979) terminology.

[10] Examples later on show that Fritz's stereotypic (repetitive) movements and habits include jumping, hitting and echoing speech. The critical feature of such activity is its fragmentary nature. Often it seems to be generated without external provocation.

scholar, preoccupied with his own thoughts and out of touch with the real world.

The mother herself was very similar to the boy. This similarity was particularly striking given that she was a woman, since, in general, one would expect a higher degree of intuitive social adaptation in women, more emotion than intellect. In the way she moved and spoke, indeed in her whole demeanour, she seemed strange and rather a loner. Very characteristic, for instance, was the situation when mother and son walked to the hospital school together, but each by themselves. The mother slouched along, hands held behind her back and apparently oblivious to the world. Beside her the boy was rushing to and fro, doing mischief. They gave the appearance of having absolutely nothing to do with each other.[11] One could not help thinking that the mother found it difficult to cope not only with her child but with the practical matters of life. She was certainly not up to running the household. Even living, as she did, in the upper echelons of society, she always looked unkempt, unwashed almost, and was always badly dressed.[12] She was also, clearly, not coping with the physical care of her son. It has to be said, however, that this was a particularly difficult problem. The mother knew her son through and through and understood his difficulties very well. She tried to find similar traits in herself and in her relations and talked about this eloquently. She emphasised again and again that she was at the end of her tether, and this was indeed obvious as soon as one saw them both together.

It was clear that this state of affairs was due not only to the boy's own internally caused problems, but also to the mother's own problems in relating to the outside world, showing as she did a limited intuitive social understanding. Take the following typical trait: whenever things became too much for her at home she would simply walk out on her family and travel to her beloved mountains. She would stay there for a week or more at a time, leaving the rest of the family to struggle for themselves.

The boy's father came from an ordinary farming family, with no reported peculiarities. He had made a successful career for himself, eventually becoming a high-ranking civil servant. He married late and was fifty-five years old when his first child was born. The father was a withdrawn and reticent man who did not give much away about himself. He clearly hated to talk about himself and his interests. He was extremely correct and pedantic and kept a more than usual distance.

---

[11] It is interesting to compare Kanner and Eisenberg's (1955) description of the autistic boy George and his mother: 'As they come up the stairs, the child trails forlornly behind the mother, who does not bother to look back'. Here the authors seem to sympathise with the child while being somewhat censorious of the mother. Asperger instead points out the similarity of mother and son in the way they ignore each other.

[12] Kanner and Eisenberg's (1955) account of George's mother is again strikingly similar: 'His mother, a college graduate, looked bedraggled at the time of the first visit. She felt futile about herself, was overwhelmed by her family responsibilities and gave the impression of drabness and ineffectualness.'

Appearance and expressive characteristics

The boy was of a rather delicate build and very tall, 11 cm above the average height for his age. He was thin, fine-boned and his musculature was weakly developed. His skin was of yellowish-grey pallor. The veins were clearly visible on the temples and upper parts of the body. His posture was slouched, his shoulders slumped, with the shoulder blades protruding. Otherwise his appearance was unremarkable. The face showed fine and aristocratic features, prematurely differentiated in a six-year-old. Any baby features had long since gone.

His eye gaze was strikingly odd.[13] It was generally directed into the void, but was occasionally interrupted by a momentary malignant glimmer. When somebody was talking to him he did not enter into the sort of eye contact which would normally be fundamental to conversation. He darted short 'peripheral' looks and glanced at both people and objects only fleetingly. It was 'as if he wasn't there'. The same impression could be gained of his voice, which was high and thin and sounded far away. The normal speech melody, the natural flow of speech, was missing. Most of the time, he spoke very slowly, dragging out certain words for an exceptionally long time. He also showed increased modulation so that his speech was often sing-song.

The content of his speech too was completely different from what one would expect of a normal child: only rarely was what he said in answer to a question. One usually had to ask a question many times before it registered. When he did answer, once in a while, the answer was as short as possible. Often, however, it was sheer luck if he reacted at all! Either he simply did not answer, or he turned away while beating a rhythm or indulging in some other stereotypic behaviour. Occasionally, he repeated the question or a single word from the question that had apparently made an impression on him; sometimes he sang, 'I don't like to say that . . .'.

Behaviour on the ward

Posture, eye gaze, voice and speech made it obvious at first glance that the boy's relations to the outside world were extremely limited. This was instantly apparent also in his behaviour with other children. From the moment he set foot on the ward he stood out from the rest of the group, and this did not change. He remained an outsider and never took much notice of the world around him. It was impossible to get him to join in group play, but neither could he play properly by himself. He just did not know what to do with the toys he was given. For instance, he put building blocks in his mouth and chewed them, or he threw them under the beds. The noise this created seemed to give him pleasure.[14]

---

[13] Kanner (1943) does not dwell much on peculiarity of gaze in his first case descriptions, but a clear reference to the same phenomenon that Asperger describes appears in the case of Virginia: 'She responded when called by getting up and coming nearer, without even looking up to the person who called her. She just stood listlessly, looking into space.'

[14] In comparison, Donald (Kanner's first case, described in 1943) 'had a disinclination to play with children and do things children his age usually take an interest in'. Further, 'he kept throwing things on the floor, seeming to delight in the sounds they made.'

While appropriate reactions to people, things and situations were largely absent, he gave full rein to his own internally generated impulses. These were unrelated to outside stimuli. Most conspicuous in this respect were his stereotypic movements: he would suddenly start to beat rhythmically on his thighs, bang loudly on the table, hit the wall, hit another person or jump around the room. He would do this without taking any notice of the amazement of those around him. For the most part, these impulses occurred out of the blue, but sometimes they were provoked, for instance, when certain demands were made which acted as undesirable intrusions into his encapsulated personality. Even when one was able to get him to respond for a short time, it was not long before he became unhappy, and there would eventually be an outburst of shouts or odd stereotypic movements. On other occasions, it was sheer restlessness which seemed to drive him to engage in stereotypic behaviour. Whenever the ward was in a noisy, happy or restless mood, for instance, when there was a competitive game going on, then one could be sure that he would soon break out of the group and start jumping or hitting.

In addition to these problems there were also various nasty and unacceptable habits. He 'ate' the most impossible things, for example, whole pencils, wood and lead, or paper, in considerable quantities. Not surprisingly, he frequently had stomach problems. He was in the habit of licking the table and then playing around with his spit. He also committed the mischievous acts which are characteristic of this type of child.[15] The same boy who sat there listlessly with an absent look on his face would suddenly jump up with his eyes lit up, and before one could do anything, he would have done something mischievous. Perhaps he would knock everything off the table or bash another child. Of course he would always choose the smaller, more helpless ones to hit, who became very afraid of him. Perhaps he would turn on the lights or the water, or suddenly run away from his mother or another accompanying adult, to be caught only with difficulty. Then again, he may have thrown himself into a puddle so that he would be spattered with mud from head to foot. These impulsive acts occurred without any warning and were therefore extremely difficult to manage or control. In each of these situations it was always the worst, most embarrassing, most dangerous thing that happened. The boy seemed to have a special sense for this, and yet he appeared to take hardly any notice of the world around him! No wonder the malicious behaviour of these children so often appears altogether 'calculated'.[16]

As one would expect, the conduct disorders were particularly gross when demands were made on him, for instance, when one tried to give him

[15] Kanner (1943) does not talk of mischievous behaviour. However, Donald showed behaviour that Asperger would almost certainly have labelled spiteful: 'He still went on chewing on paper, putting food on his hair, throwing books into the toilet, putting a key down the water drain, climbing onto the table and bureau, having temper tantrums.'

[16] One of the most controversial of Asperger's ideas is his contention that the autistic children he describes display intentionally spiteful or malicious behaviour. This idea has to be seen together with his other observations of the children's general indifference to other people's feelings. Examples that Asperger gives suggest that the child had only a physical effect in mind, not a psychological one, as, for instance, when Fritz provoked his teacher because he enjoyed seeing her display anger.

something to do or to teach him something. This was regardless of whether he was in a group with other children or on his own. It required great skill to make him join some physical exercise or work even for a short while. Apart from his intransigence to any requests, he was not good at PE because he was motorically very clumsy. He was never physically relaxed. He never 'swung' in any rhythm. He had no mastery over his body. It was not surprising, therefore, that he constantly tried to run away from the PE group or from the work-table. It was particularly in these situations that he would start jumping, hitting, climbing on the beds or begin some stereotyped sing-song.

Similar difficulties were encountered when one worked with him on his own. An example was his behaviour during intelligence tests. It turned out that it was impossible to get a good idea of his true intellectual abilities using standard intelligence tests. The results were highly contradictory. His failure to respond to particular test questions seemed to be a matter of chance and a result of his profound contact disturbance. Testing was extremely difficult to carry out. He constantly jumped up or smacked the experimenter on the hand. He would repeatedly drop himself from chair to floor and then enjoy being firmly placed back in his chair again. Often, instead of answering a question, he said 'Nothing at all, nobody at all', grinning horridly. Occasionally he stereotypically repeated the question or a meaningless word or perhaps a word he made up. Questions and requests had to be repeated constantly. It was a matter of luck to catch him at exactly the moment he was ready to respond, when he would occasionally perform considerably in advance of his age. Some examples are given below.

CONSTRUCTION TEST   (a figure made out of sticks, and consisting of two squares and four triangles, is exposed for a few seconds and has to be copied from memory). Even though he had only half-glanced at this figure, he correctly constructed it within a few seconds, or rather, he threw the little sticks so that it was perfectly possible to recognise the correct figure, but he could not be persuaded to arrange them properly.

RHYTHM IMITATION   (various rhythms are beaten out to be copied). In spite of many attempts he could not be persuaded to do this task.

MEMORY FOR DIGITS   He very readily repeated six digits. One was left with a strong impression that he could go further, except that he just did not feel like it. According to the Binet test, the repetition of six digits is expected at the age of ten, while the boy was only six years old.

MEMORY FOR SENTENCES   This test too could not be properly evaluated. He deliberately repeated wrongly many of the sentences. However, it was clear that he could achieve at least age-appropriate performance.

SIMILARITIES   Some questions were not answered at all, others got a nonsensical answer. For instance, for the item tree and bush, he just said, 'There is a difference'. For fly and butterfly, he said, 'Because he has a different name', 'Because the butterfly is snowed, snowed with snow'; asked about the colour, he said, 'Because he is red and blue, and the fly is brown and black'. For the item wood and glass, he answered, 'Because the glass is more glassy and the wood is more woody'. For cow and calf, he replied, 'lammerlammerlammer . . . '. To the question 'Which is the bigger one?' he said, 'The cow I would like to have the pen now'.

Enough examples from the intelligence test. We did not obtain an accurate picture of the boy's intellectual abilities. This, of course, was hardly to be expected. First, he rarely reacted to stimuli appropriately but followed his own internally generated impulses. Secondly, he could not engage in the lively reciprocity of normal social interaction. In order to judge his abilities it was therefore necessary to look at his spontaneous productions.

As the parents had already pointed out, he often surprised us with remarks that betrayed an excellent apprehension of a situation and an accurate judgement of people. This was the more amazing as he apparently never took any notice of his environment. Above all, from very early on he had shown an interest in numbers and calculations. He had learnt to count to over 100 and was able to calculate within that number-space with great fluency. This was without anybody ever having tried to teach him – apart from answering occasional questions he asked. His extraordinary calculating ability had been reported by the parents and was verified by us. Incidentally, we found, in general, that the parents had an excellent understanding of their child's intellectual abilities. Such knowledge as the boy possessed was not accessible by questioning at will. Rather, it showed itself accidentally, especially during his time on the ward, where he was given individual tuition. Even before any systematic teaching had begun, he had mastered calculations with numbers over ten. Of course, quite a number of bright children are able to do this before starting school at six. However, his ability to use fractions was unusual, and was revealed quite incidentally during his first year of instruction. The mother reported that at the very beginning of schooling he set himself the problem – what is bigger $\frac{1}{16}$ or $\frac{1}{18}$ – and then solved it with ease. When somebody asked for fun, just to test the limits of his ability, 'What is $\frac{2}{3}$ of 120?', he instantly gave the right answer, '80'. Similarly, he surprised everybody with his grasp of the concept of negative numbers, which he had apparently gained wholly by himself; it came out with his remark that 3 minus 5 equals '2 under zero'. At the end of the first school year, he was also fluent in solving problems of the type, 'If 2 workers do a job in a certain amount of time, how much time do 6 workers need?'

We see here something that we have come across in almost all autistic individuals, a special interest which enables them to achieve quite extraordinary levels of performance in a certain area. This, then, throws some light on the question of their intelligence. However, even now the answer remains problematic since the findings can be contradictory and different testers can come to different intelligence estimates. Clearly, it is possible to consider such individuals both as child prodigies and as imbeciles with ample justification.[17]

Now, a word about the boy's relations to people. At first glance, it seemed as if these did not exist or existed only in a negative sense, in mischief and aggression. This, however, was not quite true. Again, accidentally, on rare occasions, he showed that he knew intuitively, and indeed unfailingly, which person really meant well by him, and would even reciprocate at times. For instance, he would declare that he loved his teacher on the ward, and now and then he hugged a nurse in a rare wave of affection.

Implications of remedial education

It is obvious that in the present case there were particularly difficult educational problems. Let us consider first the essential prerequisites which make a normal child learn and integrate into school life, in terms not just of the subject matter taught, but also of the appropriate social behaviour. Learning the appropriate behaviour does not depend primarily on intellectual understanding. Well before the child can understand the spoken words of his teacher, even in early infancy, he learns to comply. He complies with and responds to the glance of the mother, the tone of her voice, the look of her face, and to her gestures rather than the words themselves. In short, he learns to respond to the infinitely rich display of human expressive phenomena. While the young child cannot understand this consciously, he none the less behaves accordingly. The child stands in uninterrupted reciprocity with his care-giver, constantly building up his own responses and modifying them according to the positive or negative outcome of his encounters. Clearly, an undisturbed relationship with his environment is an essential requirement. In Fritz's case, however, it is precisely this wonderful regulating mechanism which is severely disturbed. It is a sign of this disturbance that Fritz's expressions themselves are abnormal. How odd is his use of eye contact! Normally, a great deal of the outside world is received by the eye and communicated by the eye to others. How odd is his voice, how odd his manner of speaking and his way of moving! It is no surprise, therefore, that this boy also lacks understanding of other people's expressions and cannot react to them appropriately.[18]

[17] Asperger and Kanner were both impressed by the isolated special abilities found in almost all their cases. Fritz shows superior rote memory and calculating ability; Donald likewise has excellent rote memory and could count to 100 at the age of five.

[18] Recent findings of an impairment in the understanding of emotion in voice and face confirm Asperger's impression. See Hobson (1989) for a review of research and theoretical interpretation. Asperger believed autistic children to have a disturbed relation to the environment in general, and not merely to the social environment. It follows that their lack of emotional understanding is a consequence of the same underlying problem (that is, contact disturbance) which also results in their helplessness in practical matters of everyday life. Kanner (1943), instead, contrasts the 'excellent relation to objects with the non-existent relation to people', a highly influential view which has become the basis of many theories of autism.

Let us consider this issue again from a different point of view. It is not the content of words that makes a child comply with requests, by processing them intellectually. It is, above all, the affect of the care-giver which speaks through the words. Therefore, when making requests, it does not really matter what the care-giver says or how well-founded the request is. The point is not to demonstrate the necessity of compliance and consequence of non-compliance – only bad teachers do this. What matters is the way in which the request is made, that is, how powerful the affects are which underlie the words. These affects can be understood even by the infant, the foreigner or the animal, none of whom is able to comprehend the literal meaning.

In our particular case, as indeed, in all such cases, the affective side was disturbed to a large extent, as should have become apparent from the description so far. The boy's emotions were indeed hard to comprehend. It was almost impossible to know what would make him laugh or jump up and down with happiness, and what would make him angry and aggressive. It was impossible to know what feelings were the basis of his stereotypic activities or what it was that could suddenly make him affectionate. So much of what he did was abrupt and seemed to have no basis in the situation itself. Since the affectivity of the boy was so deviant and it was hard to understand his feelings, it is not surprising that his reactions to the feelings of his care-givers were also inappropriate.[19]

In fact, it is typical of children such as Fritz V. that they do not comply with requests or orders that are affectively charged with anger, kindness, persuasion or flattery. Instead, they respond with negativistic, naughty and aggressive behaviour. While demonstrations of love, affection and flattery are pleasing to normal children and often induce in them the desired behaviour, such approaches only succeeded in irritating Fritz, as well as all other similar children. While anger and threats usually succeed in bending obstinacy in normal children and often make them compliant after all, the opposite is true of autistic children. For them, the affect of the care-giver may provide a sensation which they relish and thus seek to provoke. 'I am so horrible because you are cross so nicely', said one such boy to his teacher.

It is difficult to know what the appropriate pedagogic approach should be. As with all genuine teaching, it should not be based primarily on logical deduction but rather on pedagogic intuition. Nevertheless, it is possible to state a few principles which are based on our experience with such children.

The first is that all educational transactions have to be done with the affect 'turned off'. The teacher must never become angry nor should he aim to become loved. It will never do to appear quiet and calm on the outside while one is boiling inside. Yet this is only too likely, given the negativism and seemingly calculated naughtiness of autistic children! The teacher must

---

[19] From Asperger's descriptions throughout it is clear that he believed autistic children to be capable of having strong feelings, and to be disturbed only in their ability to manifest such feelings appropriately.

at all costs be calm and collected and must remain in control. He should give his instructions in a cool and objective manner, without being intrusive. A lesson with such a child may look easy and appear to run along in a calm, self-evident manner. It may even seem that the child is simply allowed to get away with everything, any teaching being merely incidental. Nothing could be further from the truth. In reality, the guidance of these children requires a high degree of effort and concentration. The teacher needs a particular inner strength and confidence which is not at all easy to maintain!

There is a great danger of getting involved in endless arguments with these children, be it in order to prove that they are wrong or to bring them towards some insight. This is especially true for the parents, who frequently find themselves trapped in endless discussions. On the other hand, it often works simply to cut short negativistic talk: for example, Fritz is tired of doing sums and sings, 'I don't want to do sums any more, I don't want to do sums any more', the teacher replies, 'No, you don't need to do sums', and continuing in the same calm tone of voice, 'How much is . . .?' Primitive as they are, such methods are, in our experience, often successful.

There is an important point to be made here. Paradoxical as it may seem, the children are negativistic and highly suggestible at the same time. Indeed, there is a kind of automatic or reflex obedience. This behaviour is known to occur in schizophrenics. It could well be that these two disorders of the will are closely related! With our children we have repeatedly found that if one makes requests in an automaton-like and stereotyped way, for instance, speaking softly in the same sing-song that they use themselves, one senses that they have to obey, seemingly unable to resist the command. Another pedagogic trick is to announce any educational measures not as personal requests, but as objective impersonal law. But more of this later.

I have already mentioned that behind the cool and objective interaction with Fritz and all similar children there needs to be genuine care and kindness if one wants to achieve anything at all. These children often show a surprising sensitivity to the personality of the teacher. However difficult they are even under optimal conditions, they can be guided and taught, but only by those who give them true understanding and genuine affection, people who show kindness towards them and, yes, humour. The teacher's underlying emotional attitude influences, involuntarily and unconsciously, the mood and behaviour of the child. Of course, the management and guidance of such children essentially requires a proper knowledge of their peculiarities as well as genuine pedagogic talent and experience. Mere teaching efficiency is not enough.

It was clear from the start that Fritz, with his considerable problems, could not be taught in a class. For one thing, any degree of restlessness around him would have irritated him and made concentration impossible. For another, he himself would have disrupted the class and destroyed work done by the others. Consider only his negativism and his uninhibited, impulsive behaviour. This is why we gave him a personal tutor on the ward, with the consent of the educational authority. Even then, teaching was not easy, as should be clear from the above remarks. Even mathematics lessons were problematic when, given his special talent in this area, one might have expected an easier time. Of course, if a problem turned up which happened to interest him at that moment (see previous examples), then he 'tuned in' and surprised us all by his quick and excellent grasp. However, ordinary mathematics – sums – made for much tedious effort. As we will see with the other cases even with the brightest children of this type, the automatisation of learning, that is, the setting up of routine thought processes, proceeds only with the utmost difficulty. Writing was an especially difficult subject, as we expected, because his motor clumsiness, in addition to his general problems, hampered him a good deal. In his tense fist the pencil could not run smoothly. A whole page would suddenly become covered with big swirls, the exercise book would be drilled full of holes, if not torn up. In the end it was possible to teach him to write only by making him trace letters and words which were written in red pencil. This was to guide him to make the right movements. However, his handwriting has so far been atrocious. Orthography too was difficult to automatise. He used to write the whole sentence in one go, without separating the words. He was able to spell correctly when forced to be careful. However, he made the silliest mistakes when left to his own devices. Learning to read, in particular sounding out words, proceeded with moderate difficulties. It was almost impossible to teach him the simple skills needed in everyday life. While observing such a lesson, one could not help feeling that he was not listening at all, only making mischief. It was, therefore, the more surprising, as became apparent occasionally, for example through reports from the mother, that he had managed to learn quite a lot. It was typical of Fritz, as of all similar children, that he seemed to see a lot using only 'peripheral vision', or to take in things 'from the edge of attention'. Yet these children are able to analyse and retain what they catch in such glimpses. Their active and passive attention is very disturbed; they have difficulty in retrieving their knowledge, which is revealed often only by chance. Nevertheless, their thoughts can be unusually rich. They are good at logical thinking, and the ability to abstract is particularly good. It does often seem that even in perfectly normal people an increased distance to the outside world is a prerequisite for excellence in abstract thinking.

Despite the difficulties we had in teaching this boy we managed to get him to pass successfully a state school examination at the end of the school year. The exceptional examination situation was powerful enough to make him more or less behave himself, and he showed good concentration. Naturally, he astounded the examiners in mathematics. Now Fritz attends the third form of a primary school as an external pupil, without having lost a school year so far. Whether and when he will be able to visit a secondary school we do not know.

Differential diagnosis

Considering the highly abnormal behaviour of Fritz, one has to ask whether there is in fact some more severe disturbance and not merely a personality disorder. There are two possibilities: childhood schizophrenia and a post-encephalitic state.

There is much that is reminiscent of schizophrenia in Fritz: the extremely limited contact, the automaton-like behaviour, the stereotypies. Against this diagnosis, however, speaks the fact that there is no sign of progressive deterioration, no characteristic acute onset of alarming florid symptoms (severe anxiety and hallucinations), nor are there any delusions. Although Fritz shows a very deviant personality, his personality remains the same and can largely be seen as deriving from father and mother, and their families. In fact, his personality shows steady development, and on the whole this is resulting in improved adaptation to the environment. Lastly, the complex overall clinical impression, which cannot be pinned down further, is completely different from that of a schizophrenic. There, one has the uncanny feeling of a destruction of personality which remains incomprehensible and incalculable, even if it is perhaps possible to some extent to stave off disintegration through pedagogic means. Here, however, there are numerous genuine relationships, a degree of reciprocal understanding and a genuine chance for remedial education.

One has also to consider the possibility of a post-encephalitic personality disorder. As we shall see below, there are a number of similarities between autistic children and brain-damaged children who either had a birth injury or encephalitis. Suffice it to say here that there was no reason for thinking this applied in the case of Fritz. There were certainly none of the symptoms that are always present in post-encephalitic cases (though these are sometimes easily overlooked). There was not the slightest evidence of neurological or vegetative symptoms such as strabismus, facial rigidity, subtle spastic paresis, increased salivation or other endocrine signs.

Harro L.

Our second case is a boy who also shows the main characteristics of autism in highly typical form, except that the relationships to the outside world are not as severely disturbed as in our first case. Instead, the positive aspects of autism become more obvious: the independence in thought, experience and speech.

This eight-and-a-half-year-old boy was referred to us by his school as unmanageable.[20] He was in his third year at school, but was repeating the second year because he had failed in all subjects.[21] The teacher believed that he 'could if he only wanted to'. Occasionally, he made surprisingly clever remarks of a maturity way beyond his age. On the other hand, he often refused to co-operate, sometimes using bad language, for example, 'this is far too stupid for me', which threatened to undermine the discipline of the whole class. He hardly ever did his homework. Worse still were his

[20] As in the case of Fritz V., conduct problems seem to have been the main reason for referral.
[21] Failure to reach the required standard at the end of the school year resulted in repetition. The child was placed with a younger age group going through the same syllabus again. This would have carried a stigma for the family and the child.

conduct problems. He rarely did what he was told but answered back and with such cheek that the teacher had given up asking him so as not to lose face in front of the class. On the one hand, Harro did not do what he was supposed to do, on the other, he did exactly what he wanted to do himself and without considering the consequences. He left his desk during lessons and crawled on the floor on all fours. One of the principal reasons for his being referred by the school was his savage tendency to fight. Little things drove him to senseless fury, whereupon he attacked other children, gnashing his teeth and hitting out blindly. This was dangerous because he was not a skilled fighter. Children who are skilled fighters know exactly how far they can go and can control their movements so that they hardly ever cause real trouble. Harro was anything but a skilled fighter, and since he was very clumsy, could not control his movements and had no idea where to aim, he often allegedly caused injury to others. He was said to be extremely sensitive to teasing, and yet in many ways, with his strange and comical behaviour he directly provoked teasing.

He was said to be an inveterate 'liar'. He did not lie in order to get out of something that he had done – this was certainly not the problem, as he always told the truth very brazenly – but he told long, fantastic stories, his confabulations becoming ever more strange and incoherent.[22]

His early independence in certain things was outstanding. Since his second school year, that is, since he was only seven years old, he had travelled alone by train to school in Vienna. His parents lived in a village approximately 25 km from Vienna. The father, who wanted his son to have better opportunities, disdained the village school and therefore sent him to school in Vienna.

On a more unpleasant note, Harro also showed his social unconcern in sexual play with other boys, allegedly going as far as homosexual acts, coitus attempts.

From the family history, we note that Harro was an only child. He was a forceps delivery, but no disturbances were observed that might relate to any birth injury. His mental and physical development was unremarkable. As a small child, he was supposed to have been perfectly ordinary, except that his stubbornness and independence were evident very early.

The father, who brought the child to us, was a strange man, and very similar to his son. He appeared to be something of an adventurer. He originally came from Siebenburgen (Transylvania) and during the First World War, under great danger from the Romanian army, fled to Austria via Russia. By profession he was a painter and sculptor, but out of financial necessity he was making brooms and brushes. While there was severe unemployment at the time we saw the boy, the contrast of the two jobs was certainly striking. The father, who himself comes from peasant stock, is a typical intellectual. He professed to be completely and painfully self-

[22] Sadly, examples of fantastic stories told by Harro are not given. In their absence it is difficult to know whether these stories were imaginative in the ordinary sense of the word, that is whether Harro was fully aware of their fictitious nature. Donald (Kanner's first case) was also said by his mother to dramatise stories, again without examples to illustrate what was meant by this.

taught. One could make out from what he said that he had nothing to do with anyone in the village where he lived and where he must have been considered highly eccentric. He said himself that he was nervous and highly strung but that 'he controlled himself to such an extent that he appeared to be indifferent'.

The mother, whom we never saw (we felt that the father did not want us to see her) was also supposed to be highly strung. In both the father's and mother's families there were said to be many highly strung people. No more details were obtained.

Appearance and expressive characteristics

Harro was a rather small boy, 4 cm below average in height, and of stocky and muscular build. His arms and legs looked as if they were too short for his body. In some ways, he looked like a miniature adult, especially since his facial features were very mature. His typically lost gaze was often far away. Sometimes he appeared to be in deep thought, then he would draw together his brows and assume a strange, slightly funny dignity. His posture too was odd. He stood broadly, arms held away from the body, as a portly gentleman or a boxer might do. He had few facial expressions and gestures. His dignified seriousness was only rarely interrupted, for instance, when he secretly laughed to himself. It was usually impossible to make out what had struck him as funny at that moment.

His voice fitted this picture well. It was very deep and appeared to come from very far down, in the abdomen. He talked slowly and in a deadpan way without much modulation. He never looked at his interlocutor while talking. His gaze was far away. With a tense, even cramped, facial expression, he tried to formulate his thoughts. In this, he succeeded remarkably well. He had an unusually mature and adult manner of expressing himself, not, as one occasionally sees in children, by using ready-made copied phrases, but drawn from his own quite unchildlike experience. It was as if he coined each word to fit the moment. Often he did not *respond* to questions but let his talk run single-mindedly along his own tracks. He could describe his own experiences or feelings with an unusual degree of introspection. He could look at himself as a detached critical observer ('I am dreadfully left-handed').[23] Although he was aloof from things and people – or perhaps because of this – he had rich experiences and his own independent interests.[24] It was possible to talk to him as to an adult, and one could really learn from him. This phenomenon is well demonstrated by his behaviour during intelligence testing, as described below.

Intelligence testing

First, some general remarks about the testing methods that we use in our department. The main difference from traditional testing (for example, the

[23] 'Ich bin ein ganz fürchterlicher Linkser'.
[24] Harro's social impairment included being aloof as well as odd. He showed, for instance, aggressive disrespect for teachers, and kept himself apart from his peers.

Binet test, from which we have taken some subtests) is that we use a clinical approach where we are not interested merely in the passing and failing of single tests but, instead, in the qualitative aspects of performance. First we score the performance according to the level reached, and represent this graphically to obtain a test profile. In this way, one can see the discrepancies between the performances in various tests, which would otherwise have been submerged in the overall IQ score.[25] More importantly, we observe *how* the child solves various problems, his method of working, his individual tempo, his concentration and, above all, his ability to relate and communicate. We adapt the way we test according to the personality of the child, and we try to build up good rapport. Of course, every good tester would do this anyway. Thus, it is important to help the anxious, inhibited child who lacks self-confidence, for example, by starting off the task for him or by helping him along. The chatty and hyperactive child, or the child who does not keep a distance, on the other hand, has to be restrained and somehow made to do the required work. Obviously, any help given needs to be taken into account later when scoring, which is not easy. We also try to find out what special interests each child may have. We always let the children produce something spontaneously, and we let them expand on their responses by asking more questions. If there is a particular failure or if there are specific problems on some subtest, then we ask questions that are not part of standard procedure until we have clarified the reason for the difficulty.

This method of testing demands much greater experience than schematically laid down methods with rigid scoring. However, if carried out well, it can tell us not only about the intellectual ability of the child, but also about important personality functions.

It was almost as difficult to carry out the testing with Harro as it was with Fritz. Very often, he shut off completely when a question did not interest him. Sometimes he did not seem to hear the question. A lot of energy went into simply making him do the tasks. Again and again he went off on a tangent and had to be brought back. However, once his attention was engaged, his performance could be remarkably good.

Any tests that did not yield anything of special interest will be omitted, but I will describe in detail the results of the similarities subtest. Here, where Harro was able to produce answers spontaneously, he became lively and interested, and one even had to cut him off, since he threatened to go on for ever.

TREE/BUSH   'The bush, that is where the branches grow straight off the ground, completely jumbled up, so that it can happen that three or four cross over each other, so that one has a knot in one's hand. The tree, that is where there is first a stem and only then the branches, and not so jumbled up, and rather thick branches. This happened to me once, that is where I

[25] The examples Asperger gives of IQ test questions are chosen to illustrate the quality of the autistic child's way of thinking, but they do not go beyond a clinical impression. His colleague Elisabeth Wurst, in 1976, published profiles of IQ test performance which show a characteristically uneven pattern such as is generally found in autism. The nature of this pattern is discussed in Frith (1989).

cut into a bush, I wanted to make myself a sling, I cut off four branches and then I have an eight-part knot in my hand. This comes when two branches rub against each other, then there is a wound there, then they grow together.'

STAIRS/LADDER 'Stairs are made out of stone. One doesn't call them rungs, they are called steps, because they are much bigger, and on the ladder they are thinner and smaller and round. It is much more comfortable on the stairs than on the ladder.'

STOVE/OVEN 'The stove is what one has in the room as a firebringer(!) and the oven is where you cook something.'

LAKE/RIVER 'Well, the lake, it doesn't move from its spot, and it can never be as long and never have that many branches, and it always has an end somewhere. One can't compare at all the Danube with the Ossiach Lake in Corinthia – not in the least little bit.'

GLASS/WOOD 'Glass is transparent. Wood, if you wanted to look through it, you would have to make a hole in it. If one wants to beat on a piece of wood then one has to beat a long time until it breaks, unless it's a dry twig. Then that would break easily. With the glass you need to hit only twice and then it's broken.'

FLY/BUTTERFLY 'The butterfly is colourful, the fly is black. The butterfly has big wings so that two flies could go underneath one wing. But the fly is much more skilful and can walk up the slippery glass and can walk up the wall. And it has a completely different development! [Now he becomes over-enthusiastic, talks with exaggerated emphasis.] The fly mother lays many, many eggs in a gap in the floorboards and then a few days later the maggots crawl out. I have read this once in a book, where the floor talks – I could die laughing [!] when I think of it – what is looking out of this little tub? A giant head with a tiny body and a trunk like an elephant? And then a few days later they cocoon themselves in and then suddenly there are some dear little flies crawling out. And then the microscope explains how the fly can walk up the wall: just yesterday I saw it has teeny weeny claws on the feet and at the ends tiny little hooks; when it feels that it slips, then it hooks itself up with the hooks. And the butterfly does not grow up in the room as the fly does. I have not read anything about that and I know nothing about it (!), but I believe (!) that the butterfly will take much longer with his development.'

ENVY/MEANNESS 'The mean one has something and doesn't want to give it away, and the envious one wants to have what the other one has.'[26]

---

[26] Asperger believes that his examples of answers to the similarity questions demonstrate depth and originality of thinking. However, a striking feature of the answers is their seamless mixture of general knowledge and personal memory. Perhaps this indicates that the children had little idea of the purpose of the questions. The normal listener would realise that general questions require general answers, and refrain from recounting specific autobiographical incidents.

School attainment tests

Since most children who come to us for observation also have learning difficulties, we frequently use scholastic attainment tests. Naturally, we are aware of environmental influences here, for example, neglect of educational needs. Incidentally, when do environmental influences not play a role where test performances are concerned? It is a grave error to think that the responses to Binet tests come entirely from within the child and show no environmental effects!

READING   He read a story shoddily and with errors. However, one could notice clearly that he read for meaning and that the content of the story interested him. He wanted to read faster than he was able to and for this reason was not very accurate. As this observation suggests his *reading comprehension* was excellent. He could reproduce what he had read in his own words, and he could say what the moral of a story was even though the moral was not explicitly presented in the text (the fable of the fox who was punished for his vanity).

WRITING TO DICTATION   His handwriting, as to be expected from his general clumsiness, was very poor. He carried on writing carelessly and messily, crossing out words, lines going up and down, the slant changing. His spelling was reasonably accurate. As long as his attention was focused on a word, he knew how to spell it. It was very significant, then, that he made more spelling errors when *copying* than at dictation. Really, one would expect that copying should not present any problems at all, since, after all, the word was there in front of him; but this very simple and straightforward task simply did not interest him.

MATHEMATICS   Here his 'autistic originality' was particularly evident. A few examples:

> 27 and 12 equals 39. He spontaneously explained how he had worked this out: '2 times 12 equals 24, 3 times 12 equals 36, I remember the 3 [he means 27 is 3 more than 2 times 12], and carry on.'

> 58 plus 34 equals 92. 'Better: 60 plus 32, I always go for the tens.'

> 34 minus 12 equals 22. '34 plus 2 equals 36, minus 12 equals 24, minus 2 equals 22, this way I worked it out more quickly than any other.'

> 47 minus 15 equals 32. 'Either add 3 and also add 3 to that which should be taken away, or first take away 7 and then 8.'

> 52 minus 25 equals 27. '2 times 25 equals 50, plus 2 equals 52, 25 plus 2 equals 27.'

> A word problem (consider that the boy was only eight-and-a-half years old, and was only in the second year of the primary school!). A

bottle with a cork costs 1.10 schillings, the bottle costs just one more schilling than the cork, how much does each cost? After five seconds he gave the correct solution and explained when asked: 'When a bottle costs 1 schilling more, then you have to leave one schilling aside, and something of the 10 groschen still needs to be left, so I have to divide by 2, so the cork costs 5 groschen and the bottle costs 1 schilling and 5 groschen.'

Fascinating as his mastery of numbers may be, we can nevertheless see the disadvantages of his original methods. They were often so complicated – however ingenious – that they resulted in errors. To use the conventional methods that are taught at school, for example, starting with tens and then units when subtracting, did not occur to Harro.

Here we come to an important insight: in autism there is a particular difficulty in mechanical learning, indeed there is an inability to learn from adults in conventional ways. Instead, the autistic individual needs to create everything out of his own thought and experience. More often than not this results in defective performance, even in the more able autistic individuals.

In this way we can explain why such a bright boy as Harro was unable to attain the end of his form year and had to repeat it. Of course, in school he was more difficult than during individual testing, where we made allowances for his problems and provided an opportunity for him to give spontaneous and original answers. On the ward too, we were able to observe how much worse his performance was when he was taught in a group. Being taught in a group, of course means that everybody has to pay attention and do what the teacher asks. Harro could do neither of these. His mind wandered off on his own problems and he would not know what the lesson was about. He took away from the lesson only those things for which he had a particular affinity and could think about in his own way. According to the school report he hardly ever knew what homework he had to do, and could not therefore do the appropriate work at home despite the father's efforts. It is not surprising, then, that in the previous year he had not been able to advance to the next form despite his undoubted ability which was recognised by the school.[27]

Behaviour on the ward and educational treatment

The peculiarities of Harro's behaviour can all be explained in terms of his contact disturbance, that is, his extremely limited relationship to his environment. Through the length of his stay on the ward he remained a stranger. One would never see him join in a game with others. Most of the time, he sat in a corner buried in a book, oblivious to the noise or movement around him. Usually, of course, such fanatical reading is rare before the age of ten. The other children found him odd and he became an object of ridicule because of the way he looked and the 'dignity' that went

[27] Underachievement at school is commonly found in autistic children of both normal and high intellectual ability and this has been confirmed by recent research. For recent reviews see Gillberg (1989).

with it (children are particularly sensitive to this!). Nevertheless, they treated him with a certain shyness and respect, and with good reason. Any teasing by other children was met with brutal and ruthless aggression. He did not see the funny side of things and lacked any sense of humour, especially if the joke was on him.

He could be shamelessly recalcitrant when disciplinary requests were made. He always answered back, for example, 'I wouldn't even dream of doing this'. Even if he happened to be temporarily impressed by the teacher's authority, he would at least grumble to himself.

Harro did not form any close relationships, either with another child in the ward or with an adult. His interest could be engaged, and then it could be very stimulating to talk to him. Nevertheless, he never became warm, trusting or cheerful, just as the staff could never quite warm towards him, and he never became free and relaxed.

All his movements eloquently expressed his problem. His facial expressions were sparse and rigid. With this went a general stiffness and clumsiness. Nevertheless, there were no neuropathological symptoms indicating spasticity. The clumsiness was particularly well demonstrated during PE lessons. Even when he was following the group leader's instructions and trying for once to do a particular physical exercise, his movements would be ugly and angular. He was never able to swing with the rhythm of the group. His movements never unfolded naturally and spontaneously – and therefore pleasingly – from the proper co-ordination of the motor system as a whole. Instead, it seemed as if he could only manage to move those muscular parts to which he directed a conscious effort of will. What was true of many of his responses in general was also true here: nothing was spontaneous or natural, everything was 'intellectual'.[28]

Nevertheless, through patience and practice improvement was achieved in a number of practical skills. Like all autistic children, Harro was especially clumsy if not downright obstinate when it came to daily chores such as getting washed. One had to fight hard to teach him the important social habits of everyday life. The many practical skills needed in daily life present little problem to normal children. They can copy and learn them from adults with ease. This is, of course, what teachers expect. The teacher who does not understand that it is necessary to teach autistic children seemingly obvious things will feel impatient and irritated. Autistic children cannot cope with precisely such simple matters. It is impossible to say whether this is because of motor clumsiness or because of a failure to understand. Both seem to go together. Furthermore, they are particularly sensitive about personal demands, and it is far easier to engage their interest intellectually. It is not surprising, therefore, that autistic children

---

[28] Almost certainly, the ideas Asperger has in mind here are those discussed in a classic work of German literature, Heinrich von Kleist's (1810) essay about the puppet theatre. Kleist contrasted the natural grace of the unconsciously moving child with the artifice of mechanical puppetry. Similarly, Asperger contrasts 'intellectualised' behaviour, which is formal and stilted, with spontaneous behaviour, which is naturally graceful and appealing.

show negativism and malice to seemingly petty and routine demands, and that it is there that serious conflicts often arise.

How, then, should one treat these difficulties? We have already noted in the first case that more can be achieved by 'switching off' one's affect and by using an impersonal, objective style of instruction. Here, with the more able and less disturbed Harro, we found a way which we believe to be successful with more autistic children. The boy was more amenable when a request appeared not to be directed towards him in particular, but was verbally phrased in a very general, impersonal way, as an *objective law*, standing above the child and the teacher, for instance, '*One* always does such and such . . .', 'Now everyone has to . . .', 'A bright boy always does . . .'.

Another important point is this: normal children acquire the necessary social habits without being consciously aware of them, they learn instinctively. It is these instinctive relations that are disturbed in autistic children. To put it bluntly, these individuals are intelligent automata. Social adaptation has to proceed via the intellect. In fact, they have to learn everything via the intellect.[29] One has to explain and enumerate everything, where, with normal children, this would be an error of educational judgement. Autistic children have to learn the simple daily chores just like proper homework, systematically. With some children who admittedly were somewhat older than Harro, it was possible to achieve a relatively smooth integration by establishing an exact timetable in which, from the moment of rising at a particular time, every single occupation and duty was outlined in detail. When such children left the hospital they were given a timetable. It was, of course, made up in consultation with the parents and adapted to the individual needs of each family. The children had to give an account of how well they followed the timetable, sometimes by keeping a diary. They felt that they were firmly tied to this 'objective law'. In any case, many of them have pedantic tendencies veering towards the obsessional, and it was possible to use such tendencies for this regulatory purpose.

In this way Harro too achieved better adaptation, though not without difficulty. He certainly began to respond better to the demands of group teaching. Several months after he left, we heard that he was much happier at school. Unfortunately, we have not heard from him since, as his parents, we believe, have moved.

The difficulties these children have with instinctive adaptations are, then, amenable to partial compensation through an intellectualising approach. The better the intellectual ability the more successful this approach. Now, the autistic personality is certainly not only found in the intellectually able. It also occurs in the less able, even in children with severe mental

---

[29] Asperger frequently recommends learning through conscious intellectualising as the appropriate method in the education of autistic children. In the method of Heilpädagogik this form of compensatory learning would be taught only when it was clear that normal intuitive learning had failed.

retardation.[30] It is obvious that in the latter case adaptation is much more difficult to achieve. A further case will be given as an example.

Ernst K.

This seven-and-a-half-year-old boy was also referred to us by his school because of severe conduct and learning problems.

. The following points from the family history deserve to be mentioned. Birth and physical development were normal. Ernst was an only child. His speech was somewhat delayed (first words at the age of one-and-a-half). For a long time, the boy was reported to have had speech difficulties (stammering). Now, however, his speech was exceptionally good, he spoke 'like an adult'.

He was reported to have been a very difficult toddler, paying heed to neither his indulgent mother nor his strict father. He was said to be unable to cope with the ordinary demands of everyday life. The mother believed that it was because of his clumsiness and impracticality that he had more difficulties than other children. For instance, it was still necessary to dress him, since, by himself, he would dawdle endlessly and also make a lot of mistakes. He had learnt to eat by himself only recently and was still a messy eater. The mother also reported that occasionally he could be very naughty and would not do what he was told.

He was never able to get on with other children. It was impossible to go to a park with him, as he would instantly get embroiled in fighting. Apparently, he hit or verbally abused other children indiscriminately. This had become more of a problem since he started school. He acted like a red rag to his class and was teased mercilessly. However, rather than keeping away from the other children, he acted as a trouble-maker. For instance, he would pinch or tickle other children or stab them with his pen. He liked to tell fantastic stories, in which he always appeared as the hero. He would tell his mother how he was praised by the teacher in front of the class, and other similar tales.[31]

The report said that it was difficult to know how bright he was. Before he entered school, everyone was convinced that he would learn particularly well, since he was always making clever remarks and original observations. Moreover, he had by himself learnt to count to twenty, as well as picking up the names of various letters. At school, however, he failed miserably. He just managed to move up from the first form (wrongly, as we had cause to observe later), but now, in the second form, according to the teacher, he was not performing adequately. Instead of listening and answering when appropriate, he constantly argued with the teacher as to how to hold his pen. According to the report, he had a strong tendency to argue with

[30] The important insight that autism can occur at all levels of intellectual ability, including the subnormal range of intelligence, has often been overlooked, even by Asperger himself in his later papers.

[31] As in the case of Harro L., the information given does not tell us if Ernst himself believed his fantastic stories to be true or if he was aware that they were not and told them deliberately to mislead his mother.

everybody and to reprimand them. He was 'very precise': certain things always had to be in the same place, and certain events always had to happen in the same manner, or he would make a big scene.[32] There was an interesting contradiction here: in certain matters he was particularly messy and could not get used to things being done in an orderly fashion, but in others he was pedantic to the point of obsession.

Family history

The father was said to be very highly strung and irritable. By profession he was a tailor's assistant. Although we had known the boy for many years, we had seen the father only once. He was clearly eccentric and a loner. The mother did not like to talk about her domestic circumstances. However, it was plain that her life could not have been very happy due to the husband's difficult character.

The mother was a very bright and extremely nice woman whose life was not easy. She complained of nervousness and headaches. She was also very sensitive. She found it hard to cope with the fact that her son, who was obviously her one and only interest in life, was such an odd child and did so badly at school. She constantly tried to take his side against the school and fought desperately against a transfer into a special school for retarded children.

The rest of the family was said to be without any special peculiarities, the information being given with some reticence.

Appearance and behaviour

Ernst was tall (2 cm above average), very thin and delicate. His posture was slack, and his shoulders drooped. The face was handsome with finely chiselled features, marred only by large, sticking-out and somewhat misshapen ears. He was particularly vaso-labile, that is, when embarrassed or excited, there were bright red blotches on his face, sharply outlined, and big sweat drops on the ridge of his nose.

Again, the eye gaze was highly characteristic, far away and unfocused. The eye did not seem to grasp anything and was vaguely aimed into the distance. Mainly for this reason the boy looked as if he had just 'fallen from the sky'. His voice too fitted in with this. It was high, slightly nasal and drawn out, roughly like a caricature of a degenerate aristocrat (for example, the immortal Graf Bobby).[33]

It was not only his voice but his speech too which conveyed the impression bordering on caricature. Ernst talked incessantly, regardless of

---

[32] This observation clearly relates to the phenomenon which Kanner calls insistence on sameness, and which he believes to be a cardinal symptom of autism. Asperger observes but does not particularly focus on this symptom.

[33] Graf Bobby, the butt of popular jokes in German-speaking countries and particularly in Austria, is a refined aristocrat who constantly finds ordinary events incomprehensible. This image of the gentle innocent may well have been inspired by the existence of able autistic people.

the questions he was being asked. Everything he did was accompanied by elaborate explanations. He constantly justified why he did something in a particular way. He had to tell others at once whatever it was that captured his attention, whether or not the remark was relevant to the situation. Some of these 'asides' were quite remarkable, not only in the sense that they were very adult in diction, but also because they showed good observation. His practical skills, in sharp contrast, were highly inadequate. Even the simplest demands foiled him. He could recite in minute detail all the things he was doing when getting up and getting dressed in the morning, but in fact he was always forgetting or confusing things. While he could recite the theory, on a practical level his inadequacy was only too obvious.

In a group, which is meant to follow a common command, he behaved impossibly badly, especially in PE lessons. Ernst always stuck out from the group. This was not only because he was clumsy from a motor point of view but, above all, because he had no notion of discipline or appeal. He was a nuisance when he complained or was hurt, just as much as when he started to talk unconcernedly: 'Oh yes, I've got it, I know it already'.

To the very end of his stay on the ward he remained a stranger, walking between the other children without ever properly taking part in their games. At most, he would tell off one or other of them, or suddenly start a furious fight, either for no apparent reason or because somebody had teased him. Of course he was the perfect target for teasing, indeed, his whole demeanour was designed to provoke teasing. He was quite a spiteful boy, who pinched and pushed children secretly and spoiled their games. When the smaller children or the teacher were upset about this, he was only spurred on to further mischief.

He made life hard for himself by his awkwardness and endless hesitations. If something was only slightly different from the way that he had imagined it or from what he was used to, he was upset and confused and would go into long tirades. It was very difficult for the teacher to put a stop to this. He also tortured himself with his obsessive pedantries. For example, he had wanted a pullover for Christmas, but because this wish could not be granted, he was given a particularly nice shirt and some toys as well. He was inconsolable over this 'incorrectness'. He never even looked at the other presents, and was unhappy over the whole Christmas period.[34]

Intelligence and attainment testing

Apt as his remarks might have been occasionally, Ernst's whole behaviour spoke of such disturbed adaptation that we did not expect him to perform well on an IQ test. This was indeed the case.

Ernst lacked concentration to a high degree. This was not because he was distractible from outside (passive attention), but because his active

---

[34] By the examples he gives Asperger implies deeper links between insistence on sameness, obsessive pedantry, narrow preoccupations and tenaciously held ideas.

attention was disturbed. It was typical that during testing he seemed either to be somewhere else or as if he had just fallen from the sky. He was clearly not tuned in for proper responding and was clueless on most of the test questions. Thus he only managed a very poor performance even when one held him down long enough by look or by word.

Very characteristic again was the performance on the similarities subtest. Here are some examples:

FLY/BUTTERFLY 'The fly has wings like glass. From the wings of the butterfly you can make silk [this apparently referred to the silky shine]. They are colourful. The butterfly, when it gets colder goes down, and in the spring he turns into a caterpillar and then again a butterfly, first he is a cocoon and this is all silvery.' Then he talked about some events that had happened to him involving moths in his room and worms in the soup, which had nothing to do with the question.

RIVER/LAKE 'In the river the water flows, and in the lake it stands still, and on the top is green slime.'

WOOD/GLASS 'Glass breaks more easily and wood doesn't. Glass is a mass, wood is sappy and damp. It has marrow in the middle. Wood burns to ash, glass stretches apart and then melts.'

STAIRS/LADDER 'The ladder is leaning like this, and the stairs go like that, and up there like this [he draws steps by gesture]. The stairs have a kind of surface for treading on, the ladder has rungs.'

CHILD/DWARF 'The dwarf is small, the child big. The dwarf looks completely different. It has a pointed hat, but this is red. The child has a bonnet.'

Again, we found the peculiar signs of 'autistic intelligence'. Performance was best when he gave a spontaneous response, worst when he had to reproduce learnt material or do something in a prescribed manner. His knowledge of the world arose mainly out of his own experience and did not come from learning from others. This is, of course, precisely what makes the achievements of autistic people so often particularly original and delightful. With the less able children, who are much more disturbed, however, the answers are not so much valuable as deviant. The bits of knowledge that they gain accidentally from their own experience often miss the point. This is the same with their language. In the favourable case, we can often obtain especially apt and original verbal expressions. In the unfavourable case, however, the expressions tend towards neologisms and are often more abstruse than delightful.

With Ernst K. the negative aspects outweighed the positive ones, especially if we consider that he was a good half-a-year older than Harro L. His performance on similarities was by far the best he managed on the test, demonstrating as it did his independent powers of observation and experience. On the other tests, especially the school attainment tests, we could see the reverse side of 'autistic intelligence'. If somebody can only experience in an original way, and if he can only be 'his own self' rather than feel himself to be an integral part of the world – in other words, if he is not engaged in constant interaction – then he *is unable to learn*. He cannot assimilate the ready-made knowledge and skill that others present to him. He is also unable to build up 'automatic programmes' through practice and habit.

All autistic individuals, therefore, have their characteristic difficulties of automatisation. The cleverest among them can overcome their difficulties in the end by dint of sheer intellect. The more disturbed ones fail at school to a far worse extent than one would expect on the basis of their formally tested intelligence. Ernst belongs among these unfavourable cases. In all school subjects his performance was miserably poor. He could do arithmetic only with continuous concrete presentation. He did, however, count on his fingers quite skilfully and quite fast, so that occasionally he was able to simulate a competence that he did not have. His reading was very slow. He often confused letters and had the greatest difficulty in blending letters together. His comprehension of written text was, perhaps, slightly better. His most blatant failure was in writing. Like almost all autistic individuals, this motorically clumsy boy had atrocious handwriting. The pen did not obey him, it stuck and it spluttered; he corrected without concern for appearance and would simply write new letters on top of the old ones; he crossed out, and his letters varied in size. However, this was not the worst aspect of his writing. Even when copying – where he drew letter by letter with painful effort – he would make many spelling mistakes. In dictation, one could hardly recognise what the words were meant to be: letters were omitted, inserted, or put in the wrong order, and some could not be recognised at all.

On the basis of his performance, it was hard to understand how the boy could have advanced after the first school year to a higher form. The reason probably lies in his habit of constantly asking questions and talking about things that occasionally sounded quite clever. Thus, on the surface, his difficulties were disguised.

One could readily imagine that a teacher might have considered the boy to be essentially quite bright from the way he talked and would try to explain away his poor performance. The teacher might have blamed lack of attention and also considered that he did not yet know his pupil well enough after only a year at school, and, of course, he would have hoped for improvement.

It had become clear during testing that the boy's spelling deficiency was caused mainly by his inability to segment words into letters. He was unable to understand the structure of a word in terms of its individual elements.[35]

[35] Asperger here describes a problem that is strongly suggestive of classic dyslexia, a disorder marked by severe problems in phoneme segmentation (see Snowling (1987) for a detailed discussion). It is not known as yet whether dyslexia co-occurs with autism more than one would expect by chance.

Therefore we used the whole word method, leaving aside phonics, as an experiment when teaching him. However, when he had to read and write words in this fashion, this too proved extremely slow and tedious. Besides his specific learning difficulties, there were, of course, his general learning difficulties which resulted from his contact disturbance. Nevertheless, it was possible to demonstrate that the boy made some progress. The personal effort put in by the teacher was immense. Of course Ernst had to be taught individually, since it would have been impossible to get him to concentrate on his work in a bigger group. It was clear that the boy could not progress satisfactorily in a normal school, and that transfer to a special school was inevitable. However, since the mother considered such a transfer terribly degrading for her child, we tried the normal primary school again. Now, two years later, he attends the third class of the special school, and he certainly does not count among their best pupils. Indeed, he finds the school much harder than the typical special school pupil, who has difficulties with abstract thinking but can readily acquire the practical skills of everyday life.

It was quite difficult to decide whether Ernst was particularly able or mentally retarded, but there are numerous unequivocally retarded people who show the typical and unmistakable characteristics of autistic psychopathy: the disturbance of contact, with the typical expressive phenomena in terms of glance, voice, mimics, gesture and movement, the disciplinary difficulties, the malice, the pedantries and stereotypies, the automaton-like nature of the whole personality, the lack of ability to learn (to acquire automatic programmes), juxtaposed with relatively superior spontaneous performance. Indeed, in the mentally retarded autistic individual the impairments just mentioned are usually even more striking, since there is no counterweight of otherwise normal functions.[36]

In a reasonably sized out-patient population such cases are not particularly rare, and they are instantly recognisable to the experienced clinician. Anybody who knows such cases will immediately think of the remarkable similarity to personality disorders with an organic cause. These are disorders which are unequivocally caused by brain damage, possibly due to birth injury or to encephalitis in early childhood. Both of these clinical phenomena result in the same disturbances – whether in terms of pathological anatomy or in terms of function.

Characteristic stereotypies in particular are common to both the autistic and the brain-injured retarded child; for example, hopping, fidgeting, whirling, spinning of objects (often with surprising skill) or rhythmic rocking (for instance, of the upper body). In both groups we find a primitive spitefulness which, even with the severely retarded individual, often has the appearance of real cunning, since these children seem to sense whatever it is that might be the worst thing at any particular moment. In fact, parents often consider this ability to be proof of their child's

[36] Asperger's claim that autistic features are even more striking in retarded individuals than in those of normal intelligence is important to note. His clinical picture of autism is not limited to able children alone.

intelligence. Water supplies in the house are particularly popular targets for mischief (and one can indeed do a lot of it there!), but equally popular is throwing things out of windows, even when these are opened only for an instant. Then there is the instinctive aggression which is characteristic of both clinical groups, shown frequently in pinching, biting and scratching. Brain-injured patients often distinguish themselves by masterful spitting, especially if they have plenty of material due to hyper-salivation! In short, the disturbance of contact which we have already described in autistic children with its characteristic features can be found in a very similar form in many post-encephalitic cases.

It is often not easy to differentiate diagnostically whether, in such cases, the disturbance is constitutional (that is, autistic psychopathy), or a sequel to acquired brain damage. Important factors to consider are family history, birth history, presence of high fever with dizziness, sleepiness, vomiting, fits at any time, and other neurological symptoms. Among these are signs or hints of spastic paresis such as dysarthric speech, stuttering, oculomuscular symptoms, strabismus, vegetative signs such as increased salivation (in our experience, hardly ever absent in the brain-injured), increased eye brilliance (which, together with some other elusive features, forms the basis of the 'encephalitic glance') and profuse sweating. Lastly, there are endocrine disturbances, in particular, obesity. It is increasingly believed that endocrine disturbances are caused by primary cerebral disturbances, in particular, disturbances of the hypophysis. With endocrine disturbances go certain trophic disturbances such as double-jointedness, especially of the fingers, or a particular prominence of the middle of the face. The alveolar appendices can become enlarged and coarse, and the gums become hypertrophic. These signs are particularly striking when they are seen in children who earlier were of an elfin beauty. Three, four or five years after encephalitis, they have a badly misshapen face. As an example, another case will be described briefly.

Hellmuth L.

This boy is the fourth child of his parents, who are themselves without any peculiarities. He was born seven years after the third child, when the mother was forty-one years old. He had severe asphyxia at birth and was resuscitated at length. Soon after his birth he had convulsions, which recurred twice within the next few days, but have not since. His development was delayed and he started walking and talking towards the end of his second year. However, he then learnt to speak relatively quickly, and even as a toddler he talked 'like a grown up'.

He was always grotesquely fat, despite a strict, medically supervised diet. He gained weight without having a big appetite. When we met him six years ago, at the age of eleven, he had distinctly formed 'breasts and hips'. He has remained thus up to now (we have recently seen him again). He had bilateral cryptorchidism (for about a year he had been masturbating a good deal). The boy had been treated with hormone preparations, especially thymus and hypophysis preparations, since his early childhood but without any effect on his condition. He was double-jointed to a high degree. When one shook his hand, it seemed as if it had no bones and were made of rubber. He had knock knees and flat feet. He had noticeably increased salivation, and when he talked one could hear the saliva bubbling in his mouth.

His appearance was grotesque. On top of the massive body, over the big face with flabby cheeks, was a tiny skull. One could almost consider him microcephalic. His little eyes were closely set together. His glance was lost and absent but occasionally lit up with malice. As is to be expected from his whole appearance, he was clumsy to an extraordinary degree. He stood there in the midst of a group of playing children like a frozen giant. He could not possibly catch a ball, however easy one tried to make it for him. His movements when catching and throwing gave him an extremely comical appearance. The immobile dignity of the face which accompanied this spectacle made the whole even more ridiculous. He was said to have been clumsy in all practical matters from infancy, and has remained so ever since.

Listening to the boy talking, one was surprised how clever he sounded. He kept his immobile dignity while speaking and talked slowly, almost as if in verse, seemingly full of insight and superiority. He often used unusual words, sometimes poetical and sometimes unusual combinations. This was consistent with an interest in poetry as reported by the mother. He clearly did not have any feeling for the fact that he did not really fit into this world. Otherwise he would not have shown off in his peculiar way, especially not in front of other children. It was not surprising, then, that he was continuously taunted by other children who ran after him in the street. Of course, he could never do anything to his fleet-footed tormentors, becoming only more ridiculous in his helpless rage. This was the reason the mother had arranged for him to be taught privately over the last school years. He managed, surprisingly, to attain the fifth grade of primary school.

His school knowledge was very uneven. He was an excellent speller and never made mistakes. He also had quite a good style. On the other hand, his arithmetic was very poor, not only in terms of the mechanical aspects, but also when problems were presented in verbal form. One noticed the degree of his disability and his ignorance of worldly things when questioning him about ordinary matters of everyday life. This was where he failed abysmally, giving empty, pompous-sounding answers. The mother was quite right when she said that he was always 'in another world'. However, this did not prevent him from doing a lot of malicious things to the people he lived with and to other children. He enjoyed hiding or destroying objects, especially when he was little.

He was reported to have been pedantic from earliest childhood, for instance, he created scenes when something was occasionally placed in a slightly different position from usual. In everything he did, it was said, he had his particular rituals. He was especially concerned with his clothes, did not tolerate a grain of dirt on them, washed his hands very frequently and observed his body and its functions very closely. His pedantries tyrannised the household and he was in general very difficult to cope with.[37]

Much of his description is reminiscent of the earlier cases. This boy was 'an autistic automaton', impractical and instinctually disturbed. His relationships with the outside world were extremely limited. He did not have any genuine human relationships, was full of pedantries and also showed spiteful behaviour.

In Hellmuth's case there were clear indications that his autism was due to brain injury at birth. His medical history – asphyxia, fits, endocrine disorder, hyper-salivation, neurologically based apraxia – clearly pointed to an organic cause.

We can therefore draw the preliminary conclusion that there are cases where an organic disorder can result in a picture that, in numerous critical points, is closely similar to the picture presented by 'autistic personality disorder' of constitutional origin.[38]

The Clinical Picture of Autistic Psychopathy

Instead of describing further cases in detail, let us work out the typical characteristics that autistic children have in common. The information we draw on comes from all our cases, but, as expected with any typological approach, not every case has every feature. Nevertheless, those who know such children never cease to be surprised at the striking coincidences of detail. The autistic personality is highly distinctive despite wide individual differences. Our method would have failed if it ignored the differences and if it let each child's unique personality vanish behind the type. Autistic individuals are distinguished from each other not only by the degree of contact disturbance and the degree of intellectual ability, but also by their personality and their special interests, which are often outstandingly varied and original.

A crucial point which makes clear that the autistic personality type is a natural entity is its *persistence over time*. From the second year of life we find already the characteristic features which remain unmistakable and constant throughout the whole life-span.[39] Naturally, intelligence and personality develop and, in the course of development, certain features predominate or recede, so that the problems presented change considerably.

[37] These examples are again reminiscent of Kanner's insistence on sameness.

[38] The brevity of this case description suggests that Asperger is not as fascinated by the more severe clinical manifestations of autism as he is by the milder ones, as exemplified by Fritz V. and Harro L. In later lectures Asperger frequently refers to cases of autism reported in the American literature which are often very severely handicapped. He maintains that these cases are very different in that there is a different aetiology. Severe cases of autism, in his view, had to have brain insult rather than constitutional causes.

[39] This important statement, that symptoms are present from the second year of life, is so well buried in the text that it has often been overlooked. Instead the belief has persisted that Asperger's cases show normal development, especially in language, up to three years or later.

Nevertheless, the essential aspects of the problem remain unchanged. In early childhood there are the difficulties in learning simple practical skills and in social adaptation. These difficulties arise out of the same disturbance which at school age cause learning and conduct problems, in adolescence job and performance problems, and in adulthood social and marital conflicts. Thus, apart from its distinctiveness, it is its constancy which makes autism a highly recognisable entity. Once one has properly recognised an autistic individual one can spot such children instantly. They are recognisable from small details, for instance, the way they enter the consulting room at their first visit, their behaviour in the first few moments and the first words they utter.[40]

Physical Appearance and Expressive Characteristics

Autistic children lose their baby features very quickly. Instead of a chubby, soft and undifferentiated baby face, they have highly differentiated, finely boned features. They can be of almost aristocratic appearance, possibly somewhat degenerate. Their early thoughtfulness has formed their faces. The furrowed brow betrays the introspective worrier.[41]

The characteristic peculiarities of eye gaze are never absent. It is not only poets who know that the soul lies in the eyes. From the first moment when an infant can properly 'look', that is, from the third month of life, and well before there is any verbal expression, the majority of his social relations are based on eye gaze.[42] How the small child drinks in the world with his eyes! With his eyes he grasps things and expresses his feelings in a much less inhibited way than the adult, who has learnt to distance himself and to hide his feelings. With our children here, there is a fundamental difference. Hardly ever does their glance fix brightly on a particular object or person as a sign of lively attention and contact.[43] One can never be sure whether their

[40] A good example of give-away behaviour in the first few moments of an encounter with an autistic child is given by Kanner (1943) in his notes on Donald: 'An invitation to enter the office was disregarded but he had himself led willingly. Once inside, he did not even glance at the three physicians present . . . but immediately made for the desk and handled papers and books.'

[41] In his later textbook (1952) Asperger stresses that the appearance of autistic individuals varies greatly. The aristocratic appearance he emphasises here is not a general feature of autistic people. While many writers have commented on the beauty of young autistic children, few also mention that even captivating beauty can be lost in adolescence and adulthood. In early and middle childhood, an unchildlike, self-absorbed and socially disinterested demeanour, combined with childlike symmetrical features, may result in Asperger's attractive image of the little prince.

[42] In normally developing children socially motivated gaze can be observed in the first year of life, but it is as yet not clear whether it is absent in autistic babies. Since autism cannot be reliably diagnosed before the age of two or three, direct observations are hard to come by.

[43] Asperger's conclusion that the peculiar pattern of gaze in autistic individuals is due to the short and fleeting nature of the glance, fixing equally briefly on people as on things, is remarkable since, for decades, many professionals have held the belief that autistic children deliberately avoid looking at people. The idea of gaze avoidance may be partly responsible for the misunderstanding of autism as a state of withdrawal from social contact. Earlier awareness of Asperger's work might have prevented this misconception.

glance goes into the far distance or is turned inwards, just as one never knows what the children are preoccupied with at a particular moment or what is going on in their minds. The disturbance is particularly clear when they are in conversation with others. Glance does not meet glance as it does when unity of conversational contact is established. When we talk to someone we do not only 'answer' with words, but we 'answer' with our look, our tone of voice and the whole expressive play of face and hands. A large part of social relationships is conducted through eye gaze, but such relationships are of no interest to the autistic child. Therefore, the child does not generally bother to look at the person who is speaking. The gaze goes past the other person or, at most, touches them incidentally in passing. However, autistic children do not look with a firmly fixed glance at anything, but rather, seem to perceive mainly with their peripheral field of vision. Thus, it is occasionally revealed that they have perceived and processed a surprisingly large amount of the world around them. There is one situation, however, in which the eye gaze of these children becomes extremely expressive; their eyes light up when they are intent upon some malicious act, which is then perpetrated in an instant.

It will have become obvious that autistic children have a paucity of facial and gestural expression. In ordinary two-way interaction they are unable to act as a proper counterpart to their opposite number, and hence they have no use for facial expression as a contact-creating device. Sometimes they have a tense, worried look. While talking, however, their face is mostly slack and empty, in line with the lost, faraway glance. There is also a paucity of other expressive movements, that is, gestures. Nevertheless, the children themselves may move constantly, but their movements are mostly stereotypic and have no expressive value.[44]

Next in importance to eye gaze as a channel for expression is language.[45] As we saw with our first case, Fritz V., language expresses interpersonal relationships as much as it provides objective information. Affect, for instance, can be directly expressed in language. We can hear from the tone of voice what relationship people have to each other, for instance superior and subordinate, and whether they are in sympathy or antipathy. This is regardless of the often deceptive content of the words themselves. It is this aspect of language which tells us what someone really thinks. In this way the perceptive listener can get behind the mask. He can tell from an individual's expressions what is lie and truth, what are empty words and what is genuinely meant.

[44] While Kanner rarely mentions poverty of expression in autistic children, Asperger goes into great detail to convey the nature of this to him essential symptom of autism. It may be that the disturbance of expressive functioning that Asperger highlights is more striking in cases with fluent language and paradoxically poor communication.

[45] Asperger addresses and anticipates here that aspect of language we now know as pragmatics. It is well established that autistic individuals have a specific failure in pragmatics, that is, in the *use* of language. This is true even if their speech is otherwise linguistically sophisticated.

It is impossible to list all that can be revealed in volume, tone and flow of speech since these aspects are as varied as the human character. In any case, we do not intellectually understand many of these qualities and can only feel them intuitively.[46]

Again, it will come as no surprise that contact-creating expressive functions are deficient in people with disturbed contact. If one listens carefully, one can invariably pick up these kinds of abnormalities in the language of autistic individuals, and their recognition is, therefore, of particular diagnostic importance. The abnormalities differ, of course, from case to case. Sometimes the voice is soft and far away, sometimes it sounds refined and nasal, but sometimes it is too shrill and ear-splitting. In yet other cases, the voice drones on in a sing-song and does not even go down at the end of a sentence. Sometimes speech is over-modulated and sounds like exaggerated verse-speaking. However many possibilities there are, they all have one thing in common: the language feels unnatural, often like a caricature, which provokes ridicule in the naive listener. One other thing: autistic language is not directed to the addressee but is often spoken as if into empty space. This is exactly the same as with autistic eye gaze which, instead of homing in on the gaze of the partner, glides by him.

In a wider sense, the choice of words too must be considered among the expressive functions of language. This will become clear in the following section.

Autistic Intelligence

The skills that a child acquires grow out of a tension between two opposite poles: one is spontaneous production, the other imitation of adult knowledge and skills. They have to balance each other if the achievement is to be of value. When original ideas are lacking achievement is an empty shell: what has been learnt is merely a superficial and mechanical copy. Autistic intelligence is characterised by precisely the opposite of this problem. Autistic children *are* able to produce original ideas. Indeed, they can *only* be original, and mechanical learning is hard for them. They are simply not set to assimilate and learn an adult's knowledge. Just as, in general, somebody's good and bad sides are inextricably linked, so the special abilities and disabilities of autistic people are interwoven.

This becomes clearer when we look at the language production of autistic children. They, and especially the intellectually gifted among them, undoubtedly have a special creative attitude towards language. They are

---

[46] In Asperger's remarks about expressive functions the influence of Ludwig Klages (for example, 1936) is strongly evident. Klages was a widely read author of the time who attempted to find a scientific basis for character-reading from phenomena observed in each person's style of behaviour. Target behaviour included voice, movement, facial expression and also handwriting.

able to express their own original experience in a linguistically original form. This is seen in the choice of unusual words which one would suppose to be totally outside the sphere of these children. It is also seen in newly formed or partially restructured expressions which can often be particularly accurate and perspicacious, but also, of course, often quite abstruse.[47] It is worth mentioning here that all young children have a spontaneous way with words and can produce novel but particularly apt expressions. This is what makes for the charm of child language. Beyond the toddler age, in our experience at least, such spontaneously formed expressions are found only in autistic children. As an example, we can mention a six- to seven-year-old autistic boy who defined the difference between stairs and ladders as 'The ladder goes up pointedly and the stairs go up snakedly'.[48]

Especially rich in original language productions was an eleven-year-old autistic boy: 'I can't do this orally, only headily.'[49] (He wanted to say that he had understood something but could not express it verbally.) 'My sleep today was long but thin.' (This is also an example of autistic introspection.) 'To an art-eye, these pictures might be nice, but I don't like them.'[50] 'I don't like the blinding sun, nor the dark, but best I like the mottled shadow.' To the question whether he was religious: 'I wouldn't like to say I'm unreligious, but I just don't have any proof of God.'[51]

Behind the originality of language formulations stands the originality of experience. Autistic children have the ability to see things and events around them from a new point of view, which often shows surprising maturity.[52] The problems these children think about are usually far beyond the interests of other children of the same age.[53] A good example for this is our second

---

[47] The original words and phrases produced by autistic children are more often than not characterised by a disregard for the listener's ability to comprehend their meaning, and particularly the reason for their use. Asperger tends to stress the originality and overlook the inappropriateness of idiosyncratic language.

[48] 'Die Leiter geht so spitz und die Stiege so schlangenringelich'.

[49] 'Mündlich kann ich das nicht, aber köpflich.'

[50] 'Fur ein Kunstauge sind solche Bilder vielleicht schön, aber mir gefallen sie nicht.'

[51] 'Ich möcht nicht sagen dass ich unfromm bin, aber ich hab so kein Merkmal von Gott.'

[52] An interesting example of a seven-and-a-half-year-old boy quoted by Asperger in his 1952 textbook also serves to illustrate the capacity to make original observations and the ability to draw causal inferences that one can find in bright autistic children: GLASS/MIRROR 'A mirror is not much different, a sheet of glass that is painted with mercury on the back; it mirrors back the picture before the glass; why mercury is able to do this, I don't know, perhaps because it is so dark. I have found out that you can see yourself when there is something dark behind the glass. When there was light behind it, I have never been able to see myself. In our house we have a glass door; you can see yourself in it only when the light behind it is not switched on.' Incidentally, this example shows the same mixture of personally remembered episodes and factual knowledge as is found in the answers given by Fritz and Harro.

[53] Very often the interests of autistic children cannot be described as advanced; rather they are outside the interests of their normal peers. However, their reasoning with biological or physical concepts appears to be ahead of their reasoning with psychological concepts (Baron-Cohen, 1989) while the opposite is true of normal children.

case, Harro L. Often a very narrow, circumscribed and isolated special area can show hypertrophic development.

We know an autistic child who has a particular interest in the natural sciences. His observations show an unusual eye for the essential. He orders his facts into a system and forms his own theories even if they are occasionally abstruse. Hardly any of this has he heard or read, and he always refers to his own experience. There is also a child who is a 'chemist'. He uses all his money for experiments which often horrify his family and even steals to fund them. Some children have even more specialised interests, for instance, only experiments which create noise and smells. Another autistic boy was obsessed with poisons. He had a most unusual knowledge in this area and possessed a large collection of poisons, some quite naively concocted by himself. He came to us because he had stolen a substantial quantity of cyanide from the locked chemistry store at his school! Another, again, was preoccupied by numbers. Complex calculations were naturally easy for him without being taught. We are reminded here of our first case, Fritz V., which, however, also shows us the possibility of failure. The same child who astounded others by solving complex maths problems had the most serious learning disabilities at school, and could not learn the simple calculation methods that were taught there. Another autistic child had specialised technological interests and knew an incredible amount about complex machinery. He acquired this knowledge through constant questioning, which it was impossible to fend off, and also to a great degree through his own observations. He came to be preoccupied with fantastic inventions, such as spaceships and the like, and here one observes how remote from reality autistic interests often are.[54]

Another distinctive trait one finds in some autistic children is a rare maturity of taste in art.[55] Normal children have no time for more sophisticated art. Their taste is usually for the pretty picture, with kitschy rose pink and sky blue. The artfully stylised children's books, so fashionable fifteen to twenty years ago, are therefore as unchildlike as possible. Fortunately, matters have now improved in this respect. Autistic children, on the other hand, can have a surprisingly sophisticated understanding, being able to distinguish between art and kitsch with great confidence. They may have a special understanding of works of art which are difficult even for many adults, for instance Romanesque sculpture or paintings by Rembrandt. Autistic individuals can judge accurately the events represented in the picture, as well as what lies behind them, including the character of

[54] About ten years later, Asperger points out in his textbook (1952) that spaceships are no longer a fantastic invention. He jokingly suggests that the inventors might have been autistic.

[55] The claim that autistic children have a special gift for art appreciation is very surprising. One can imagine, however, that bright autistic children may well give refreshingly unconventional responses to high art and literature.

the people represented and the mood that pervades a painting. Consider that many normal adults never reach this mature degree of art appreciation.

Related to this skill is the autistic person's ability to engage in a particular kind of introspection and to be a judge of character.[56] While the normal child lives unself-consciously and appropriately interacts with others as an integrated member of his community, these children observe themselves constantly. They are an object of interest to themselves, and they direct their attention towards the functions of their body. Here is an example: a nine-year-old autistic boy suffered badly from homesickness[57] in the evening (homesickness always being worst at this time), saying: 'If one lays one's head on the bolster, then there is such a strange noise in the ear and one has to lie very quietly for a long time and that is nice.' The same boy also described an occasional micropsy: 'At school, I sometimes see that teacher has a tiny head, then I don't know what it is; it is very unpleasant to me that I see this way. Then I press my eyes very hard [demonstrates how he does this], and then it gets better.'

These peculiarities lead us to a digression. As always, the miraculous automaticity of vegetative life is at its best when left unconscious. When attention is directed towards it we invariably find disturbances of these functions. Hamburger has always emphasised that educators should never direct the child's attention towards eating, sleeping or elimination, since this would only disturb these automatic functions.[58] With autistic children, however, their own bodily functions are in the forefront of their consciousness anyway. The functions are not only registered and taken seriously, but they are also often disturbed. Especially frequent are eating and sleeping difficulties, which can lead to serious conflicts within the family.

Just as these children observe themselves to a high degree, so they also often have surprisingly accurate and mature observations about people in their environment. They know who means well with them and who does not, even when he feigns differently. They have a particular sensitivity for

---

[56] Introspection and self-reflection usually refer to mental rather than physiological processes. Asperger's examples all pertain to observations of physiological states. If the autistic child has difficulty in conceiving of mental states, then biological concepts might well take on special prominence in such a child's life. The idea of personality that would follow from a biological theory would be quite different from that derived from a psychological one. From this viewpoint the claim that autistic children can read character in others is a most unlikely one. However, autistic children may unerringly know which person really loves them precisely because they tend to be behaviourists. They would ignore the person who merely talks sweetly but does not in fact help them.

[57] Experience in boarding schools for autistic children over many years confirms that severe homesickness can occur but is not particularly common. Asperger later on suggests a reason for the type of homesickness he observed: the missing of daily routines. As highlighted by Kanner, great unhappiness can result from even apparently trivial changes in familiar habits.

[58] Asperger pays homage here to his mentors at the University Paediatric Clinic where he was trained. Hamburger was the director at the time this work was carried out and no doubt influenced it.

the abnormalities of other children. Indeed, abnormal as they themselves may be, they are almost over-sensitive in this respect.

Here we have to solve an apparent contradiction, which will, however, lead us directly on to a very important point. We want to demonstrate that the essential abnormality in autism is a disturbance of the lively relationship with the whole environment. We claim that this disturbance explains all peculiarities shown by autistic individuals. Now, how can one reconcile this contact disturbance with the special clear-sightedness which is implicit in the examples just described? How can somebody with disturbed relationships experience so much so consciously? The contradiction is only apparent. The normal child, especially the young one, who stands in a proper relation to the environment, instinctively swims with the tide. Conscious judgement does not come into this and in fact can occur only when one has some distance from the world of concrete objects. Distance from the object is the prerequisite of abstraction of consciousness, and of concept formation. Increased personal distance which characterises autistic individuals and which is also at the heart of their disturbed instinctive affective reactions, is, in a sense, responsible for their good intellectual grasp of the world. This is why we can speak of 'psychopathic clarity of vision' in these children, since it is seen only in them. This ability, which remains throughout life, can in favourable cases lead to exceptional achievements which others may never attain. Abstraction ability, for instance, is a prerequisite for scientific endeavour. Indeed, we find numerous autistic individuals among distinguished scientists. The contact disturbance which gives rise to a helplessness in the matters of practical life is typical of the absent-minded professor, and has made him immortal in jokes and cartoons.[59]

Unfortunately, in the majority of cases the positive aspects of autism do not outweigh the negative ones. We have mentioned repeatedly that autism occurs at different levels of ability. The range encompasses all levels of ability from the highly original genius, through the weird eccentric who lives in a world of his own and achieves very little, down to the most severe contact-disturbed, automaton-like mentally retarded individual. Our third case, Ernst K., may give an idea of people in the middle group. A further example for this group is an eight-to-nine-year-old boy who, when asked 'What is the difference between wood and glass?', replied 'The wood grows and gets a dirty skin, it attracts the dirt from the soil, and it gets so hard that it sticks to the tree and does not go away any more. This is how the soil fixes itself to the tree. If one drops glass, then it breaks even though it has been welded together, because the stickiness which is welded in lets go, and then it breaks.' Clearly this abstruse theory is weird rather than original!

[59] The image of the unworldly professor is indeed reminiscent of autism. Kanner too evokes this image when describing parents of autistic children: 'Many of the fathers remind one of the popular conception of the absent-minded professor who is so engrossed in lofty abstractions that little room is left for the trifling details of everyday life.'

From this middle group there is a smooth transition further along the range to those mentally retarded people who show highly stereotyped automaton-like behaviour. Sometimes they have crackpot interests which are of no practical use. They also include 'calendar people', who know the name of the saint for every day of the year, or children who, long before they enter a special school, know all the tram lines of Vienna with their terminals, or children who show other feats of rote memory.[60]

So far, we have looked at the intelligence of autistic children from the point of view of their own spontaneous productions and their own interests. Now we shall turn to learning and schooling. Obeying only spontaneous impulses and never paying attention to social demands may well lead to originality but will also lead to learning failure. The truth of this statement is borne out in almost all our cases. The very same children who can astonish their teachers with their advanced and clever answers fail miserably at their lessons. What they find difficult are the mechanical aspects of learning which the least clever, even somewhat retarded, pupils find easy, in other words, reading, writing and arithmetic (multiplication tables!). Sometimes, school subjects happen to coincide with the child's special interest. For instance, some of these children may learn to read particularly easily because they absorb all reading material from an unusually early age, say six or seven years (normally, children become bookworms around the age of ten).[61] 'Savant' calculators can certainly do well at school arithmetic, although there are some noticeable paradoxes here. The obsession to go his own way in all circumstances and the exclusive use of his own self-invented procedures can prevent the child from assimilating the calculation methods the school wishes to instil. These children make life difficult for themselves. They are bound to make errors and to arrive at the wrong results. Examples are described in the first case (Fritz V.) and the second (Harro L.). Another example is of an autistic boy who was just starting school, but could pose and solve the problem of how many seconds there are in two hours. However, when asked to work out 5 plus 6, he said, 'I don't like little sums, I'd much rather do a thousand times a thousand.' After he had produced his 'spontaneous' calculations for a while, we insisted that he solve the given problem. He then presented the following original, but awkward method: 'Look, that's how I work it out. 6 and 6 equals 12 and 5 and 6 is 1 less, therefore 11.' This boy was also particularly prone to being distracted, that is, distracted from within. This type of distraction impairs the performance of many autistic children.

---

[60] Why special skills in autistic individuals so often involve feats of rote memory is as yet unexplained. The spontaneous predilection for calendar skills and transport is also an unsolved mystery. Through Asperger's observations we know that these odd interests were as conspicuous then as they are now.

[61] Asperger himself is known to have read all of the works of Grillparzer, one of Austria's greatest playwrights, by the time he was nine.

We regularly find a disturbance of active attention in autistic children. Here we are not, or not only, talking about the common-or-garden problems of concentration. These are problems that we find in many neurologically disordered children who are constantly distracted from work by external stimuli, especially restlessness or movement. Autistic children on the other hand are, from the start, not interested in directing their attention to outside stimuli, in this case, what the school wants them to attend to. They follow their own ideas, which are mostly far removed from ordinary concerns, and do not like to be distracted from their thoughts. Nevertheless, autistic children can often be quite easily influenced from outside, in this as well as in other matters.[62]

It is little wonder, then, that most autistic children have severe learning difficulties. With the cleverest children, teachers may overlook the problems in mechanical learning. Usually, however, teachers despair at the tortuous efforts required of them and of the children themselves. In many cases, there are also characteristic conflicts between teacher and parents. Parents are generally inclined to judge their children favourably, and if the child shows original and inventive ideas then they will often believe him to be particularly intelligent. Teachers tend rather to see the failure in the taught school subjects and give bad marks. This easily leads to conflict where both parties are to some extent right.

At this juncture, another point concerning the practice of intelligence testing needs to be made. Most intelligence tests, especially those devised by Binet and subsequent modifications, deliberately avoid testing school knowledge because this is thought to depend largely on exogenous factors. Instead, the tests exclude tasks where learning and environment play a role. Strictly speaking, this is, of course, impossible. Now, the Binet test, especially at older age levels, involves above all logical, abstract thinking. Since this is what autistic children often find congenial, they may achieve a high score, which would give a false picture of their intelligence. The difficulties of these children will, however, be revealed in tests involving learning. Here one can readily witness the particular kind of learning failure that has just been described. We therefore use learning tests to tell us not only about the scholastic knowledge of these children, but also about their methods, attention, concentration, distractibility and persistence.[63] Clearly there are influences of exogenous factors, for instance the possibility of teaching neglect, and one has to be aware of them. Of course, this is also true for IQ tests if their results are to be of real value. To mention just one

[62] Asperger's observations on disturbance of active attention in autistic children are interesting and deserve to be followed up by systematic investigation. An obvious question is whether links could be made from attention disorders to narrow preoccupations. Those autistic individuals with strong special interests might, for instance, also show a pronounced lack of distractibility.

[63] Unfortunately, we are not given any examples of such learning tests. Innovative as the idea is, it is difficult to evaluate the evidence for Asperger's claims of mechanical learning failure.

example: the verbal fluency of socially advantaged children can often produce deceptively high test results.

Behaviour in the Social Group

It has been my aim to show that the fundamental disorder of autistic individuals is the limitation of their social relationships. The whole personality of these children is determined by this limitation. So far, we have looked at the children by themselves and seen how the disorder affects expressive functions and intellectual performance. However, the nature of these children is revealed most clearly in their behaviour towards other people.

Indeed, their behaviour in the social group is the clearest sign of their disorder and the source of conflicts from earliest childhood. These conflicts are especially pronounced in the smallest social unit, that is, the family. The fact that schizophrenics too suffer their worst conflicts within the family provides a parallel example. The reason is simple: the family unit is based on the emotional bonds of the members to each other. The children in the family are influenced strongly by these feelings, by the interplay of feeling between parents and children. Neither the schizophrenic, with limited affect, nor the autistic individual knows what to do with these particular feelings. They face them with incomprehension and even rejection. Thus parents suffer deeply from the unfeeling behaviour of their children.

It is thus mainly within the family that 'autistic acts of malice' occur. These acts typically appear to be calculated. With uncanny certainty, the children manage to do whatever is the most unpleasant or hurtful in a particular situation. However, since their emotionality is poorly developed, they cannot sense how much they hurt others, either physically, as in the case of younger siblings, or mentally, as in the case of parents.[64] There can sometimes be distinctly sadistic acts. Delight in malice, which is rarely absent, provides almost the only occasion when the lost glance of these children appears to light up.

Similarly, there are negativistic reactions, as we saw in the case of Fritz V.[65] These can often be caused by failure and frustration in the practical matters of life. We have already discussed the gaucheness of autistic children and their need to learn by way of intellectual effort. They can learn only with the help of elaborate rules and laws and are unable to pick up all those things that other children acquire naturally in unconscious imitation of

---

[64] Again, we hear about acts of malice; this time, however, Asperger suggests that the cause might be a poorly developed sense of how much another person may be hurt. This idea fits well with the hypothesis that autistic individuals usually fail to take account of mental states. For further discussion of this topic see chapter 1.

[65] Negativistic reactions include refusing to do what one is required to do or doing exactly the opposite.

adults. Parents find the learning problems particularly hard to understand. They expect compliance in the daily routines of washing, dressing and eating. Therefore it is precisely these situations which give rise to scenes and to the negativistic and malicious reactions.

Having just considered aggressive reactions within the social unit of the family, we have to take into account the isolation of the autistic child within the family. This isolation occurs when there are siblings, but it applies equally to only children, which autistic children usually are. 'It is as if he were alone in the world' is a common enough description. 'He dwells among people as if a stranger', 'he seems to take no notice of what happens around him'. Of course, one is sometimes surprised at how much is absorbed of what goes on despite the apparent lack of interest. The child sits preoccupied, perhaps apart in a corner, or even in the middle of a happy, noisy group of siblings or peers. He is like an alien, oblivious to the surrounding noise and movement, and inaccessible in his preoccupation. He is irritated only if someone breaks into his isolation.

The young autistic child is often engaged in stereotypic activity. Sometimes we find the simplest movement sterotypies, such as rhythmic rocking. Sometimes there is monotonous play with a shoelace which goes on for hours or with a particular toy, for instance, a whip or an old doll, which is treated almost like a fetish. The children often enjoy rhythmical beating and hitting, and forming patterned rows with their toys, for instance, they sort toy bricks according to colour, form or size, or according to some other unfathomable rule rather than building with them. It is usually impossible to tear them away from their play or their preoccupations. A seven-year-old autistic boy showed severe eating problems because he never stopped looking at the little specks of fat that were swimming on the surface of his soup. They interested him excessively, to look at, to move to and fro or to blow at. Seemingly, the changing forms were alive and meaningful to him.[66]

In everything these children follow their own impulses and interests regardless of the outside world. In the family one can largely adjust to these peculiarities in order to avoid conflict, and simply let these children go their own way. Only when it comes to the daily chores of getting up, getting dressed, washing and eating do we get characteristic clashes. In school, however, the freedom to indulge in spontaneous impulses and interests is heavily curtailed. Now the child is expected to sit still, pay attention and answer questions. Autistic children can do none of these things, or do them only with great difficulty. Causes for open conflict are now multiplied. While parents can often cope with the oddities of small autistic children on

[66] The appearance of rapt attention and deep absorption in their own preoccupations may be partly responsible for the belief that autistic children have a rich inner imagination. However, there is little evidence to suggest that autistic children have the same sort of fantasy life as normally developing children.

their own, at school they are almost always referred to child guidance centres because they cannot be handled in the ordinary way.

In the first two cases we pointed out the learning and conduct problems in school that are due to autism. It was also mentioned that autistic children are often tormented and rejected by their classmates simply because they are different and stand out from the crowd. Their conduct, manner of speech and, not least, often grotesque demeanour cries out to be ridiculed. Children in general have a good eye for this and show great accuracy in their mocking of conspicuous character peculiarities.

Thus, in the playground or on the way to school one can often see an autistic child at the centre of a jeering horde of little urchins. The child himself may be hitting out in blind fury or crying helplessly. In either case he is defenceless. The situation can be so bad that the mother must accompany the child to protect him from this sort of cruelty. The child may need a minder to the end of his school years and often beyond.[67] In favourable cases, however, it is possible for autistic children to earn respect, even if it is mixed with ridicule, either through sheer intellectual prowess or through particularly ruthless aggression.

Drive and Affect in the Autist

It will be clear by now that the personality of the children presented here lacks, above all, harmony between affect and intellect. While intellect may often be above average, drives and instincts are often severely disturbed. This is shown in the failure of instinctive situational adaptation and when faced with the practical demands of ordinary life. It is also shown in the expressive aspects of behaviour. We will now go on to look at these disturbances of drive and feeling one by one.

We start with sexuality. The picture is by no means uniform. Some individuals, throughout their childhood, and also beyond puberty, are sexually uninterested. They have a weak drive and never achieve healthy sexuality even in later life. However, in the majority of cases, there are early signs of strong sexual activity. In many cases, this is shown in masturbation which appears early, is practised intensively and obstinately, and is not amenable to change. Since any feelings of shame or guilt are largely absent, the children may masturbate in public, exhibitionistically, and they cannot be made to desist. One also hears of homosexual acts in relatively young children, as in case 2.

Sadistic traits are frequently reported. As an example, we mention some remarks of a seven-year-old boy with strongly autistic features: 'Mummy, I

---

[67] A delightful example mentioned by Asperger at a later date (1952) was that of a boy who regularly dived into a watchmaker's shop, which was situated right next to the school gate, to escape his tormentors. The watchmaker got to like the boy and the two of them spent much time together discussing philosophical questions.

shall take a knife one day and push it in your heart, then blood will spurt out and this will cause a great stir.' 'It would be nice if I were a wolf. Then I could rip apart sheep and people, and then blood would flow.' Once, when the mother cut her finger, 'Why isn't there more blood? The blood should run!' When he injured himself on one occasion, he was said to have been utterly thrilled, so that the doctor who tended the wound remarked on the child's state as extremely odd. At the same time, the boy was particularly anxious. He was afraid to fall over in his chair and extremely afraid of fast-moving vehicles on the road. There is also not infrequently a tendency to use obscene words which may stand in strange contrast to the otherwise often stilted language of these children.

Thus, with the sexual aspect of affective life there is often a definite disharmony, either a weakness or precocity and perversion, but no harmonious integration of sexuality into the developing personality. The same is also true for other areas of affective life. Over-sensitivity and blatant insensitivity clash with each other. Here are some examples.

In the sense of taste we find almost invariably very pronounced likes and dislikes. The frequency of this phenomenon provides yet more proof of the unity of the type. There is often a preference for very sour or strongly spiced food, such as gherkins or roast meat. Often there is an insurmountable dislike of vegetables or dairy produce.[68] It is no different with the sense of touch. Many children have an abnormally strong dislike of particular tactile sensations, for example, velvet, silk, cotton wool or chalk. They cannot tolerate the roughness of new shirts, or of mended socks. Cutting fingernails is often the cause of tantrums. Washing water too can often be a source of unpleasant sensations and, hence, of unpleasant scenes. In the hospital we have observed hypersensitivity of the throat which was so strong that the daily routine inspection with the spatula became an increasingly difficult procedure. There is hypersensitivity too against noise. Yet the same children who are often distinctly hypersensitive to noise in particular situations, in other situations may appear to be hyposensitive. They may appear to be switched off even to loud noises.[69]

The impression of disharmony and contradiction only increases when we consider the higher feelings as they are manifested in relationships to objects, to animals and to other people. As soon as one starts to work with these children, one is struck by a distinctive emotional defect which one may well consider an ultimate cause of their social disturbance. This defect is apparent in their isolation while they are in the midst of other people and in their contrariness with their environment and especially their closest family.

[68] It is possible that food allergies, if investigated, might have had links with some of the aversions mentioned.
[69] In contrast to Kanner (1943) Asperger remarks on the paradoxical phenomenon of hyper- and hyposensitivity to sound, light and touch. This phenomenon has since been observed in autistic children of all ability levels. No consensus has been reached, however, on the diagnostic value or meaning of this feature.

They lack the displays of affection which normally make life with a small child so richly rewarding. One never hears that they try to flatter or try to be nice. Indeed, they often turn nasty when one tries to be nice to them. Their malice and cruelty too clearly arise from this impoverished emotionality.

Autistic children are egocentric in the extreme. They follow only their own wishes, interests and spontaneous impulses, without considering restrictions or prescriptions imposed from outside. They lack completely any respect for the other person. They treat everyone as an equal as a matter of course and speak with a natural self-confidence. In their disobedience too their lack of respect is apparent. They do not show deliberate acts of cheek, but have a genuine defect in their understanding of the other person.

For personal distance too they have no sense or feeling. Just as they unconcernedly lean on others, even complete strangers, and may run their fingers over them as if they were a piece of furniture, so they impose themselves without shyness on anybody. They may demand a service or simply start a conversation on a theme of their own choosing. All this goes, of course, without any regard for differences in age, social rank or common courtesies.[70]

Autistic children's relations to *objects*, too, are abnormal. With the normal child, particularly the infant, things become alive because he fills them with life through his vivid relationship with the world around him. He gains experience and maturity through lavishing his attention and love on objects. This does not happen with autistic children. Either they take no notice of the objects in their environment, for instance, they take little interest in toys, or they have abnormal fixations. Perhaps they fixate on a whip or a wooden brick or a doll that they never let out of their sight, and cannot eat or sleep when the 'fetish' is not there. There can be the most severe tantrums at any attempt to take away the object of such passionate attachment.[71]

Very often, the relationship of autistic children to things is limited to *collecting*, and here again, instead of the harmonious order and richness of a normally balanced affective life, we find deficiencies and empty spaces, in

---

[70] All the autistic features which Asperger considers in the three preceding paragraphs can be explained by the theory that autistic individuals lack a proper conception of mental states: first, they do not display affection or try to be nice, because they do not try to manipulate other people's feelings towards them; secondly, they are totally egocentric because they do not distinguish their own from other people's mental states and do not recognise that they may differ; thirdly, they appear to be rude because they are unaware of the social niceties that allow smooth mutual understanding. Likewise, the disobedience and bad behaviour that seemed to be the major reasons for referral of Asperger's cases may arise from a defect in understanding the effect of their behaviour on another person's mental state.

[71] The potential link between disturbance of active attention, attachment to objects and narrow preoccupations is referred to by Asperger as a poor relationship to the world of objects. While Kanner makes a distinction between poor relations to people and good relations to objects, Asperger points out examples of poor relations in both spheres.

which singular areas develop to an excessive extent. The collections that are favoured by autistic children appear like soulless possessions. The children accumulate things merely in order to possess them, not to make something of them, to play with them or to modify them. Thus, a six-year-old-boy had the ambition to collect 1,000 matchboxes, a goal which he pursued with fanatical energy. The mother, however, never saw him play trains with them as other children do. Another boy collected cotton threads; a third 'everything' that he found on the street, but not like the street urchin, who has everything in his trouser pocket that he might need for his pranks. The autistic individual just stacks boxes full of useless junk. He constantly orders things and watches over them like a miser. Thus, there are serious rows when the mother dares to throw anything away. In adulthood the passion for collections often becomes more interesting and selective, in short more 'rational', and their mental attitude to collecting improves. The real collector-type is often an eccentric with pronounced autistic traits.[72]

Autistic children also do not have a proper attitude towards their own bodies. It is often well nigh impossible to teach them the numerous requirements of cleanliness and physical care. Even as adults they may be seen to walk about unkempt and unwashed, including those who have taken up an academic career. Up to the end of their childhood autistic children tend to be extremely messy eaters. They may smear or 'paint' with their food while being preoccupied with some strange problem of their own.

Another characteristic of autistic children is the *absence of a sense of humour*.[73] They do not 'understand jokes', especially if the joke is on them. This is another reason for their often being the butt of teasing: if one can laugh at oneself, one can take the edge off ridicule. However, autistic children are rarely relaxed and carefree and never achieve that particular wisdom and deep intuitive human understanding that underlie genuine humour. When they are in a merry mood, as sometimes happens, then this often strikes one as unpleasant. The mood is exaggerated and immoderate. They jump and rampage around the room, infringe other people's space, are aggressive and annoying. When making puns, however, autistic people sometimes shine, and may even be highly creative. This can range from simple word-play and sound associations to precisely formulated, truly witty remarks.

Nevertheless, if one focused only on the features just described, one would gain a false impression of the emotional side of autistic individuals.

---

[72] Later examples of collections mentioned by Asperger include collecting toys and collecting sewing thread. Collecting as a peculiarly autistic feature is not mentioned in Kanner's original paper. This has since been frequently documented in autistic individuals of all levels of ability.

[73] This original observation of Asperger's has been amply confirmed by later case descriptions. A sense of humour depends crucially on an intact ability to understand the use of language in communication, that is, pragmatics.

There are also observations that do not show such a decidedly negative picture.

Again and again, we have been surprised by the severe bouts of homesickness of autistic children when newly admitted to the ward. At first, this phenomenon did not seem to us to fit at all with the otherwise blatant signs of emotional poverty. Ordinary children, even those who have a very strong and genuine emotional bond to their family, adapt to their new environment after a short period of grief. This is because they can soon feel the love and care offered to them, and because they increasingly become interested in the new environment and the various activities that fill their days. Autistic children suffer from homesickness much more severely. For days they may cry desperately, especially in the evenings, when the pain always breaks out anew. They talk about their poor tormented parents and about their home with the tenderest words – with the mature language that we have already mentioned – and also with an exceptionally differentiated emotion, which children of that age cannot usually express. In a peculiar mixture of naivety and sophistication they give reason upon reason why they cannot stay, why they definitely have to go home today. They write imploring and quite shattering letters home. This all lasts very much longer than the homesickness of normal children, until at last they too get used to us and start to feel happy under the inescapable structure and guidance that we impose. It is possible that an exceptional degree of bonding to the objects and habits of the home, bordering on the obsessional, causes these children to suffer so much at separation. Therefore, it may be their general limitation in the normal freedom of action which lies at the root of this reaction. Nevertheless, the phenomenon of severe homesickness shows that autistic children are capable of strong feelings.

There are other examples. One boy, whose highly creative verbal expressions have already been quoted, had two white mice for which he cared tenderly, and which he preferred to all human beings, as he frequently pointed out. This boy deeply upset his parents by his spitefulness and cruelly tormented his little brother. There are similar examples of undoubted emotional attachments to animals and also to particular people which can regularly be observed in autistic children.

In view of these facts, the problem of the emotionality of autistic children is made extremely complicated for us. In any case, the children cannot be understood simply in terms of the concept 'poverty of emotion', used in a quantitative sense. Rather, what characterises these children is a qualitative difference, a disharmony in emotion and disposition. They are full of surprising contradictions which makes social adaptation extremely hard to achieve.

Genetic and Biological Factors

Given that the autistic personality type is both circumscribed and persistent, the questions of heredity must arise. The idea that psychopathic states are constitutional and, hence, inheritable has long been confirmed. However, it is a vain hope to think there may be a clear and simple mode of inheritance. These states are undoubtedly polygenetic, but it is as yet impossible to know whether such a trait is dominant or recessive.

The task of tracing the pedigrees of our children will have to remain for a later investigation. We want only to state briefly that over the course of ten years we have observed more than 200 children who all showed autism to a greater or lesser degree. We have been able to discern related incipient traits in parents or relatives, in *every* single case where it was possible for us to make a closer acquaintance.[74] Usually certain autistic peculiarities were present, but often we also found the fully fledged autistic picture starting with abnormalities of expressive functions and gaucheness up to the higher level of 'integration difficulties'. If it is the father who has transmitted the autistic traits, then he will in most cases have an intellectual profession. If one happens to find a manual worker among them, then it is probably someone who has missed his vocation (see case 2). In many cases the ancestors of these children have been intellectuals for several generations and have been driven into the professions by their nature. Occasionally, we found among these children descendants of important artistic and scholarly families. Sometimes it seems as if of the former grandeur only the eccentricity remains – which often also characterises great scientists. Many of the fathers of our autistic children occupy high positions, despite their noticeable peculiarities. This testifies to the social value of this personality type.

The familial findings we have sketched here certainly suggest a dominant mode of inheritance. They also suggest specificity since there is astonishing similarity between autistic individuals.

It is fascinating to note that the autistic children we have seen are almost exclusively *boys*. Sometimes girls had contact disturbances which were reminiscent of autism, and there were also girls in whom a preceding encephalitis had caused the state (as in case 4, Hellmuth L.). However, we never found the fully formed picture as shown in cases 1 to 3. How can this be explained? There is certainly a strong hint at a sex-linked or at least sex-limited mode of inheritance.

The autistic personality is an extreme variant of male intelligence.[75] Even

[74] Unfortunately, a pedigree study was never completed, and the summary statement that autistic traits were always present in a relative of the child was never backed by data. Gillberg (chapter 4), however, provides detailed evidence for the heritability of Asperger syndrome in six family studies.

[75] This provocative idea deserves to be re-examined in the light of neurobiological theories on sex differences in brain maturation (for example, Geschwind and Galaburda, 1985).

within the normal variation, we find typical sex differences in intelligence. In general, girls are the better learners. They are more gifted for the concrete and the practical, and for tidy, methodical work. Boys, on the other hand, tend to have a gift for logical ability, abstraction, precise thinking and formulating, and for independent scientific investigation. This is the reason, too, why in general boys at older age levels do better than girls in the Binet test. The narrowly logical and abstract items which start at the ten-year level are simply more congenial to boys! In the autistic individual the male pattern is exaggerated to the extreme. In general, abstraction is congenial to male thought processes, while female thought processes draw more strongly on feelings and instincts. In the autistic person abstraction is so highly developed that the relationship to the concrete, to objects and to people has largely been lost, and as a result the instinctual aspects of adaptation are heavily reduced.[76]

While we have never met a girl with the fully fledged picture of autism, we have, however, seen several mothers of autistic children whose behaviour had decidedly autistic features. It is difficult to explain this observation. It may be only chance that there are no autistic girls among our cases, or it could be that autistic traits in the female become evident only after puberty. We just do not know.[77]

When surveying our case material, we found that more often than not autistic children were *only children*.[78] This is noticeable even after allowing for urban population trends. Precise numbers have to await further investigation. An observer coming from a background of 'individual psychology' ('Individual-psychologie') would naturally explain the whole clinical picture out of the situation of the only child, and see in this proof for an exogenous cause of autism. He would explain the disturbed social relations, as well as the precocious speaking and thinking, simply from the fact that only children grow up among adults and never learn to adjust to siblings. Parents and teachers too often tend to explain the typical difficulties by referring to the notion of the only child. However, here as so often, this particular psychological approach confuses cause and effect. If one sees how autistic children grow up autistic from babyhood, and if one sees that those who grow up among siblings develop in exactly the same

---

[76] Asperger's comparison of the sexes in terms of underlying thought processes and interests is very much in accord with cultural stereotypes. As yet we have little scientific basis for these widely held beliefs. So far there is no empirical evidence to suggest that autistic boys differ from autistic girls in terms of abstract thinking.

[77] In his textbook (1952) Asperger still maintains that the only young girls he has seen with the full clinical picture of autism are those who have acquired autism after presumed encephalitis. That young girls too can show the typical Asperger variant of autism has been well established. Several cases are described elsewhere in this volume. It remains true, however, that girls are vastly outnumbered by boys. A sex-linked mode of inheritance is compatible with this pattern.

[78] Epidemiological studies have not confirmed that autistic children are predominantly only children.

way as those who are only children, then an explanation in terms of exogenous causes must seem absurd. Autism does not arise because there are unfavourable developmental influences for a siblingless child, but because there is an inherited disposition. It may be an expression of autism in the parents that they have brought into the world only one child. Undoubtedly, there are many reasons for the wish to have children, and this is subject to change by outside forces. An excellent example of such change can be seen most recently in Germany.[79] The variations of the human character suggest, however, that the wish for children, or its converse, has a deep biological basis. A lack of or reduction of this wish is a characteristic trait in most autistic personalities and can be considered another symptom of their hyposexual, instinctually disturbed nature. Many autistic people lead solitary lives and do not marry and have children. Many of those who do marry show tensions and problems in their marriage. In such a marriage the proper harmony between mind and body cannot be found and there is little space for raising large numbers of children. One is reminded here of Ludwig Klages who said 'the intellect is the enemy of life'. We need to emphasise, then, that being an only child is a symptom rather than a cause of the autistic condition.

In our description of the cases, especially the first, we saw that there were a number of similarities between autistic psychopathy and schizophrenic states. Indeed, the question arises whether a child as deviant as Fritz V. suffers from childhood schizophrenia. We considered this question and rejected the diagnosis of a schizophrenic psychosis in this case. The same applies to the others, who were less deviant in any case.

We now need to turn to another question. Could it be that at least some of the cases described are precursors of schizophrenia? The answer is again no. Our cases here do not show the progressive deterioration that would be expected for psychosis. In essence, they remain the same throughout their life, though there is often improved adaptation, and many can achieve a reasonable degree of social integration. I know of only one case, first considered to be severely autistic, in which, two years later, a progressive destruction of the personality occurred, and hebephrenia was diagnosed. In all other cases, some of which I have observed for twenty years or longer, I have not seen a transition of autistic personality disorder into genuine schizophrenia.[80]

Concerned with this, we now need to ask whether autistic psychopathy derives, perhaps partially, from a genetic disposition to schizophrenia. If we

[79] This refers to the pressure which the fascist regime then put on families to produce more children. This single remark is the only one in the whole paper to refer to a point of fascist ideology at a time when it would have been opportune to make many more such references. Apparently, acceptance of Asperger's thesis was delayed because he was not a party activist.

[80] It has recently been shown that superimposition of schizophrenia on autism can occur. A specific case is described by Tantam (chapter 5).

presuppose polygenetic inheritance for schizophrenia, are autistic individuals carriers of single genes which, in combination, would cause schizophrenia, or is autism a sign of disposition towards schizophrenia which has failed to manifest itself? These questions can be clarified only by means of exact family studies. It would be necessary to find an excess of schizophrenics in the blood relations of autistic children. We can give no conclusive answers at present but have to refer again to future studies. Meanwhile, it should be pointed out that we do not believe that there is an excess of schizophrenics in the families of autistic children, and thus the autistic personality is neither biologically nor genetically related to schizophrenia.[81] This would be consistent with Schröder's view of personality disorder or psychopathy; he maintained that psychopaths are *not* mad, nor half nor quarter mad.

The Social Value of the Autistic Psychopath

The aim of this paper was to report on a personality disorder already manifest in childhood which to my knowledge has not yet been described.[82] In the following section we try to go beyond this aim and consider what will become of autistic children. At the same time, we shall consider their potential value to society. This question is important enough to be discussed in spite of the limitations of this paper, which can deal only with autism in childhood.

One might expect from much that has been said so far that social integration of autistic people is extremely difficult if not impossible. After all, we have pointed out that the essential feature of the condition is a disturbance of adaptation to the social environment. This bleak expectation, however, is borne out only in a minority of cases and, in particular, almost exclusively in those people with considerable intellectual retardation in addition to autism.

The fate of the latter cases is often very sad. At best they may get into a low-level odd job, often only on a temporary basis. In the less favourable cases, they roam the streets as 'originals', grotesque and dilapidated, talking loudly to themselves or unconcernedly to passers-by as autistic individuals would. They are taunted by urchins and react to this with wild but ineffectual outbursts.

This is not so with intellectually intact autistic individuals, and in particular those of above-average intelligence. Of course, in adulthood too their relationships to others are as disturbed as they are in childhood when they produce the same characteristic conflicts. An old definition of psycho-

---

[81] Asperger's view is identical to that of Kanner and has been confirmed by epidemiological studies: schizophrenia is not seen in increased numbers in the families of autistic children.

[82] Kanner's classic paper on autism was published a year earlier but would not have come to Asperger's notice during the war years.

pathy is that psychopaths are people who suffer from themselves, and from whom the environment suffers in turn. The latter part of the saying certainly applies to autistic individuals but it is hard to know whether they suffer from themselves. They *are* strangely impenetrable and difficult to fathom. Their emotional life remains a closed book. Given their behaviour problems in childhood, it is to be expected that their closest relatives or spouses find them difficult to get on with. However, it is a different matter where their work is concerned.

In the vast majority of cases work performance can be excellent, and with this comes social integration. Able autistic individuals can rise to eminent positions and perform with such outstanding success that one may even conclude that only such people are capable of certain achievements. It is as if they had compensatory abilities to counter-balance their deficiencies. Their unswerving determination and penetrating intellectual powers, part of their spontaneous and original mental activity, their narrowness and single-mindedness, as manifested in their special interests, can be immensely valuable and can lead to outstanding achievements in their chosen areas. We can see in the autistic person, far more clearly than with any normal child, a predestination for a particular profession from earliest youth. A particular line of work often grows naturally out of their special abilities.

Here is an example. For almost three decades we were able to observe an autistic individual from boyhood to manhood. Throughout his life he showed grossly autistic behaviour. It was as if he never took any notice of other people. He behaved so absent-mindedly that he often did not recognise his closest acquaintances. He was extremely clumsy and gauche, and there were all the difficulties we described earlier in learning to deal with the practical chores of daily life. He remained awkward and socially unconcerned in his demeanour. For instance, one could see him as a young man sitting in the tram and picking his nose with great care and persistence! When he was at school there were constant serious difficulties; he learnt or did not learn as the whim took him. For languages he had no talent at all. In secondary school he never advanced beyond the elementary grade of Greek and was able to get by only on the basis of his other abilities.

Even as a toddler, one could see in him a most unusual and spontaneous mathematical talent. Through persistent questioning of adults he acquired all the necessary knowledge from which he then worked independently. The following scene is reported from his third (!) year of life. The mother had to draw for him, in the sand, a triangle [Dreieck or three-corner], a square [four-corner] and a pentangle [five-corner]. He then took a stick himself, drew a line and said 'And this is a two-corner [Zwei-eck], isn't it?', then made a dot and said 'And this one is a one-corner [Ein-eck]'. All his play and all his interest centred on mathematics. Before he even started school he was able to work out cubic roots. It must be emphasised that the parents had never drilled the child in calculating skills, but that the boy quite spontaneously, sometimes against the wishes of his teachers, forced them to teach him these skills. In secondary school he surprised his teachers by his specialised mathematical knowledge which had already advanced to the most abstract areas. Thanks to this extraordinary talent, and despite his impossible behaviour and failure in other subjects, he managed to advance without having to repeat classes, and was able to take the university entrance examinations. Not long after the start of his university studies, reading theoretical astronomy, he proved a mathematical error in Newton's work. His tutor advised him to use this discovery as the basis for his doctoral dissertation. From the outset it was clear that he was destined for an academic career. In an exceptionally short time he became an assistant professor at the Department of Astronomy and achieved his Habilitation.[83]

This case history is by no means exceptional. To our own amazement, we have seen that autistic individuals, as long as they are intellectually intact, can almost always achieve professional success, usually in highly specialised academic professions, often in very high positions, with a preference for abstract content. We found a large number of people whose mathematical ability determines their professions: mathematicians, technologists, industrial chemists and high-ranking civil servants. We also found some unusual specialisations. For instance, there is a heraldry expert who is said to be an authority in his field. There are also several musicians of considerable stature who were observed by us when children. The superficially surprising fact that such difficult and abnormal children can achieve a tolerable, or even excellent, degree of social integration can be explained if one considers it a little further.

A good professional attitude involves single-mindedness as well as the decision to give up a large number of other interests. Many people find this a very unpleasant decision. Quite a number of young people choose the wrong job because, being equally talented in different areas, they cannot muster the dedication necessary to focus on a single career. With the autistic individual, on the other hand, the matter is entirely different. With collected energy and obvious confidence and, yes, with a blinkered attitude towards life's rich rewards, they go their own way, the way to which their talents have directed them from childhood. Thus, the truth of the old adage is proved again: good and bad in every character are just two sides of the same coin. It is simply not possible to separate them, to opt for the positive and get rid of the negative.

We are convinced, then, that autistic people have their place in the organism of the social community. They fulfil their role well, perhaps

---

[83] Asperger notes in 1952 that the young man in question has long since become a university professor. Interestingly, the following sentence, which here states that the case is by no means exceptional, is changed in the 1952 volume to say that this *is* a very exceptional case.

better than anyone else could, and we are talking of people who as children had the greatest difficulties and caused untold worries to their care-givers.[84]

The example of autism shows particularly well how even abnormal personalities can be capable of development and adjustment. Possibilities of social integration which one would never have dreamt of may arise in the course of development. This knowledge determines our attitude towards complicated individuals of this and other types. It also gives us the right and the duty to speak out for these children with the whole force of our personality. We believe that only the absolutely dedicated and loving educator can achieve success with difficult individuals.

Conclusion

Now, at the end of the paper, one ought to discuss the literature, but this would not be very fruitful at present. One should investigate in what way the type of child described here relates to existing typologies. While I do not believe in a perfect systematic typology, the concept of type can be useful in certain cases, and this I have tried to prove in the present investigation.

The literature on personality types certainly includes those who show similarities to the autistic personality. There is E. Kretschmer's schizo-thymous personality, E. R. Jaensch's disintegrated personality and, above all, the introverted personality described by C. G. Jung. In the description of the introvert, in particular, there is much that is reminiscent of the children described here. Introversion, if it is a restriction of the self and a narrowing of the relations to the environment, may well be autism in essence.[85] However, none of the authors mentioned has anything to say about the behaviour of their particular personality types in childhood. Hence the basis for comparison is largely lacking, and the descriptions are situated on quite a different level from ours. The debate will undoubtedly become more fruitful when we know what becomes of our autistic children when they are adults. This awaits a later comprehensive study, in which we intend not only to research more fully the biological and genetic basis, but also to look at development beyond childhood. This, then, will offer the opportunity to

---

[84] The historical background to this passionate defence of the social value of autism was the very real threat of Nazi terror which extended to killing mentally handicapped and socially deviant people.

[85] The remark that introversion may in essence be the same as autism is odd but also fascinating in view of the fact that Asperger considered himself, and was considered by others, to be a typical introvert. Aspects of autism are not alien to normal experience and comparison to introversion may be relevant. However, it should not be overlooked that there is a world of difference between a well-adjusted introverted personality (who does not have to try hard to adapt) and an essentially no more than precariously adjusted autistic personality (who is constantly struggling).

compare autism in more detail with the characterisations of personality types reported by other authors.[86]

In the present study, our purpose was to report on one type of abnormal child, both because we have first-hand experience of such children, and also because we have a deep commitment to their education. This type of child is of interest not only because of its peculiarities and difficulties, but also because of its relevance to central psychological, educational and sociological problems.

Asperger's References

Bleuler, E. (1922). *Das autistisch-undisziplinierte Denken in der Medizin und seine Ueberwindung.* Berlin: Springer.

Bleuler, E. (1930). *Lehrbuch der Psychiatrie.* 5th edn. Berlin: Springer.

Hamburger, F. (1939). *Die Neurosen des Kindesalters.* Vienna and Berlin: Urban & Schwarzenberg.

Heinze, H. (1932). Freiwillig schweigende Kinder. *Zeitschrift für Kinderforschung,* 40, 235–56.

Jaensch, E. R. (1929). *Grundformen menschlichen Seins.* Berlin: Elsner.

Jaensch, E. R. (1936). *Der Gegentypus.* Leipzig: Barth.

Jung, C. G. (1926). *Psychologische Typen.* Zurich and Leipzig: Rascher.

Klages, L. (1936a). *Grundlegung der Wissenschaft vom Ausdruck.* 5th edn. Leipzig: Barth.

Klages, L. (1936b). *Die Grundlagen der Charakterkunde.* Leipzig: Barth.

Kretschmer, E. (1928). *Körperbau und Charakter.* Berlin: Springer.

Schneider, K. (1934). *Die psychopathischen Persönlichkeiten.* Leipzig and Vienna: Deuticke.

Schröder, P. (1931). *Kindliche Charaktere und ihre Abartigkeiten, mit erläuternden Beispielen von Heinze.* Breslau: Hirth.

Schröder, P. (1938). Kinderpsychiatrie. *Monatsschrift für Psychiatrie und Neurologie,* 99, 269–93.

References

Asperger, H. (1944). Die 'Autistischen Psychopathen' im Kindesalter. *Archiv für Psychiatrie und Nervenkrankheiten,* 117, 76–136.

Asperger, H. (1952). *Heilpädagogik.* Berlin: Springer.

Baron-Cohen, S. (1989). Are autistic children 'behaviourists'? An examination of their mental–physical and appearance–reality distinctions. *Journal of Autism and Developmental Disorders,* 19, 579–600.

Bleuler, E. (1916). *Lehrbuch der Psychiatrie.* Trans. A. A. Brill (1951), *Textbook of psychiatry.* New York: Dover.

---

[86] Sadly, Asperger never carried out this promised study. His later work was almost solely concerned with consolidating his views and propagating the approach of remedial pedagogics (Heilpädagogik).

Bleuler, E. (1919). *Das autistisch–undisziplinierte Denken in der Medizin und seine Ueberwindung.* Berlin: Springer.

Frith, U. (1989). *Autism: explaining the enigma.* Oxford: Blackwell.

Geschwind, N. & Galaburda, A. (1985). Cerebral lateralization: biological mechanisms, associations, and pathology. *Archives of Neurology,* 42, 428–62, 521–56, 634–54.

Gillberg, C. (ed.) (1989). *Assessment and diagnosis in autism.* New York: Plenum.

Hobson, P. (1989). Beyond cognition: a theory of autism. In G. Dawson (ed.), *Autism: new perspectives on diagnosis, nature and treatment.* New York: Guilford.

Kanner, L. (1943). Autistic disturbances of affective contact. *Nervous Child,* 2, 217–50. Reprinted in L. Kanner (1973), *Childhood psychosis: initial studies and new insights.* Washington: Winston.

Kanner, L. & Eisenberg, L. (1955). Notes on the follow-up studies of autistic children. In P. H Hoch & J. Zubin (eds.), *Psychopathology of childhood.* New York: Grune & Stratton. Reprinted in L. Kanner (1973), *Childhood psychosis: initial studies and new insights.* Washington: Winston.

Klages, L. (1936). *Grundlegung der Wissenschaft vom Ausdruck.* 5th ed. Leipzig: Barth.

Kleist, H. von (1810). Ueber das Marionetten-theater. *Berliner Abendblätter.*

Snowling, M. (1987). *Dyslexia: a cognitive developmental perspective.* Oxford: Blackwell.

Wing, L. & Gould, J. (1979). Severe impairments of social interaction and associated abnormalities in children: epidemiology and classification. *Journal of Autism and Developmental Disorders,* 9, 11–29.

Wurst, E. (1976). *Autismus.* Berne: Huber.

3

The relationship between Asperger's syndrome and Kanner's autism

LORNA WING

A year before Asperger's first on 'autistic psychopathy' appeared, Kanner (1943) published his famous first account of eleven children with a pattern of abnormal behaviour that he decided to call 'early infantile autism'. He began as follows: 'Since 1938, there have come to our attention a number of children whose condition differs so markedly and uniquely from anything reported so far, that each case merits – and I hope will eventually receive – a detailed consideration of its fascinating peculiarities.'

The characteristics of Kanner's syndrome

Kanner pointed out that these children had a number of characteristics in common. Kanner and Eisenberg (1956) selected five diagnostic criteria from Kanner's descriptions. Kanner's own words are given in quotation marks. The expansions and examples are based on his descriptions and my clinical experience.

1. 'A profound lack of affective contact with other people'. When young, the children appear aloof and indifferent to other people, especially other children. Kanner wrote: 'There is, from the start, an extreme autistic aloneness that, wherever possible, disregards, ignores, shuts out anything that comes to the child from outside.' Their parents describe them as 'self-sufficient', 'like in a shell', 'acting as if people weren't there', 'happiest when alone'.

2. 'An anxiously obsessive desire for the preservation of sameness'. This is shown especially in resistance to change in the daily routine (for example, absolute insistence on a lengthy bedtime ritual) or in repetitive activities invented by the child (for example, playing a set of records in the same sequence over and over again) or in the arrangement of furniture, ornaments, curtains, other household items or the child's own toys.

3. 'A fascination for objects, which are handled with skill in fine motor movements'. Some children become intensely attached to specific objects or collections of similar objects such as empty detergent packets, tin lids, dead holly leaves, and show resistance to any interference with these possessions. These objects are used only for repetitive activities such as making them spin with amazing dexterity, twisting them into identical complex shapes or arranging them in long straight lines, or are amassed for no obvious purpose. Normal pretend play is conspicuous by its absence, or, if present, is narrow, limited and repetitive in form.

4. 'Mutism, or a kind of language that does not seem intended to serve interpersonal communication'. The latter includes immediate and delayed echolalia, the reversal of pronouns ('you want biscuit' meaning 'I want . . .') and the idiosyncratic use of words or phrases, often due to irrelevant associations formed by one chance incident and remaining fixed thereafter. Kanner (1943) gave the example of a child who invariably exclaimed 'Peter-eater' when he saw a saucepan. This association began at two years old when his mother accidentally dropped a saucepan at the same time as reciting a nursery rhyme to him, beginning 'Peter, Peter, pumpkin eater'. Sometimes autistic children invent new words or adapt names, such as the child, known to me, who called a dish-washing machine a 'gaslectric dish-pie-er'.

Those who have at least some comprehension of language tend to make literal interpretations of the meaning. For example, a boy, when asked 'Have you lost your tongue?' anxiously looked around for it, and a little girl, being told to 'walk on ahead', stopped and touched her head as if wondering how it was possible to obey that instruction.

Those who have speech use it repetitively and those with large vocabularies tend to be long-winded and pedantic in their utterances. Kanner quoted one child who asked endless questions about light and darkness. When persuaded to answer some questions his replies were 'painstakingly specific'. For example, he defined a balloon as 'made out of dried rubber and has air in it and some gas and sometimes they go up in the air and sometimes they can hold up and when they get a hole in it they'll bust-up; if people squeeze they'll bust. Isn't it right?'

5. 'The retention of an intelligent and pensive physiognomy and good cognitive potential manifested, in those who can speak, by feats of memory or, in the mute children, by their skill on performance tests, especially the Séguin form board'. Kanner explained failure on intelligence tests or subtests as due to lack of co-operation. The islets of ability, as the special skills came to be called, also include a remarkable memory for music, the ability to play musical instruments, drawing with accurate perspective, calculations based on calendars for past and sometimes future years, and unusual skill in mental arithmetic, even, in some cases, extending to negative numbers. These skills can be manifested from an early age.

In his early writings Kanner stated that the behaviour pattern was present from birth, though he later modified this view (see below).

Additional clinical features

Kanner also described other abnormalities but did not include them in the list of essential diagnostic criteria that he distilled from the complex clinical picture. These additional features include the following:

1.   There is impairment of non-verbal aspects of communication and social responsiveness, manifested by lack of facial expression, poor eye contact, monotonous or peculiar vocal intonation, little or no use of gesture to supplement or substitute for speech. Autistic infants and toddlers typically fail to adopt a posture showing readiness and desire to be picked up.

2.   Although some autistic children appear agile in large movements and indulge in hair-raising feats of balancing if they escape supervision, such as walking along the top of the house roof, others are clumsy and ill co-ordinated despite their dextrous manipulation of objects and are nervous even of simple motor tasks such as descending stairs.

3.   Stereotyped movements of limbs and body are common, such as finger-flicking, arm-flapping, tip-toe walking, jumping and complex whole-body movements.

4.   Odd responses to sensory stimuli are frequent in young autistic children and include, for example, intense dislike or fear of some loud noises, fascination with lights or spinning objects, indifference to quite severe pain, heat or cold.

5.   In some the ability to imitate is very poor or absent, but others show a remarkable capacity to mimic exact tones of voice, accents, movements or whole sequences of actions performed by other people. There is no impression of deliberate teasing in this mimicry – rather a quality of automatic action without understanding the meaning of that which is copied.

6.   Though some will eat anything, including non-edible objects, problems affecting feeding are described in some autistic infants and young children. These can lead to extraordinary limitations of the types of food that will be accepted. One child known to me lived for months on bananas and lettuce leaves.

7.   Temper tantrums, aggressiveness, destructiveness, without any apparent awareness of the effects on others, are common, especially in response to interference with repetitive activities or changes in the environment. In some children, this type of behaviour disturbance seems to be associated with high levels of anxiety, hence Kanner's reference to an 'anxiously obsessive desire for the preservation of sameness'. Autistic children often appear to react negatively to every approach except from people who understand how to elicit their co-operation.

Kanner's and Asperger's accounts compared

Comparison of Asperger's writings (1944, 1979) with the above summary of Kanner's early papers shows many striking similarities between the children described by the two authors.

1. Both emphasised the marked excess of males over females. Asperger originally believed that his syndrome never occurred in pre-pubertal girls.

2. Social isolation, egocentricity and lack of interest in the feelings or ideas of others characterise both syndromes. Asperger described how his children would 'finger strangers as if they were a piece of furniture'.

3. The same problems in the way language is used were described by both authors (Asperger, 1944, 1979; Kanner, 1946), including the lack of use of language for interchange with others; the reversal of pronouns, especially in the early years; the peculiar, long-winded, pedantic speech in Asperger's children and in those with Kanner's syndrome who have enough speech; the tendency to invent words and to use language in idiosyncratic ways; the repetitive questioning.

4. Impaired non-verbal aspects of communication were noted by both authors, including poor eye contact, poverty of expressive gestures and movements, peculiar vocal intonation.

5. Both authors described the lack of flexible imaginative play.

6. A repetitive pattern of activities was described by both authors as a major feature, including dislike of environmental change shown as intense homesickness in Asperger's children, stereotyped play with fixation on some objects while others are ignored, the collecting of objects, stereotyped bodily movements.

7. Both wrote of the odd responses to sensory stimuli, including hypersensitivity to noise, love of strong-tasting foods and fascination and skill with spinning objects (Asperger, 1979).

8. Kanner described clumsiness in gait and gross motor performance in 'several' of his first eleven children, and Asperger remarked on this as a general characteristic, but both noted the dexterity with which special skills are performed (Kanner, 1943; Asperger, 1979).

9. Both authors noted behaviour problems such as apparent negativism, aggressiveness to people, destructiveness to objects and general restlessness. Asperger's comment concerning one child that 'he was abandoned to his spontaneous impulses' would apply equally to Kanner's children.

10. Special abilities, in contrast to learning problems in other areas, especially skill with numbers and good rote memory, were mentioned for both groups.

There are also certainly some differences in the accounts. The children described by Asperger all developed speech before school age. They typically had large vocabularies and reasonable grammar and some were described as 'talking like grown-ups' in early childhood, although they tended to ramble on, sometimes on fantastic themes. Although they were socially isolated, they were not unaware of the existence of others, but their approaches tended to be inappropriate and sometimes malicious in effect. Asperger described them as odd in appearance in contrast to the alert, attractive look often mentioned as typical of Kanner's children. He also commented on their 'originality of thought' and the frequency with which their interests were 'canalised into rather abstract subjects of little practical use' (Asperger, 1979).

Asperger, unlike Kanner, did not compile a list of essential diagnostic criteria for his syndrome. The features mentioned here are extracted from his clinical descriptions and discussions of cases.

From my own case material I include as illustration one case (already published, Wing, 1981a) which is a typical example of Asperger syndrome, showing social ineptness, communication problems and peculiar interests. (Reprinted by permission of the publishers, Cambridge University Press.)

The case of the train enthusiast

Mr K. N. first presented as a psychiatric out-patient when he was twenty-eight, complaining of nervousness and shyness.

As a baby he was always placid and smiling, and rarely cried. He used to lie in his pram for hours, laughing at the leaves on the trees. His mother remembered that he did not point things out for her to look at, in contrast to his sister. He continued to be quiet and contented as a toddler. If other children took his toys he did not protest. Walking was somewhat delayed, and he was slow in acquiring self-care skills, though not enough for his parents to worry.

He began to talk around the age of one. He had several words at this time, but after seeing and hearing a car crash which startled him, he stopped talking and did not begin again until he was three. His parents thought his understanding of speech was normal. K. developed good grammar, though he referred to himself in the third person till he was four or five. He has never been communicative. Even as an adult he gives information only if questioned and then replies as briefly as possible. His facial expression and gestures are limited, and his voice is monotonous.

As a child he was attached to his mother, never made any friends and was much teased at school. He remains a shy and socially isolated person though he would like to be able to make social contact.

K. has no stereotyped movements, but has always been ill co-ordinated and very poor at games. He does not swing his arms when he walks. He attended a private school and did well in subjects needing a good rote memory, such as history and Latin, but fell behind at the stage when comprehension of abstract ideas became necessary. He was in the army for a short time, but was not allowed to take part in marches and parades because of his clumsiness and inability to do the right thing at the right time. He was discharged because of these peculiarities.

K. did not object to changes imposed by others but was, and still is, orderly in his own daily routines and in arranging his possessions.

From early in his life he liked toy buses, cars and trains. He amassed a large collection and would notice at once if a single item were missing. He would also make models with constructional kits. He played with such toys on his own for as long as he was allowed to. He had no other pretend play and never joined in with other children. The interest in means of transport has remained with him. In his spare time he reads factual books on the subject, watches cars and trains and goes on trips to see trains with fellow train enthusiasts. He has no interest in fiction or any other type of non-fiction.

K. has been employed for many years in routine clerical work. He enjoys his job and his hobby, but is very sad and anxious because he is aware of his social ineptness and would like to have friends and to marry. He writes many letters to advice columns in magazines, hoping for help with these problems. His concern over what he terms his 'shyness' finally made him ask for help from a psychiatrist.

The WAIS gave K. an IQ in the low normal range, with similar verbal and non-verbal scores. He was particularly poor at subtests requiring comprehension of a sequence of events.

The relationship between the syndromes

In their original papers, written towards the end of the Second World War, neither Kanner nor Asperger referred to each other. As far as I am aware, Kanner never referred to Asperger's writings in any of his papers on autism. Asperger, on the other hand, in his paper published in 1979, did discuss Kanner's early infantile autism and its relationship to 'autistic psychopathy'.

Asperger wrote of the 'astonishing similarities within these two groups which accounted for the same choice of name. The two types are at once so alike and yet so different.' However, in his 1979 paper, he described far more similarities than differences and even those differences he did find he tended to argue away. Thus, although he said that children with his syndrome tended to develop grammatical speech even before they could walk, he qualified this with the comment that, like Kanner's children, they did not use the speech they had for purposes of interpersonal communication, but held forth on their own interests regardless of the listener.

Asperger's final conclusions are not completely clear, but seem to be that autism can be the end result of a variety of causes and that Kanner's syndrome is a much more severe form than 'autistic psychopathy'. He refers to Kanner's syndrome as a 'near psychosis or psychosis', which virtually meaningless terms add nothing of significance to the discussion.

Evidence for separation of the syndromes

The reader of Asperger's first paper cannot fail to be impressed by the close similarities to Kanner's case descriptions and the relatively few differences. When other clinicians became interested in Asperger's work, some adopted the position that the two syndromes were different in nature. Van Krevelen (1971) produced a scheme of the points he considered to be the major distinguishing features that, in his opinion, 'made it unmistakably clear that early infantile autism and autistic psychopathy are two entirely different nosological syndromes'. These points were: early infantile autism is manifested in the first month of life, whereas autistic psychopathy is not manifested until the third year of life or later; the child with early infantile autism walks earlier than he speaks, speech is retarded or absent, and language is not used to communicate, whereas in autistic psychopathy the child walks late but speaks earlier and tries to communicate although in a one-sided manner; in early infantile autism, eye contact is poor because, for the child, other people do not exist and he lives in a world of his own, whereas the child with autistic psychopathy evades eye contact and lives in our world but in his own way; early infantile autism is a psychotic process and the social prognosis is poor, whereas autistic psychopathy is a personality trait and the social prognosis is rather good.

The major problem with this formulation is that, in clinical practice, the features are not neatly divided as in this account; many, perhaps even most, individuals manifest elements from both lists (this point is pursued in detail in other parts of this chapter). Van Krevelen went on to suggest, on the basis of Asperger's and his own observations of the personalities of the parents, especially the fathers, that autistic psychopathy is a familial trait transmitted via the male line and that early infantile autism occurs when a child who inherits the trait also suffers organic brain damage. Thus, he recognised a relationship between the two conditions even though he considered them to be entirely different.

Wolff and Chick (1980) described a group of children with an abnormal pattern of behaviour that they classified as schizoid personality disorder. They defined the core characteristics as solitariness, rigidity of mental set and an unusual or 'odd' style of communication, and considered the group to resemble Asperger's syndrome in all respects except that a small minority were girls. Wolff and Chick stated that, although there were similarities to Kanner's autism, children with schizoid personality never showed what they considered were the essential features of autism, namely, absent or impaired language development with echolalia, lack of emotional responsiveness with gaze avoidance, ritualistic and compulsive behaviour, all beginning under thirty months of age. They agreed with Van Krevelen that Asperger's syndrome is an unchanging personality trait, whereas changes can be seen in autistic children over the years. Unfortunately, Wolff and Chick did not give any details of the pre-school years of their 'schizoid' subjects, so it is difficult to tell whether any typical autistic behaviour was present or absent at that age.

Wolff and Barlow (1979) compared eight matched pairs of 'schizoid' and well-functioning autistic children. They also included eight matched control children attending normal schools. The subjects were given tests of intelligence, language, memory, cognitive processes and emotional constructs. The results showed that there were some differences and some similarities between the 'schizoid' and the autistic children and that, in general, the 'schizoid' group were intermediate in function between the autistic and the normal children. The authors concluded that the study confirmed their hypothesis that the two handicapped groups are distinct from each other and from normal children, though the results could be interpreted as evidence for the hypothesis of a continuum of autistic disorders, as discussed later in this chapter.

Kay and Kolvin (1987), in their discussion of the borderlands of childhood psychosis, considered that Asperger's syndrome was biologically linked to childhood autism. However, they also hypothesised that the syndrome was a type of 'personality disorder' whereas autism was a 'psychosis', but they did not define the meaning of these terms.

Nagy and Szatmari (1986) considered that Asperger's syndrome was the same as schizotypal personality disorder found in adults (American Psychiatric Association, 1980) but with onset in childhood. They also equated it with the clinical picture in the group studied by Wolff and her colleagues (Wolff and Barlow, 1979; Wolff and Chick, 1980) although these workers used the term 'schizoid'. Nagy and Szatmari carried out a case record study of twenty children with social isolation and oddities of behaviour. They concluded that these children could be diagnosed as having pervasive developmental disorders as well as fitting the criteria for schizotypal personality. They noted that a subgroup may represent a mild form of infantile autism despite the fact that the children concerned did not meet the *DSM-III* criteria for this condition. (Nagy and Szatmari also suggested that some of the children displayed symptoms of schizophrenia, which raises questions concerning the specificity of the criteria used by the authors for this diagnosis – but that is another story.) However, in a later paper, Szatmari *et al.* (1986) argued for the retention of the term Asperger's syndrome, at least for the present, since firm evidence for the unity of Kanner's infantile autism and Asperger's syndrome was not yet available. They suggested that Asperger's group might comprise a subtype of children with similarities to and differences from classic autism. Retaining the former term would have the advantage of opening up a wider field of enquiry than autism alone.

Evidence for a close relationship

Other authors argued from clinical evidence that there is a close relationship between Kanner's and Asperger's syndromes and that they should be classified as the same, or at least as in the same general category.

In 1962 the German psychiatrist Bosch published a book on infantile autism, which appeared in English translation in 1970. This comprised mainly a fascinating though abstruse discussion of the nature and implications of language disturbances in autism, but also contained a comparison of Asperger's and Kanner's syndromes. The author noted that Asperger initially believed the two syndromes to be identical but later revised this opinion. Bosch pointed out that among the people known to him who were diagnosed as having typical Asperger's syndrome, there were some who, if they had been seen in their early years, would at that time certainly have been regarded as having Kanner's syndrome. Conversely, some children diagnosed as having early infantile autism began to make progress and gradually revealed more and more a picture of 'autistic or schizoid psychopathy'. Bosch discussed the views of various authors and concluded that doubt remained as to whether the difference between the two syndromes was fundamental or only one of degree. His own view seemed to be that Kanner tended to describe more severely affected cases while Asperger described those with milder problems, but there was an overlap between the two, giving some central cases which both authors would have accepted as within their respective groups. The Russian psychiatrists Isaev and Kagan (1974) also regarded Asperger's syndrome and early infantile autism as subgroups within the wider range of the autistic syndromes.

Schopler (1985), in an editorial comment on some published papers, pointed out that Asperger's syndrome, higher level autism and some cases of 'learning disability' converged in their clinical pictures, and emphasised that no behavioural distinction between the first two had yet been demonstrated. Volkmar, Paul and Cohen (1985) made the same point, giving a case history as illustration.

Tantam (1988a, 1988b) studied a group of adults in touch with psychiatric services selected for lifelong eccentricity and difficulties with social relationships. He found that the majority had childhood histories, dating from their early years, of abnormal behaviour and developmental deviances like those found in autism. The behaviour in adult life was like that described by Asperger. A minority of the subjects in the study developed eccentric behaviour in adolescence, and some of these could best be classified as schizoid and others as borderline personality disorders. Tantam emphasised the close relationship between autism and Asperger's syndrome. He considered these conditions to lie on a continuum of severity. He also discussed their relationship with schizoid personality disorder, but concluded that, despite some similarities, the evidence did not justify including this last condition within the autistic spectrum. More work was needed to clarify the reasons for the similarities and differences.

A study of the 929 first- and second-degree relatives of fifty-one children with autism or other pervasive developmental disorder was carried out by DeLong and Dwyer (1988). They found, among other results, that there was a high incidence of Asperger's syndrome in the families of children with IQs above 70, but not in those with lower IQs. Fifteen of the nineteen probands with IQs above 70 had the clinical picture of Asperger's syndrome as well as showing the *DSM-III* criteria for autism or pervasive developmental disorder. The authors suggested that high- and low-functioning autism are different conditions; Asperger's syndrome and high-functioning autism are largely equivalent and have a predominantly familial aetiology, in contrast to low-functioning autism in which there is a high incidence of evidence of neuropathology.

Gillberg and Gillberg (1989) examined all six-year-old children who were not mentally retarded living in Gothenburg in 1977. They found fourteen individuals who had a combination of deficits in attention, motor control and perception, referred to as the DAMP syndrome. The group was followed up at ten, thirteen and sixteen years of age. Eight of the fourteen children showed 'autistic type traits', that is, impairments of social relationships, speech and language and stereotyped behaviours or interests. One had the *DSM-III-R* criteria for autism, three had all the six diagnostic features of Asperger's syndrome listed by the authors, and four had three or four of these features. The authors reported that among mentally retarded children in the same area studied in 1984, the only child found with the diagnostic features of Asperger's syndrome was one mildly retarded boy. The authors suggested that the clinical findings fitted the hypothetical construct of a continuum of disorders with, at one extreme, severely or profoundly retarded children with the triad of impairments described by Wing and Gould (1979) (see below), followed by Kanner's syndrome, then Asperger's syndrome and, towards the mildly handicapped end of the scale, the DAMP syndrome (see chapter 4 for further details of this argument).

The idea of a continuum fits very well with findings of family-genetic studies. Burgoine and Wing (1983) published a clinical account of teenage identical male triplets diagnosed as having Asperger's syndrome but who had some typically autistic features in their histories and current behaviour. They differed along a continuum in the severity of their impairments, the degree to which they showed autistic features and the amount of peri- and post-natal trauma each had experienced. Bowman (1988) described a family in which two of the four sons satisfied the diagnostic criteria for autism except that one had no history of speech delay, a third son had the features of Asperger's syndrome, and the father was a loner with circumscribed interests and odd language-use. Only the mother and the eldest son did not show any clinical features of either syndrome. All the family were of normal overall intelligence but all the males, including the eldest son, had an unusually wide scatter of subtests on WISC or WAIS performance scores, with highest scores on block design and object assembly and lowest on digit symbol and picture arrangement. In the case of the two boys with the autistic clinical picture, the mother had had ante-partum haemorrhages, but she had had no problem with the births of the other two sons. A similar family (the case of the lawyer) is presented in chapter 4.

Perhaps the strongest argument for a seamless continuum from Kanner autism to Asperger's syndrome comes from clinical case material where the same individual was typically autistic in his early years but made progress and as a teenager showed all the characteristics of Asperger's syndrome. The following (earlier published in Wing, 1981a) is such a case. (Reprinted by permission of the publishers, Cambridge University Press.)

The case of the late talker

C.B. at age thirteen. His mother dates C.'s problems from the age of six months when his head was accidentally bruised. From this time he became socially aloof and isolated and spent most of his time gazing at his hands, which he moved in complicated patterns in front of his face. At the age of one he began to watch the passing traffic but still ignored people. He continued to be remote, with poor eye contact, until he was five. He passed his motor milestones at the usual ages and, as soon as he was physically able, spent hours running in circles with an object in his hand, and would scream if attempts were made to stop him. At the age of three he began to be able to recognise letters of the alphabet and rapidly acquired skill at drawing. He then drew the salt and pepper pots, correctly copying the names written on them, over and over again. For a time this was his sole activity. After this, he became fascinated with pylons and tall buildings and would stare at them from all angles and draw them.

He did not speak till the age of four and then for a long time used single words. After this, he acquired repetitive phrases and reversed pronouns. C. had many stereotyped movements as a young child, including jumping, flapping his arms and moving his hands in circles.

After the age of five, C.'s speech and social contact improved markedly. He attended a special school until the age of eleven, where they tolerated a range of bizarre, repetitive routines. At one point, for example, he insisted that all his class and the teacher should wear watches that he had made from plasticine before lessons could begin. Despite all the problems, he proved to have excellent rote memory, absorbed all that he was taught and could reproduce facts verbatim when asked. C. was transferred to a normal comprehensive school at the age of eleven. He has good grammar and a large vocabulary, though his speech is naive and immature and mainly concerned with his own special interests. He has learnt not to make embarrassing remarks about other people's appearances, but still tends to ask repetitive questions. He is not socially withdrawn but prefers the company of adults to that of children of his own age, finding it difficult to understand the unwritten rules of social interaction. He said of himself, 'I am afraid I suffer from bad sportsmanship.' He enjoys simple jokes but cannot understand more subtle humour. He is often teased by his classmates.

At the age of eighteen C. still has social and communication impairments. He has developed two circumscribed interests, namely, maps and citizens' band radio. Using the latter, he enjoys talking to a wide circle of fellow enthusiasts despite his problem in sustaining face-to-face interactions. He has no other friends and leads an isolated life.

Variations in diagnostic criteria

As can be seen from the literature reviewed above, the distinction between Kanner's and Asperger's syndromes is not, in practice, as clear as some writers (for example, Van Krevelen) believe.

Definitions of Kanner's syndrome

The blurring of the borderlines is not confined to the interface between the two conditions. In 1956 Kanner and Eisenberg modified the criteria for autism given by Kanner in 1943, thereby shifting the parameters within which the syndrome could be diagnosed. They noted that their case material had expanded to include some children reported to have developed normally for the first eighteen to twenty months of life before becoming autistic. They also selected two of Kanner's original five criteria as being of primary diagnostic importance and sufficient for identification of autism, namely extreme self-isolation and obsessive insistence on the preservation of sameness. They went on to say that the preservation of sameness must be manifested as preoccupation with 'elaborately conceived rituals' since simple repetitive activities may be present in severely retarded children. The authors did not offer any operational criteria for distinguishing these two types of repetitive activities.

In 1973 a collection of Kanner's papers on autism was published, together with some additional material. The last chapter comprised Kanner's brief descriptions of thirty-four 'psychotic' children, fifteen of whom he diagnosed as having early infantile autism, seven as 'childhood schizophrenia' and the rest as 'disorders with evidence of organicity'. Kanner noted that the grouping reflected 'the frequently apparent perplexities of nosological nomenclature'. The discussions of the individual children showed how difficult it was even for Kanner himself to apply his own diagnostic criteria precisely and consistently. Autistic features appeared to be scattered at random among the children in the different groups. The reasons for classifying some as schizophrenic were obscure, and it was not clear why Kanner felt that some had an organic aetiology and others did not, since no positive neurological findings were available for any of the children, but all had marked cognitive abnormalities.

The definitions of infantile autism officially adopted by the World Health Organization (1978, 1990) and the American Psychiatric Association (1980, 1987) differ between the two organisations and in different editions of the relevant manuals within each organisation. However, in their latest editions, both the WHO and the APA emphasise the importance for diagnosis of impairments of social interaction and communication and the presence of repetitive stereotyped routines. In contrast, the definition adopted by the Autism Society of America stresses disturbances in the rate of appearance of physical, social and language skills; abnormal responses to sensations; speech and language absence or delay; and abnormal ways of relating to people, objects and events. This definition overlaps with the WHO and APA systems, but would produce some significant differences in deciding which children should be included as autistic and which excluded (see table 3.3).

Definition of Asperger's syndrome

Asperger also subtly changed his descriptions of his syndrome over the years, perhaps affected by the opinions of other authors. In his later paper (1979) he emphasised the high intelligence and special abilities in areas of logic and abstraction, whereas, in 1944, he had specified that his syndrome could be found in people of all levels of intelligence, including those with mental retardation. In 1979 he stated that his children developed highly grammatical speech before they could walk. But, among the four early case histories given as representative of 200 children (1944), one child (Fritz V.) fitted this picture, talking at ten months and walking at fourteen months, one (Harro L.) was said to be 'unremarkable' in his early development, one (Ernst K.) was delayed in speech and did not talk till eighteen months but his age of walking was not given, and the last (Hellmuth L.) was said to have walked and talked when nearly two years old.

Until now, no English-language translation of Asperger's original paper has been published. Also, as mentioned previously, Asperger himself did not lay down specific criteria for the diagnosis of his syndrome. In consequence, variations in ideas concerning the parameters of Asperger's syndrome can be found in the literature, for example, that it is always associated with normal or high intelligence, that development is normal for the first three or more years (whereas Asperger said it was rarely *diagnosed* in the pre-school years) and that the social, language and behavioural abnormalities seen in Kanner's syndrome do not occur.

In the draft of the tenth edition of the World Health Organization's *International classification of diseases* (World Health Organization, 1990) Asperger's syndrome is included for the first time in this classification system; it appears as a subgroup of the pervasive developmental disorders. Alternative labels mentioned are 'schizoid disorder of childhood' and 'autistic psychopathy'. As can be seen in table 3.3, the only essential diagnostic criteria listed are a lack of clinically significant general delay in language or cognitive development apart from possibly motor delay and clumsiness; qualitative impairments in reciprocal social interaction, as for autism; restricted, repetitive and stereotyped interests and activities, as for autism. Circumscribed intellectual interests, so much emphasised by Asperger, are not mentioned specifically, but are included by implication in a reference to abnormal preoccupations, and in the list of possible types of repetitive activities given for autism. No mention is made of the abnormalities of verbal and non-verbal communication (as distinct from the formal aspects of language) so graphically described by Asperger.

It is to be hoped that the material presented in this book will provide a more informed basis for discussion of the issues involved in diagnosis and classification.

Other relevant clinical pictures

Children with impairments of social interaction, abnormalities of interpersonal communication and a behavioural repertoire dominated by repetitive stereotyped activities have been described by a number of writers both prior to and since the work of Kanner and Asperger. Some authors considered that all these could be grouped together as one single condition, namely, childhood psychosis, which they regarded as the childhood variant of schizophrenia (Bender, 1947, 1961; Rank, 1949; Szurek, 1956; Goldfarb, 1970; O'Gorman, 1970; Creak, 1961, 1964).

Other authors attempted to identify specific syndromes. De Sanctis (1906, 1908) applied the terms 'dementia precocissima' and 'dementia precocissima catatonica' to conditions characterised by social and cognitive deterioration and stereotyped behaviour following a varying period of normal development. Heller (translated by Hulse, 1954) described similar conditions for which the term 'dementia infantilis' was used. Some of the children these authors wrote about died within a few years following the regression, but, in others, their condition stabilised at a low level of function. In these, the clinical pictures were strongly reminiscent of severe autism associated with severe retardation. Earl (1934) wrote a vivid account of a group of adolescents and adults who functioned as severely or profoundly mentally retarded with no speech or self-care but with some motor skills, who were indifferent to people and absorbed in repetitive, stereotyped movements of fingers, limbs and body. He referred to this clinical picture as the 'primitive catatonic psychosis of idiocy'. Mahler (1952) described a group of children with abnormal social relationships, especially 'empty clinging' to adults, echolalia and repetitive speech on bizarre themes, to which she gave the name 'symbiotic psychosis'. Newson (1983) wrote about children with what she called the 'demand avoidance syndrome' with some features reminiscent of Mahler's group. They had repetitive speech and play, accurately mimicking people, inappropriate social interaction and a marked tendency to react to any demand from others by tactics of avoidance, which appeared to be manipulative, although in fact they lacked real social skills.

The patterns of impairment described above tend to be associated with moderate, severe or profound mental retardation. Social and communication problems with odd behaviour can also be found among those with borderline or normal intelligence. Weintraub and Mesulam (1983) described adults with a clinical picture similar to that of Asperger's syndrome, although they did not mention circumscribed interests. They referred to this picture as 'developmental learning disabilities of the right hemisphere'. Rourke *et al.* (1986) wrote of 'central processing difficulties' in a group of children with abnormalities of social behaviour, repetitive speech and specific learning problems affecting arithmetic and visuo-spatial skills. Sparrow *et al.* (1986) reported follow-up findings on 'atypical' children who had odd social interaction, were awkward and clumsy in motor skills and, while not typically autistic nor fitting all aspects of Asperger's syndrome, nevertheless had features of both conditions. The same or similar clinical pictures can be found among children and adults given different psychiatric diagnoses. As already discussed, 'schizoid' and 'schizotypal' personality disorders are relevant examples.

The literature on language disorders includes accounts of children whose speech and behaviour is remarkably like that found in children with autism or Asperger's syndrome. Blank, Gessner and Esposito (1979) considered this type of speech problem to be 'a marked discrepancy between the conceptual and the social-interpersonal aspects of verbal behaviour' which is precisely the problem identified by Asperger in his group of children. Rapin and Allen (1983) coined the term 'semantic–pragmatic disorder' for a problem affecting language and behaviour, the features of which closely resemble – in fact, are virtually identical with – Asperger's syndrome. More recently, Rapin (1987) has modified her views. She now suggests that autism and semantic–pragmatic disorder are not mutually exclusive diagnoses, but are terms describing impairments of different aspects of psychological function (sociability and communication respectively) and can and do occur together.

Creating order out of chaos

The history of diagnosis and classification in this field can be expressed in an analogy from music. It is as if some groups of people believe they are singing the same song but each singer has chosen a different key and some have changed their keys over time, while other groups are really singing the same song but each singer has called it by a different name.

The questions that need to be answered concern the relationships among all the 'syndromes' (not just those of Kanner and Asperger) in which impaired social interaction is a feature, and the relationships of these syndromes to mental retardation, other childhood disorders affecting cognitive, language and social functions, personality variations and disorders and the psychoses usually occurring in adult life (Waterhouse, Wing and Fein, 1989).

The last question was dealt with by Kolvin and his colleagues (Kolvin, 1971; Kolvin et al. 1971a–e). In a study of a series of children presenting with childhood psychoses, these authors found that, on the basis of the clinical phenomena, intelligence testing and personal and family history, they could differentiate between children with autism and autistic-like conditions on the one hand and on the other those with symptoms of the adult psychoses, especially schizophrenia. The latter were rare and were virtually never seen before seven years of age, while the former were comparatively much more frequent and, in almost all cases, began before three years of age.

With regard to the relationship to mental retardation, a number of studies have shown that the clinical phenomena of infantile autism and of autistic-like conditions can occur in association with any level of intelligence as measured on standardised tests, though the majority of those affected are mentally retarded, more than half being in the severely retarded range, even though they may have isolated skills at a higher level (DeMyer et al., 1974; Lockyer and Rutter, 1969; Wing and Gould, 1979).

A population study

In order to tackle the questions that were still unanswered and still the subject of debate, workers in the MRC Social Psychiatry Unit decided to carry out a study of children from one geographical area, Camberwell in south-east London (Wing and Gould, 1979; Wing, 1981b, 1988).

The aim was to examine the full range of clinical phenomena in the children in order to see if the syndromes named in the literature could be identified and separated from each other and from other childhood disorders. The children were then followed-up into adolescence or early adult life to observe any changes that might occur over time. The children selected were aged under fifteen years and were functioning as severely mentally retarded (that is, were catered for or known to the services for severe mental retardation) or were of any intelligence level and in any service but had any one or more of the features described as occurring in autism or autistic-like conditions.

The details of the method used are given in other papers (Wing and Gould, 1978, 1979). The results showed that the children studied could be divided into two main groups. Some were on the borderlines and were difficult to classify but most could be assigned to one or other category with reasonable confidence. One group comprised children who were normally sociable in the light of their mental ages, although, because of the method of selection for the study, they were all functioning as severely mentally retarded even if they had IQs of 50 or above on some tests (see table 3.1).

The other group contained the children whose social interaction was impaired and would have been abnormal for any mental age. This group included all those with any autistic features and, because of the method of selection, their intelligence levels covered the whole range from profoundly retarded to normal, although most were mentally retarded. Most were also especially impaired in language development, and examples of all kinds of other specific developmental delays in cognitive and motor skills could be found scattered among the children.

It was found that social impairment was closely associated with impairment of two-way social communication and impairment of the development of imaginative activities, especially those related to social understanding, referred to by the authors as a 'triad' of impairments. Furthermore, when these problems were present, the pattern of activities, instead of being flexible and creative, was rigid, repetitive and stereotyped.

Each of these abnormalities was manifested in different ways in different children. Impairment of social interaction could be shown as aloof indifference to others, passive acceptance of approaches, or active but odd, repetitive one-sided approaches. Impairment of communication (as distinct from formal language skills) varied from absence of any attempts to communicate, through communication of needs only, to repetitive questioning or lengthy monologues regardless of the responses of the listener. Imaginative activities could be totally absent, copied from other children in a meaningless way, or spontaneous but carried out repetitively in an identical fashion regardless of suggestions from other children. The rigid repetitive pattern of behaviour could be manifested as simple bodily directed stereotypies such as rocking or tooth-grinding, collecting and organising objects into meaningless patterns or insistence on repetition of sequences of actions or routines, or they could be verbal or abstract such as repetitive questioning or concentration on circumscribed interests in specific subjects such as railway timetables, calendars, chemistry, complex arithmetical calculations. No subject was too abstruse or bizarre to become a special interest of someone in this group.

An attempt was made to identify the named syndromes and to fit each socially impaired child into some diagnostic group. All the syndromes mentioned in this chapter were represented among the socially impaired children in the study but this exercise highlighted a number of problems. First, the longer the list of essential diagnostic criteria, the fewer the children that were eligible. Thus, as shown in table 3.1, seventeen children fitted Kanner and Eisenberg's (1956) two criteria for infantile autism (see page 104) but only seven out of the seventeen fitted Kanner's original five criteria (see page 93). Secondly, although it was possible to identify the diagnostic criteria when present in typical form, for every item there were problems of delimiting the borderlines. Thirdly, the criteria for different syndromes overlapped so much that some children could be given two or more

Table 3.1. *Camberwell children's study (fully ambulant children surviving to age 16+)*

IQ (non-verbal tests)	Kanner's syndrome (two criteria)	Kanner's becoming Asperger's	Asperger's syndrome	Other socially impaired	Sociable, functioning as severely retarded	Total in study
< 50	6	—	—	40	33	79
50–69	6	—	2	13	23	44
70+	2	3	2	4	—	11
Total	14	3	4	57	56	134

Notes:
1. The total population of children aged under 15 years numbered approximately 35,000 at the time of the study.
2. There were 29 non-ambulant children not included in the above table, 16 of whom were also socially impaired.
3. The use of non-verbal tests gave, in most, though not all, cases, higher estimates of levels of abilities than verbal tests.
4. The number of children with Asperger's syndrome with normal level of ability was an underestimate (degree unknown).

diagnoses. Fourthly, many children had mixtures of features from different syndromes and could not be fitted precisely into any diagnostic category. The more narrowly the criteria were defined the fewer the children that could be included.

One limitation of this study was that eligible children were sought only among those attending special schools or special classes. Any children with Asperger's syndrome attending normal school and not given any special educational help would not have been found. Nevertheless, there were four children who, when first seen, had odd social interaction, grammatical but pedantic language, circumscribed interests and motor clumsiness and who could be given the diagnosis of Asperger's syndrome, as shown in table 3.1.

The follow-up into adolescence or early adult life showed some changes in the manifestations of social impairment in about one-fifth of all the socially impaired children. Most of those who changed became passive or odd rather than aloof, though none became appropriately sociable. A minority tended to become more aloof with the passing years.

Of particular relevance to the present discussion is that three who, when first seen in childhood were aloof and fitted into Kanner's syndrome, on follow-up in late adolescence had all the features of Asperger's syndrome, including the odd, naive social approaches to others. Thus, at follow-up a total of seven children fitted the criteria for this syndrome.

Twenty of those in the study who were socially impaired but not classically autistic had some, but not all, of the characteristics of Asperger's syndrome.

The increase in social interaction found in some adolescents and young adults diagnosed as autistic in early childhood, though they still remained socially impaired, is similar to that described by Kanner (1973) in his follow-up studies. Eleven of Kanner's ninety-six autistic adults had improved sufficiently to maintain themselves in society. They all remained socially odd. One was described as gifted in mathematics and as 'awkward and intellectual'. In his spare time he did some composing and built a telescope. Kanner does not mention their motor co-ordination or give all the relevant details, but his accounts of these individuals suggest that some at least might be recognised by Asperger as members of his group.

The autistic continuum

The findings from research and clinical work are best explained on the hypothesis of a continuum of impairments of the development of social interaction, communication and imagination and consequent rigid, repetitive behaviour. To quote Kanner (1973): 'It is well known in medicine that any illness may appear in different degrees of severity, all the way from the so-called *formes frustes* to the most fulminant manifestations. Does this possibly apply also to early infantile autism?'

The continuum ranges from the most profoundly physically and mentally retarded person, who has social impairment as one item among a multitude of problems, to the most able, highly intelligent person with social impairment in its subtlest form as his only disability. It overlaps with learning disabilities (Shea and Mesibov, 1985) and shades into eccentric normality. It is approximately equivalent to 'pervasive developmental disorder' as defined in *DSM-III-R* (American Psychiatric Association, 1987). Another name for it is the 'autistic continuum' (Wing, 1988).

But it is necessary to emphasise that this triad of social impairments, though of primary importance, is not the only variable involved in the clinical pictures. Language, non-verbal communication, reading, writing, calculation, visuo-spatial skills, gross and fine motor co-ordination and all other aspects of psychological and physical function may be intact or may be delayed or abnormal to any degree of severity in socially impaired people. Any combination of skills and disabilities may be found and any level of overall intelligence. The overt clinical picture depends upon the pattern seen in each individual. (See Anderson (1986) for a discussion of a theory which combines the notion of general intelligence with that of various cognitive processes each having some degree of independence.) Table 3.2 summarises the manifestations at different levels of severity of the diagnostic criteria for the autistic continuum. Table 3.3 shows the variations in the criteria used to define 'typical' autism adopted by different authors or groups.

This view of multiple impairment was discussed by Wing and Wing in 1971 in relation to Kanner's autism. At that time, the idea of specific

Table 3.2. *The autistic continuum (features most often used in diagnosis[a])*

Item	Manifestations[b]			
	1 Tend to be seen in the most severely handicapped/retarded	2	3	4 Tend to be seen in the least severely handicapped/retarded
a Social interaction	Aloof and indifferent	Approaches for physical needs only	Passively accepts approaches	Makes bizarre one-sided approaches
b Social communication (verbal and non-verbal)	No communication	Needs only	Replies if approached	Spontaneous, but repetitive, one-sided, odd
c Social imagination	No imagination	Copies others mechanically	Uses dolls, toys correctly but limited, uncreative, repetitive	Acts out one theme (e.g. Batman) repetitively, may use other children as 'mechanical aids'
d Repetitive pattern of self-chosen activities	Simple, bodily directed (e.g. face-tapping, self-injury)	Simple, object-directed (e.g. taps, spins, switches lights)	Complex routines, manipulation of objects, or movements (e.g. bedtime ritual, lining up objects, attachment to objects, whole-body movements)	Verbal, abstract (e.g. timetables, movements of planets, repetitive questioning)
e Language-formal system	No language	Limited – mostly echolalic	Incorrect use of pronouns, prepositions; idiosyncratic use of words/phrases; odd constructions	Grammatical but long-winded, repetitive, literal interpretations
f Responses to sensory stimuli (over-sensitive to sound, fascinated by lights, touches, tastes, self-spinning; smells objects or people; indifferent to pain, cold, etc.)	Very marked	Marked	Occasional	Minimal or absent

	Very marked	Marked	Occasional	Minimal or absent
g Movements (flaps, jumps, rocks, tiptoe-walking, odd hand postures, etc.)				
h Special skills (manipulation of mechanical objects, music, drawing, mathematics, rote memory, constructional skills, etc.)	No special skills	One skill better than others but all below chronological age	One skill around chronological age – rest well below	One skill at high level, well above chronological age, very different from other abilities

[a] There are other clinical features seen in disorders in the autistic continuum, but they are not mentioned in the various sets of criteria considered essential for diagnosis.
[b] The manifestations of each item (numbered 1 to 4 under each heading) are arbitrarily chosen points along a continuum. In reality, each shades into the next without any clear divisions.

Table 3.3. *Comparison of essential diagnostic criteria (the numbers refer to the features listed in table 3.2)*

Abnormalities of	Typical autism[a]						Asperger's syndrome		Autistic continuum
	Kanner 1943	Lotter 1966	Rutter 1978	Draft ICD-10 WHO, 1990[b]	DSM-III[c] APA, 1980	DSM-III-R[d] APA, 1987	Wing 1981a	Draft ICD-10 WHO, 1990	Wing and Gould 1979
a Social interaction	1,2	1,2	1,2	1,2,3,4	1,2,3	1,2,3,4	3,4	1,2,3,4	1,2,3,4
b Social communication	1,2	1,2	1,2,3,4	1,2,3,4	1,2,3	1,2,3,4	3,4	—	1,2,3,4
c Social imagination	—	—	1,3	1,2,3,4	—	1,2,3,4	3,4	—	1,2,3,4
d Repetitive activities	3	3	3,4	2,3,4	2,3,4	1,2,3,4	4	3,4	1,2,3,4
e Language	1,2,3	—	1,2,3	—	1,2,3	—	4	—	—
f Sensory responses	—	—	—	—	1,2	—	—	—	—
g Movements	—	—	—	—	1,2	—	—	—	—
h Special skills	3	—	—	—	4	—	4	—	—
i Other	Attractive appearance no organic aetiology	—	—	—	No delusions or hallucinations	—	Clumsy	May be clumsy No language or cognitive delay	—
Age of onset of signs of abnormal development	0–2½	—	0–2½	0–3	0–2½	—	—	3+, but may be earlier motor delay	—

[a] Most workers imply that the characteristic features have to be present in early life, but may become less obvious or change in manifestation in middle or later childhood. However, none has specified precisely the age up to which the features must be present to make a diagnosis, except Lotter, who specified up to 7 or 8 years, and Rutter who specified up to around 5 years.

[b] At least *three* examples from a, *two* from b or c and *two* from d must be present.

[c] Examples (number unspecified) from a and b or e and d or e and d or f or h must be present.

[d] At least *eight* examples, including at least *two* from a, *one* from b or c and *one* from d must be present.

impairments of the skills of social interaction, communication and imagin-ation had not been formulated, so the list of the fundamental impairments and the secondary abnormalities of behaviour now seems inappropriate and inadequate. Nevertheless, the basic premise remains unchanged: the various clinical pictures of autism and related disorders depend upon the combinations of different impairments, which vary in severity independ-ently of each other, though they interact to produce the overt behaviour pattern.

The nature of the social impairment is still the subject of debate and research. Are social interaction skills inborn attributes of humans and other animals that are inherited as an indivisible package, or do they depend upon a set of simpler psychological functions? Are the skills best classified as cognitive, affective or conative, or are these terms outdated and irrelevant in relation to social interaction? These issues are discussed elsewhere in this book (see chapters 1 and 6).

Discussion and conclusions

From the review in this chapter, it can be seen that most workers who have, to date, published results of research work in this field conclude that there is a close relationship between Kanner's and Asperger's syndromes, even if they differ in their ideas on the nature of that relationship.

Given the available evidence, Kanner's and Asperger's syndromes are best regarded as falling within the continuum of social impairment (of which they form only a part) but characterised, at least in the earlier years of childhood, by somewhat differing profiles of cognitive, language and motor functions. Thus, to emphasise the differences, the young classic Kanner's child has good visuo-spatial skills, good manual dexterity when engaged in his or her preferred activities but has delayed and deviant language development as well as social impairment of the aloof kind. Those with typical Asperger's syndrome have good grammatical speech from early in life, passive, odd or subtly inappropriate social interaction and poor gross motor co-ordination shown in gait and posture. They also tend to be in the mildly retarded, normal, or superior range of intelligence, while Kanner's group covers a wider range of the IQ scale with many being severely retarded on standardised tests, although on non-verbal tests some are in the mildly retarded, normal or even superior range. However, the more able among Kanner's group can, over the years, develop the characteristics, including the types of social interaction, of people with Asperger's syn-drome and become indistinguishable from them in adult life.

There is much to be said for equating Asperger's syndrome with high-functioning Kanner's autism, since the two syndromes shade into each other and into other parts of the social impairment continuum. But the danger of taking this view without further questioning is that the interesting differences that do exist between typical examples of each of the so-called syndromes will be overlooked instead of being investigated for the clues they might provide concerning underlying causes and dysfunctions. However, there should be no conflict between accepting that Asperger's syndrome is part of the autistic continuum and, at the same time, studying the variations in ways in which the autistic pattern can be manifested.

The classification of Asperger's syndrome as a personality disorder raises the question of the meaning of this term. Wolff and Chick (1980) emphasised that personality traits are enduring characteristics of the individuals concerned and argued, like Van Krevelen (1971), that Asperger's syndrome must be a personality disorder because it is lifelong. This view ignores the fact that developmental impairment of any specific skill can be lifelong. This is the case, for example, for reading disability, speech disorder and motor co-ordination disorder. The permanence of underlying social impairment and its accompanying pattern of odd behaviour do not preclude its classification as a disorder of the development of a particular aspect of psychological function.

Placing Asperger's syndrome in the continuum of autistic developmental disorders has useful practical implications for management and prognosis, whereas the use of the ill-defined blanket term 'personality disorder' does not. The word 'schizoid', with its overtones of a relationship with adult schizophrenia, is particularly unhelpful with regard to management and for the families concerned, since few if any people with developmental social impairments develop clinically recognisable adult schizophrenia.

It is, of course, possible that Kanner and Asperger each identified clusters of psychological and behavioural features that will be shown to have some independent validity, but solid evidence is still lacking. Future advances in techniques of examining the central nervous system and its functioning may enable new reliable, valid and useful schemes of subclassification to be devised. The plural is used advisedly, since it is possible that subgroupings based on different levels of analysis (gross organic aetiology, neurological dysfunction, psychological impairment or overt behaviour) may have little or only a partial relationship with each other, but each would have value for different purposes (Waterhouse, Wing and Fein, 1989). In the meantime, the best way to help any socially impaired child is to recognise the social impairment, examine for and, as far as possible, treat or alleviate any identifiable underlying cause or associated conditions, assess specific skills and disabilities and overall level of intelligence, then use this information to plan an individual programme. Identification of any of the eponymous behavioural syndromes within the full range of developmental social impairment (the autistic continuum) is not of any practical help in this process.

At this point we must raise the question whether the term Asperger's syndrome is of any value, or whether as Schopler (1985) suggested, it should be discarded to avoid diagnostic confusion. In replying to Schopler (Wing, 1986), I agreed that the syndromes within the autistic continuum could not be clearly differentiated, but put forward two main reasons for the limited usefulness of the label Asperger's syndrome in current clinical practice. The first, also emphasised by Szatmari *et al.* (1986), is that the diagnosis of autism is, in the minds of many lay people, synonymous with total absence of speech, social isolation, no eye contact, hyperactivity, agility and absorption in bodily stereotypies. There is a lack of understanding of the wide range of severity and the widely differing manifestation of the basic impairments. For this reason, parents without special experience tend to overlook or reject the idea of autism for their socially gauche, naive, talkative, clumsy child, or adult, who is intensely interested in the times of tides around the coast of Great Britain, the need for the abolition of British Summer Time, or the names and relationships of all characters who have ever appeared in a television soap opera, such as 'Coronation Street'. The suggestion that their child may have an interesting condition called Asperger's syndrome is much more acceptable. That this is closely related to autism and is in the autistic continuum can be explained gradually over the course of time, and the parents can then be introduced to their proper reference group of other families with similar problems through the National Autistic Society.

The second reason is that professional workers without special experience of autism, including psychiatrists working with adults, also tend to have a narrow view of the clinical picture. Many of them think of autism as a condition of childhood and do not automatically include it as a possible diagnosis when seeing adults. The various recent papers on Asperger's syndrome have attracted attention from adult as well as child psychiatrists because of its novelty value in English-language publications, whereas papers on autism would probably have been read only by people working with children. As a result of using the Asperger label there has been an increase in awareness that an autistic person of normal intelligence can be undiagnosed in childhood but be referred to a psychiatrist in adult life. Attention has also been drawn to the fact that such people can develop psychiatric illnesses and that the presence of the developmental disorder as well as the adult illness complicates treatment and management.

To quote the final sentence of my reply to Schopler: 'It is indeed a pity to introduce yet more terminological confusion into the field of autism (itself a term subject to muddled interpretation) but the discussion of Asperger's work has been of help to many families who previously believed they were alone in their problems.' This controversy will have served a useful purpose if it leads to more clinically and theoretically appropriate descriptions of the disorders comprising the autistic continuum that take into account the variations related to differences in severity and the changes that occur with age, and to more reliable and valid ways of subgrouping these conditions.

When these aims are achieved it would be preferable to find new diagnostic terms since those in current use overlap sufficiently to cause confusion, as can be seen from the variations in definitions in different diagnostic systems (see table 3.3).

Social interaction, communication and imagination are just three of a large number of developmental skills, any of which can be absent, delayed or deviant on their own or in combination with others. Impairment in any such skill causes problems for the individuals concerned, so why should particular attention be paid to abnormalities of social interaction? The reason is that any degree of impairment of the social skills has a particularly profound effect upon the development of the child as a whole person and upon his or her chances of becoming an independent adult, able to work, marry and raise a family. Only those socially impaired people who have few or no other disabilities and who have sufficient skills and determination to compensate for their problems manage to become reasonably well-functioning and even, in a few cases, markedly successful as adults. The majority need help and guidance in sheltered settings for all their lives.

References

American Psychiatric Association. (1980). *Diagnostic and statistical manual of mental disorders.* 3rd edn. Washington: APA.

American Psychiatric Association. (1987). *Diagnostic and statistical manual of mental disorders.* 3rd edn, revised. Washington: APA.

Anderson, M. (1986). Understanding the cognitive deficit in mental retardation. *Journal of Child Psychology and Psychiatry*, 27, 297–306.

Asperger, H. (1944). Die 'Autistischen Psychopathen' im Kindesalter. *Archiv für Psychiatrie und Nervenkrankheiten*, 117, 76–136.

Asperger, H. (1979). Problems of infantile autism. *Communication*. 13, 45–52.

Bender, L. (1947). Childhood schizophrenia: clinical study of 100 schizophrenic children. *American Journal of Orthopsychiatry*, 17, 40–56.

Bender, L. (1961). The brain and child behaviour. *Archives of General Psychiatry*, 4, 531–47.

Blank, M., Gessner, M. & Esposito, A. (1979). Language without communication: a case study. *Journal of Child Language*, 6, 329–52.

Bosch, G. (1970). *Infantile autism.* New York: Springer.

Bowman, E. P. (1988). Asperger's syndrome and autism: the case for a connection. *British Journal of Psychiatry*, 152, 377–82.

Burgoine, E. & Wing, L. (1983). Identical triplets with Asperger's syndrome. *British Journal of Psychiatry*, 143, 261–5.

Creak, E. M. (Chairman) (1961). Schizophrenic syndrome in childhood: progress report of a working party (April 1961). *Cerebral Palsy Bulletin*, 3, 501–4.

Creak, E. M. (1964). Schizophrenic syndrome in childhood: further progress report of a working party (April 1961). *Developmental Medicine and Child Neurology*, 6, 530–5.

DeLong, G. R. & Dwyer, J. T. (1988). Correlation of family history with specific autistic subgroups: Asperger's syndrome and bipolar affective disease. *Journal of Autism and Developmental Disorders*, 18, 593–600.

DeMyer, M., Barton, S., Alpern, G., Kimberlin, C., Allen, J., Yang, E. & Steele, R. (1974). The measured intelligence of autistic children. *Journal of Autism and Childhood Schizophrenia*, 4, 42–60.

De Sanctis, S. (1906). Sopra alcune varieta della demenza precoce. *Rivista Sperimentale di Freniatria e di Medicina Legale*, 32, 141–65.

De Sanctis, S. (1908). Dementia praecocissima catatonica oder katatonie des fruheron kindesalters? *Folia Neurobiologica*, 2, 9–12.

Earl, C. J. C. (1934). The primitive catatonic psychosis of idiocy. *British Journal of Medical Psychology*, 14, 230–53.

Gillberg, I. C., & Gillberg, C. (1989). Asperger syndrome – some epidemiological considerations: a research note. *Journal of Child Psychology and Psychiatry*, 30, 631–8.

Goldfarb, W. (1970). Childhood psychosis. In P. H. Mussen (ed.), *Carmichael's manual of childhood psychology*. New York: Wiley.

Hulse, W. C. (1954). Dementia infantilis. *Journal of Nervous and Mental Diseases*, 119, 471.7.

Isaev, D. N. & Kagan, V. E. (1974). Autistic syndromes in children and adolescents. *Acta Paedopsychiatrica*, 40, 182–90.

Kanner, L. (1943). Autistic disturbances of affective contact. *Nervous Child*, 2, 217–50.

Kanner, L. (1946). Irrelevant and metaphorical language in early infantile autism. *American Journal of Psychiatry*, 103, 242–6.

Kanner, L. (1973). *Childhood psychosis: initial studies and new insights*. New York: Winston/Wiley.

Kanner, L. & Eisenberg, L. (1956). Early infantile autism 1943–1955. *American Journal of Orthopsychiatry*, 26, 55–65.

Kay, P. & Kolvin, I. (1987). Childhood psychoses and their borderlands. *British Medical Bulletin*, 43, 570–86.

Kolvin, I. (1971). Studies in the childhood psychoses: I. Diagnostic criteria and classification. *British Journal of Psychiatry*, 118, 381–4.

Kolvin, I., Garside, R. F. & Kidd, J. S. H. (1971a). Parental personality and attitude and childhood psychoses. *British Journal of Psychiatry*, 118, 403–6.

Kolvin, I., Humphrey, M. & McNay, A. (1971b). Cognitive factors in childhood psychoses. *British Journal of Psychiatry*, 118, 415–21.

Kolvin, I., Ounsted, C., Humphrey, M. & McNay, A. (1971c). The phenomenology of childhood psychoses. *British Journal of Psychiatry*, 118, 385–95.

Kolvin, I., Ounsted, C., Richardson, L. & Garside, R. F. (1971d). The family and social background in childhood psychoses. *British Journal of Psychiatry*, 118, 396–402.

Kolvin, I., Ounsted, C. & Roth, M. (1971e). Cerebral dysfunction and childhood psychosis. *British Journal of Psychiatry*, 118, 407–14.

Lockyer, L. & Rutter, M. (1969). A five to fifteen year follow-up study of infantile psychosis: III. Psychological aspects. *British Journal of Psychiatry*, 115, 865–82.

Lotter, V. (1966). Epidemiology of autistic conditions in young children: I. Prevalence. *Social Psychiatry*, 1, 124–37.

Mahler, M. S. (1952). On child psychoses and schizophrenia: autistic and symbiotic infantile psychoses. *Psychoanalytic Study of the Child*, 7, 286–305.

Nagy, J. & Szatmari, P. (1986). A chart review of schizotypal personality disorders in children. *Journal of Autism and Developmental Disorders*, 16, 351–67.

Newson, E. (1983). Pathological demand-avoidance syndrome. *Communication*, 17, 3–8.

O'Gorman, G. (1970). *The nature of childhood autism*. London: Butterworth.

Rank, B. (1949). Adaptation of the psycho-analytical technique for the treatment of young children with atypical development. *American Journal of Orthopsychiatry*, 19, 130–9.

Rapin, I. (1987). Developmental dysphasia and autism in pre-school children: characteristic and sub-types. In *Proceedings of the first international symposium on specific speech and language disorders in children, Reading University, England*. London: AFASIC.

Rapin, I. & Allen, D. (1983). Developmental language disorders. In U. Kirk (ed.), *Neuropsychology of language, reading and spelling*. New York: Academic.

Rourke, B. P., Young, G. C., Strange, J. D. & Russell, D. L. (1986). Adult outcome of central processing deficiencies in childhood. In I. Grant & K. M. Adams (eds.), *Neuropsychological assessment of neuropsychiatric disorders*. Oxford: Oxford University Press.

Rutter, M. (1978). Diagnosis and definition of childhood autism. *Journal of Autism and Childhood Schizophrenia*, 8, 139–61.

Schopler, E. (1985). Convergence of learning disability, higher level autism, and Asperger's syndrome. (Editorial.) *Journal of Autism and Developmental Disorders*, 15, 359.

Shea, V. & Mesibov, G. B. (1985). The relationship of learning disabilities and higher level autism. *Journal of Autism and Developmental Disorders*, 15, 425–36.

Sparrow, S. S., Rescorla, L. A., Provence, S., London, S. O., Goudreau, D. & Cicchelti, D. V. (1986). Follow-up of 'atypical' children. *Journal of the American Academy of Child Psychiatry*, 25, 181–5.

Szatmari, P., Bartolucci, G., Finlayson, A. & Krames, L. (1986). A vote for Asperger's syndrome. (Letter to the editor.) *Journal of Autism and Developmental Disorders*, 16, 515–17.

Szurek, S. A. (1956). Psychotic episodes and psychotic maldevelopment. *American Journal of Orthopsychiatry*, 26, 519–43.

Tantam, D. (1988a). Lifelong eccentricity and social isolation: I. Psychiatric, social and forensic aspects. *British Journal of Psychiatry*, 153, 777–82.

Tantam, D. (1988b). Lifelong eccentricity and social isolation: II. Asperger's syndrome or schizoid personality disorder? *British Journal of Psychiatry*, 153, 783–91.

Van Krevelen, D. A. (1971). Early infantile autism and autistic psychopathy. *Journal of Autism and Childhood Schizophrenia*, 1, 82–6.

Volkmar, F. R., Paul, R. & Cohen, D. J. (1985). The use of 'Asperger's syndrome'. (Letter to the editor.) *Journal of Autism and Developmental Disorders*, 15, 437–9.

Waterhouse, L., Wing, L. & Fein, D. (1989). Re-evaluating the syndrome of autism in the light of empirical research. In G. Dawson (ed.), *Autism: perspectives on diagnosis, nature and treatment*. New York: Guilford.

Weintraub, S. & Mesulam, M. M. (1983). Developmental learning disabilities of the right hemisphere. *Archives of Neurology*, 40, 463–8.

Wing, L. (1981a). Asperger's syndrome: a clinical account. *Psychological Medicine*, 11, 115–29.

Wing, L. (1981b). Language, social, and cognitive impairments in autism and severe mental retardation. *Journal of Autism and Development Disorders*, 11, 31–44.

Wing, L. (1986). Clarification on Asperger's syndrome. (Letter to the editor.) *Journal of Autism and Developmental Disorders*, 16, 513–15.

Wing, L. (1988). The continuum of autistic characteristics. In E. Schopler & G. B. Mesibov (eds.), *Diagnosis and assessment in autism*. New York: Plenum.

Wing, L. & Gould, J. (1978). Systematic recording of behaviours and skills of retarded and psychotic children. *Journal of Autism and Childhood Schizophrenia*, 8, 79–97.

Wing, L. & Gould, J. (1979) Severe impairments of social interaction and associated abnormalities in children: epidemiology and classification. *Journal of Autism and Childhood Schizophrenia*, 9, 11–29.

Wing, L. & Wing, J. K. (1971). Multiple impairment in early childhood autism. *Journal of Autism and Childhood Schizophrenia*, 1, 256–66.

Wolff, S. & Barlow, A. (1979). Schizoid personality in childhood: a comparative study of schizoid, autistic and normal children. *Journal of Child Psychology and Psychiatry*, 20, 29–46.

Wolff, S. & Chick, J. (1980). Schizoid personality in childhood: a controlled follow-up study. *Psychological Medicine*, 10, 85–100.

World Health Organization. (1978). *International classification of diseases: ninth revision*. Geneva: WHO.

World Health Organization. (1990). *International classification of diseases: tenth revision*. Chapter V. Mental and behavioural disorders (including disorders of psychological development). Diagnostic criteria for research (May 1990 draft for field trials). Geneva: WHO (unpublished).

4

Clinical and neurobiological aspects of Asperger syndrome in six family studies

CHRISTOPHER GILLBERG

Introduction

Asperger syndrome – whatever it is – cannot be dismissed at the drop of a hat as 'mild autism' and thereby relegated to the status of eccentricities in a textbook on child psychiatry. Since the seminal paper by Wing (1981), interest and work in the field have so grown that one senses the presence of a true diagnostic entity – at least from the clinical point of view – which for many years has haunted child and adult psychiatrists alike, variously alluded to as 'autism in high-functioning individuals', 'MBD (minimal brain dysfunction) with autistic traits', 'borderline personality', 'schizoid personality disorder' or 'schizotypal personality disorder'.

Hans Asperger, in his original 1944 paper (see chapter 2), described a group of patients suffering from 'the autistic psychopathy of childhood' who in some respects (particularly with regard to superior language skills, perhaps also with respect to worse motor skills) appeared to differ markedly from the group of cases described by Kanner in 1943. Van Krevelen, in 1971, made a devoted attempt to conceptualize autistic psychopathy as a separate disorder. Nevertheless, Asperger's original descriptions did not, as it were, catch on, until Lorna Wing drew attention to them in her 1981 paper, in which she acknowledged the usefulness of the term Asperger syndrome while at the same time announcing that she considered it to be one among several entities within the 'autism spectrum disorders'. Since then, Schopler (1985) has argued against the use of the term, while Nagy and Szatmari (1987) and Gillberg and Gillberg (1989) have – albeit on different grounds – made claims for its usefulness.

In Gothenburg we recently carried out a clinical and neurobiological study of twenty-three children (twenty-one boys and two girls) with Asperger syndrome who were diagnosed according to specific criteria (Gillberg, 1989). The criteria are outlined in tables 4.1 and 4.2. We

Table 4.1. *Asperger syndrome.*
Gillberg and Gillberg's 1989
diagnostic criteria at a glance

1. Social impairment (extreme egocentricity)
2. Narrow interest
3. Repetitive routines
4. Speech and language peculiarities
5. Non-verbal communication problems
6. Motor clumsiness

Table 4.2. *Asperger syndrome. Gillberg and Gillberg's 1989 diagnostic*
criteria elaborated

1. Severe impairment in reciprocal social interaction
   (at least two of the following):

   (a) Inability to interact with peers
   (b) Lack of desire to interact with peers
   (c) Lack of appreciation of social cues
   (d) Socially and emotionally inappropriate behaviour

2. All-absorbing narrow interest
   (at least one of the following):

   (a) Exclusion of other activities
   (b) Repetitive adherence
   (c) More rote than meaning

3. Imposition of routines and interests
   (at least one of the following):

   (a) on self, in aspects of life
   (b) on others

4. Speech and language problems
   (at least three of the following):

   (a) Delayed development
   (b) Superficially perfect expressive language
   (c) Formal, pedantic language
   (d) Odd prosody, peculiar voice characteristics
   (e) Impairment of comprehension including misinterpretations of literal/implied meanings

5. Non-verbal communication problems
   (at least one of the following):

   (a) Limited use of gestures
   (b) Clumsy/gauche body language
   (c) Limited facial expression
   (d) Inappropriate expression
   (e) Peculiar, stiff gaze

6. Motor clumsiness

   Poor performance on neuro-developmental examination

Table 4.3. *Infantile autism.* DSM-III *(1980) diagnostic criteria at a glance*[a]

A. Onset before 30 months
B. Pervasive lack of responsiveness to other people (autism)
C. Gross deficits in language development
D. Peculiarities in speech pattern (if speech is present, e.g. echolalia, pronominal reversal, idiosyncratic language)
E. Bizarre responses (resistance to change, peculiar interests, attachments)
F. Absence of schizophrenic symptoms (hallucinations, delusions, incoherence)

[a] For full diagnostic criteria of infantile autism, with examples of behaviours see *DSM-III* (American Psychiatric Association, 1980), pp. 87–90.

Table 4.4. *Autistic disorder.* DSM-III-R *(1987) diagnostic criteria at a glance*[a]

A. Qualitative impairment in reciprocal social interaction
B. Qualitative impairment in verbal and non-verbal communication, and in imaginative activity
C. Markedly restricted repertoire of activities and interests
D. Onset during infancy or childhood

[a] For full diagnostic criteria of autistic disorder with examples of behaviours see *DSM-III-R* (American Psychiatric Association, 1987), pp. 38–9. Autistic disorder is classified as a severe form of pervasive developmental disorder with onset in infancy or childhood (pp. 33–9).

compared them with twenty-three sex-, age- and IQ-matched children who had been diagnosed as autistic on *DSM-III* criteria (table 4.3). These autism cases also fulfilled *DSM-III-R* criteria for autistic disorder (table 4.4). The present chapter examines three of the Asperger cases from this sample and three more recent cases in detail. These cases and their families provide a basis for discussion which is complementary to group studies. The paper goes on to discuss the implications of the cases as regards the arguments on Asperger syndrome as a clinical entity. Delineations *vis-à-vis* autism, and the possible neurobiological basis of the disorder are also discussed.

In our study there were no requirements regarding the child's intellectual level. This is in line with Asperger's own viewpoint, as is evident from the clinical status of the patients he described. However, the six cases, with their families, presented here are all of rather high general ability. This allows one to see the most subtle features of Asperger syndrome unconfounded by additional handicaps. For purposes of cross-reference the cases are given *aide-mémoire* labels.

Family 1. The case of the lawyer

II:4 in this family is now thirty-three years old. He is an unmarried man with all the classical traits of Asperger syndrome. I have had irregular

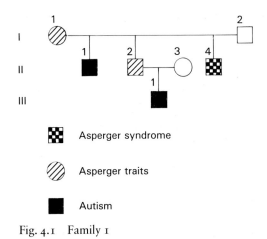

Asperger syndrome

Asperger traits

Autism

Fig. 4.1 Family 1

contact with him for just over twenty years, from the time when he was pre-pubertal. He was then a highly intelligent but very peculiar, tall and skinny boy of twelve. He had no friends and did not seem to care. He had the most amazing interest and knowledge in the field of Rommel's desert wars: he knew the 'exact' numbers of soldiers who had been killed in various battles and would enact the major battles in the same fashion over and over again using a set of tin soldiers. His speech was almost hilariously formal, and children and adults who did not know him often burst out laughing on hearing him for the first time, believing him to be joking and putting on a show (which, of course, he was not). His gait was stiff and all his motor movements were awkward and ill co-ordinated.

He had been slow to start walking (sixteen months) and comparatively slow as regards speech development. He did not say much until almost three years of age, when in a very short space of time he started saying long and complicated sentences. These perfectly echoed things he had heard his mother say during the day. He never showed an interest in anything but mechanical toys and electric equipment of various kinds. The parents state that they never noticed any kinds of stereotypies but, at the age of thirty-three, it is plain that II:4 shows highly stereotyped repetitive spreading of the fingers, hundreds of times each day, and has a tendency to make slight but clearly stereotyped nods for no obvious reason. These repetitive movements have been present since I first saw him. II:4 does not like water and the parents had a tough time trying to teach him to swim when he was nine years old. However, he learnt to swim (in a very stiff manner) one afternoon at 5 o'clock. The parents remember this very clearly because, since that day, whenever he has been to their summer house he has gone for a swim at 5 o'clock sharp.

He was perceived as odd by his parents – in particular the father – from around the time when he was five years old and did not want to mix with age-peers. Throughout childhood, adolescence and early adult life he has remained completely without friends. He is now a lawyer and has to meet people every day. This works out all right, he thinks, because he is very interested in their 'cases' (various economical and financial problems). He does not participate in social gatherings at or in connection with his work. He has had one 'girl-friend', when he was twenty-three – a fellow student whom he once invited for a Saturday to the parents' summer house, but with whom he has had no further contact since. At the age of thirty-three he seems to be perfectly happy with his job, his very restricted daily routine and visiting his parents once a month. He has a small flat which he keeps very neat and tidy. He is always clean and well dressed. His voice is a high-pitched monotone, and his speech is still almost unbearably pedantic. II:4 is of normal appearance and right-handed.

Unfortunately, it has never been possible to make a complete neurobiological work-up in his case. However, the case is of great interest because the family history reveals both Asperger syndrome and autism among its members.

His eldest brother, II:1, ten years his senior, has Kanner-type autism and mild mental retardation. He was first diagnosed when he was four years old. He now lives in a group home for mildly mentally retarded people. He belongs to that group of autistic individuals who are passive and friendly (Wing, 1983). The mother had rubella during the first trimester of this brother's pregnancy. The mother herself has several Asperger-type traits: she does not have any friends, is very formal, pedantic, obsessive and has difficulty understanding some abstract expressions in spite of overall very good intelligence (she took a Ph D in history at the age of sixty, after having been a housewife for twenty-five years). However, her personality would probably have been seen as on the extreme end of a normality continuum had it not been for her sons, one with autism, the other with Asperger syndrome.

The middle brother, II:2, also has several traits suggestive of Asperger syndrome: formal, pedantic and staccato-type speech; difficulty mixing socially with other people; and stiff, awkward gait. He is married and works as a chief dentist in a laboratory. Tragically, his first-born son by a healthy unrelated woman shows at the age of three all the signs of infantile autism (and probably normal intelligence). This boy had severe perinatal asphyxia.

The father of II:4, I:2, a very distinguished civil servant with a lifelong interest in geography, is a quiet, warm but socially rather shy person with a few very good friends with whom he has kept in contact throughout his life (he is now seventy-two years old).

This family history suggests that there may be important genetic links between Asperger syndrome and autism, at least in some cases. There are similarities between this family and the one recently described by Bowman (1988), in which there seemed to be a continuum of disorders ranging from Asperger-type traits to typical Asperger syndrome and autism.

If Asperger-type traits have indeed been inherited in this family, pure X-linked inheritance is excluded as a candidate mode of transmission unless II:2 has more than one X-chromosome. The fragile-X abnormality could not otherwise account for these findings. The physical phenotype in all cases in this family is very dissimilar from that described as typical of this chromosomal abnormality. Nevertheless, since no chromosomal cultures were performed in this family, conclusions cannot be definite in this respect. The presence of Asperger traits in the mother, I:1, is unusual, but has been described by Asperger himself (1944) and also by Wing (1981).

Otherwise, clinical experience (for example, Gillberg, 1989) abounds with examples of Asperger males having Asperger-type fathers. From the very limited data so far available a (perhaps atypical) dominant mode of heritability seems to be the most likely candidate, but this cannot be regarded as even near settled. The two cases of autism in this family were both associated with brain-damaging factors (maternal rubella and perinatal asphyxia), while no such factors were present in the Asperger case.

Family 2. The case of the one-dress girl

IV:1 is a fourteen-year-old girl with high intelligence (full scale WISC at the age of twelve 120, verbal IQ 127, performance 110, poorest performance on picture arrangement, digit span and parts of the comprehension subtest, average on block design), whom I have followed regularly at least twice a year from before her first birthday. She was born after a normal pregnancy, and birthweight, length, head circumference, and peri- and neonatal periods were all normal. She was a very 'good' baby, not demanding much. When I first saw her in connection with a routine health control at the age of ten months, I made a note in the record that she seemed 'very serious', 'a little late in gross motor development' and 'slightly hypotonic'. She started walking at the age of fifteen months. At eighteen months she had acquired a few single words. At thirty months she seemed a bit slow in language development but by the age of four years she was speaking at an age-appropriate level (no test performed).

She was described as 'day-dreaming' and 'never listening' by the parents, and this impression was substantiated in connection with a routine health check. She had no peers with whom she would play, and was totally uninterested in other children except one particular girl who was a year her junior. One day she demanded that her parents ask this little girl to come over. When she came, she was in complete control of all situations and IV:1 remained passive. IV:1 was uninterested in all toys, except a particular doll which she would dress and undress endlessly. She demanded that her parents buy unreasonable quantities of clothes for this doll and they complied lest she throw a severe tantrum. She spent some time in a day nursery but had to be taken out of it because she refused to mix with the other children.

At the age of six years, she was talking in a shrill, monotonous voice, endlessly about clothes. A ten-year-old girl who lived in the neighbourhood selected IV:1 to be her 'slave', a role she performed without complaint for at least two years until the older girl grew tired of the situation. IV:1 gradually developed a strong interest in paper bags which she would collect

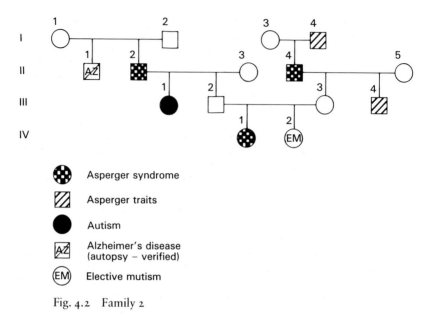

Fig. 4.2   Family 2

and store in the attic with such fervour that her parents became extremely concerned. This interest was at its peak from the age of eight to ten years and was then replaced, rather suddenly, by an almost fanatic preoccupation with the idea that research on animals must be prohibited. She would write long letters on this subject to various state officials, but would not expect an answer. She had a pet, a guinea pig which she treated in a rather careless fashion and which eventually died, presumably because of starvation in connection with a family holiday when it had been left behind for several days.

Throughout her early school years, IV:1 insisted on wearing the same dress every day (except at Christmas and Easter). Her mother had to wash the garment secretly at night and then try to make it smell 'non-clean' in order for the girl not to notice and throw a tantrum.

She had a very formal and repetitive way of responding to questions and always ended each statement on a very high note. Much of what she said spontaneously seemed to be exact repetitions of what she had heard other people say. If asked 'What do you think?' she would invariably respond 'Oh, I don't know'. She had several 'friends' at the age of twelve but never made any demands on them, except in so far as animal research was discussed. She passively accepted what her peers proposed. She was well liked but the parents saw how her friends marvelled at her complete lack of intuitive notions about other people and deficient appreciation of irony and her inability to understand such concepts. She was clumsy and her gestures and movements ill co-ordinated. She got very poor reports for PE but participated seemingly without self-criticism in spite of the fact that her performance was 'comical' to say the least. She also had problems with mathematics but otherwise performed as expected in all school subjects given her relatively good IQ. She looks normal and is right-handed.

The girl represents a case which, scrutinised this way, is a typical example of Asperger syndrome. The fact that she has several 'friends' may at first seem to detract from the possibility of this diagnosis. However, this case demonstrates clearly that reports about existing interactions with age-peers have to be analysed very carefully before they can be accepted as indicative of normal socialisation. This girl at the age of fourteen in the middle of her pubertal period, has interactions with other people that are either obsessive or passive. Indeed IV:1 shows many of the characteristics of the passive and friendly autism group described by Wing (1983).

The case is particularly interesting in that it illustrates that Asperger syndrome can occur in girls. It suggests that, on the surface, symptoms of impairment of social interaction might be less conspicuous than corresponding symptoms in boys.

As in the case of family 1, she has never been referred for child psychiatric treatment or help. Both her parents are dentists and have been able to cope with the problems partly because of personal contacts with psychiatrists and psychologists, and their almost incredible patience, and also to some extent because of their respective family histories (see the pedigree). Since IV:1 has taken part in various research projects, I have been in a position to obtain the necessary information which has allowed at least tentative diagnoses. I have made a point of meeting and talking to all the members of the family shown in the pedigree, except the paternal uncle who died of Alzheimer's disease many years ago.

The paternal grandfather is a very tall and thin man, very formal, pedantic and socially inept. Furthermore, he is clumsy and ill co-ordinated. He is without doubt one of the most clear-cut examples of Asperger syndrome I have met. The paternal aunt, III:1, was diagnosed in childhood as suffering from psychosis. In retrospect it is clear that she must have fulfilled current *DSM-III-R* criteria (American Psychiatric Association, 1987) for autistic disorder. Her mother, II:3, in the third month of gestation, had a temperature, a rash and arthralgia. Rubella infection was not then considered a plausible aetiological agent, and in retrospect it has not been possible to confirm or refute this diagnosis. III:1 is of low or borderline normal intelligence. At the age of forty she has half-sheltered work and is treated by an adult psychiatrist with lithium because of frequent mood swings.

IV:1's younger sister, now five years old, has shown some features suggestive of Asperger syndrome but also fulfils *DSM-III-R* criteria for elective mutism. The maternal grandfather and uncle both represent mild but clear variants of Asperger syndrome. Both parents, although friendly and cheerful people, have problems identifying with the feelings and perspectives of other people. The mother fulfills criteria for histrionic personality disorder according to *DSM-III-R* (American Psychiatric Association, 1987).

With regard to neurobiological examinations, IV:1 has a normal karyotype and no fragile-X positive cells, a normal CT of the brain but a bilateral pathological prolongation of the I–V interval on auditory brainstem response (ABR) examination.

Like family 1, this family illustrates that Asperger syndrome can cluster in families and that autism too can occur in the same family. Autism can be the outcome perhaps if brain damage is added to the genetic predisposition. There is the possibility – although in this case we have no hard evidence to support it – that a viral infection (perhaps rubella?) in the first trimester tipped the balance negatively for III:1 so that what might have turned out to be a mild case of Asperger syndrome (or an extreme of normal social-cognitive functioning) developed into autism instead.

There is double genetic loading in this case, with both parents having family histories of Asperger syndrome. It is of considerable interest that the parents themselves do not show obvious outward signs of the disorder. Therefore a genetic rather than a psychosocial mode of transmission seems likely.

Finally, the prolonged brainstem transmission time in the index case might be taken to indicate brainstem-vestibular dysfunction. Unfortunately we do not have data on any of the other family members in this respect.

Family 3. The case of the amateur actor

III:1 is an eighteen-year-old young man of good intelligence (full scale WISC 118, verbal IQ 130 (poor performance on comprehension), performance IQ 108 (top performance on block design)) who was a typical case of Asperger syndrome when I first met him when he was twelve years old, a year before he entered puberty. He was first seen by a child psychiatrist at the age of seven, when his mother had applied for help for him because of difficulties adjusting socially with age-peers at school. He was described as 'eccentric, monotonously and repetitively talking in a shrill voice and yet giving a naive impression'. The mother described him as a 'problem child' from the start, who screamed a lot and needed little sleep. He did not seem to listen and was regarded as unduly active. He was stubbornly fixed in various routines by the age of three. He spoke long and complicated sentences before the age of two and was already, by that time, imitating television reporters, which has remained his favourite activity to this day. He imitates them very well but can never improvise. Instead, he has to say everything the reporter said in the same tone of voice and sitting in exactly the same posture. If interrupted, he got – and still gets – furious. Already, before the age of two years he shunned body contact and, at playgrounds or family gatherings, would stand isolated with his back towards other people, usually doing nothing at all. He has never shown major motor stereotypies but from very early in childhood has had a strong wish to wave objects. Now, at the age of eighteen, he almost constantly plucks at his fingers in various odd ways.

His mother insisted that as a baby, before he started walking, he had been cuddly. There is no reason to doubt this information since she was a trained nurse and had been working with small children for many years.

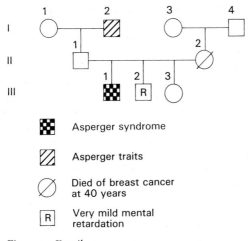

Asperger syndrome

Asperger traits

Died of breast cancer
at 40 years

R   Very mild mental
retardation

Fig. 4.3   Family 3

From about the age of two years, it became obvious that III:1 was
extremely pedantic in all his undertakings. He always demanded to sit in
exactly the same position at the breakfast table and to wear the same red
trousers every day. His mother had to wash them at night when he had
gone off to sleep. Afterwards, he would complain for hours that the
trousers smelt and felt 'wrong'.

From around the age of four years he began to concentrate on
circumscribed interests, first aeroplanes, then trams then trains and now
chess and stage productions. These interests have always excluded all other
activities, at least until very recently when he had – to some extent,
successfully – taken part in an amateur actors' group.

His manner of speech is very pedantic and formal. Up till about the age
of fourteen he always echoed by whisper what people said to him.
Nowadays he always hums before he answers a question. Asked why, he
says that 'under the hum' he repeats your question.

Children at school have always found him strange and even 'weird'.
Adult people such as the parents' friends, on the other hand, have always
found him amicable.

At eighteen he has no friends, attends a normal school (achieving like
average teenagers) and considers going on to university to study trains! He
shuts himself in his room most of the time when he is not at school, except
when he goes out to his actors' group.

He is the firstborn of three. His younger brother has very mild mental
retardation, an operated cleft palate and a tendency towards both
hyperactivity and obsessional traits. His sister, who is ten years younger, is
healthy in all respects. Sadly, his mother died of cancer when he was fifteen
years old. Before she died he said to her in his very formal way: 'How
unfortunate that you should have cancer.' His father has mild Asperger

traits and is a bit of a loner. He is easily moved by human suffering and misses his wife to the point of utter despair.

After the death of his mother, when people asked III:1 how he was doing, he usually answered: 'Oh, I am all right. You see I have Asperger syndrome which makes me less vulnerable to the loss of loved ones than are most people.'

A full neurobiological work-up, including an EEG and a chromosomal culture in a folic-acid depleted medium, has shown normal results throughout. The boy is of normal weight and height and is good looking. He is right-handed. There are many relatives (all male) on the paternal side of the family who show many features suggestive of Asperger syndrome. A paternal uncle has a grandson with epilepsy and a paternal cousin (female) is mentally retarded. The maternal grandmother has a sister who has a daughter and a granddaughter both of whom have epilepsy.

Family 4. The case of the little frog expert

III:2 is a six-year-old boy of normal intelligence whom I have known since he was four years old. He is a typical case of Asperger syndrome, but equally a case could have been made for a diagnosis of autistic disorder (*DSM-III-R*, American Psychiatric Association, 1987), at least before the age of five.

His parents describe him as 'good and undemanding' in his first year of life, much easier to manage than his older brother, who craved more attention. He had appeared to be particularly content with being left in his bed. He started walking at fourteen months and had full bowel and bladder control by the age of twenty months. From about eighteen months of age, he gradually began to need less and less sleep, until eventually he slept only five or six hours out of twenty-four. He got out of bed after midnight and stayed up for many hours wandering about the house. During this period he was considered 'totally impervious to distraction' by his parents.

At twelve months he stayed with his maternal grandparents for a week. Exactly a year later, he again visited his grandparents together with his parents but this time he stubbornly refused to get out of the car. His refusal was so serious and had such fervour that the parents had to bring him home again without leaving the car. From around the age of thirty months he was perceived by his parents as turning 'hyperactive' and 'obviously uninterested in other children'. He 'communicated' with loud noises but had no speech whatsoever before the age of three years. He was very destructive and all sorts of household equipment was destroyed by him. Every summer the family went on a sailing trip in their boat and III:2 was then (and has been since the age of two) very different: calm, insisting on routine and very careful not to damage anything on board.

At the age of three and a half years, when his expressive speech development was still limited to a few single words, he was admitted to a full-time day nursery. His behaviour did not change much and his language development appeared to be unaffected.

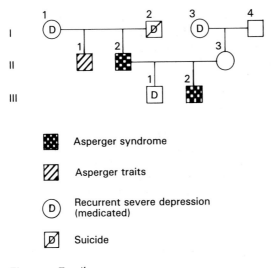

Fig. 4.4   Family 4

At four years he started relatively quickly to use long sentences. These were almost always perfect imitations (with regard to content, pronunciation, pitch and inflection) of what he had heard some grown-up say seconds or hours earlier. Both the parents and staff came to regard him as exceptionally gifted in many ways, both because this manner of speech seemed to them to be much more mature than that of his age-peers and because he led his peers in various technical games (he managed to build ingenious trains out of chairs, saucepans or empty boxes). However, everyone thought he was odd in that he still seemed to be almost completely unaware of the other children (and most of the grown-ups too). He began to develop a special interest in trains and aeroplanes just before his fifth birthday. He would enquire endlessly about makes and details of engines and cabins. For almost a year he was totally preoccupied with these two areas of interest and would talk about them in a monotonous, hoarse voice at the dinner table, at the day nursery or to nobody in particular at the tram station. Suddenly, just before his sixth birthday, these interests were abandoned and he started to accumulate facts about frogs. In this connection he quickly learnt the letters of the alphabet and acquired some reading skills to the extent that he could amass new knowledge out of encyclopedias concerning frogs. Asked to read other texts he refused, but also seemed unable to manage it. Now, at the age of six years and four months, his main interest is in frogs. He demands to go the library every day to take down all the books with information about frogs from the shelves. He is also concerned with various minute technical details at the day nursery (for example, connecting wires inside the telephone). He knows the names of his age-peers but does not play with them. They are interested in him, but he does not show any interest in them. He still echoes (often whispering) everything said by adults. If what he just echoed was a question directed at him, he sometimes answers in a very matter-of-fact way. He does not display any emotions except anger (when he doesn't want to accept demands). He still sleeps very little (around five hours out of the twenty-four).

The boy's mother first contacted a child guidance clinic when III:2 was three years and eleven months of age. A Griffiths test at that stage revealed him to have an overall developmental quotient (DQ) of 82 with very poor results on hearing and language (DQ 69) and practical reasoning (DQ 65) but age-appropriate skills in the gross motor, eye–hand co-ordination, performance and ADL (activities of daily life) domains. A speech therapist made a diagnosis of 'echolalia' when he was four and a half years old. At four years eight months he was referred to the special autism diagnosis centre where I work. Testing with the Griffiths scale again at the age of five years five months yielded a DQ of 89, but this time hearing and language was on a par with other functions. Only practical reasoning still came out poorly (DQ 74). On the Leiter test he obtained an IQ of 85. A year later his Leiter IQ was 95. On the ITPA (Illinois Test of Psycholinguistic Abilities) his scores ranged from 120 to 77. He was best at auditory reception, auditory sequencing and expressive language skills, and worst at visual reception and visual analogy. It is the clinical impression that once he can be tested with the WISC he will show an uneven profile with scores ranging from mild mental retardation to much above average intellectual functioning.

A full medical work-up has shown him to have a large head (99th centile), be slightly overweight (80th centile), of normal height (50th centile) and without obvious physical stigmata. He has two small pendunculated fibromas (2 × 5 mm), one near the left ear and one on the left shoulder. He is clumsy in all his movements. The auditory brainstem response (ABR) examination showed a pathological prolongation of the brainstem transmission time on the left side. All other examinations (CT scan, chromosomal culture (including fragile-X), EEG, ophthalmological examination, audiometry and CSF) were normal. However, his CSF-HVA: HMPG quotient was relatively high (7.1:1; cf. Gillberg and Svennerholm, 1987). He is right-handed.

The mother had slight toxaemia signs in pregnancy (oedema and mild proteinuria), but otherwise, the boy's intrauterine and intrapartal/neonatal periods seem to have been uneventful (medical record data).

The boy's father has typical Asperger syndrome as manifested in the following features. He has a monotonous voice, a circumscribed interest in electronics (runs an electronics firm), and a sincere wish to understand other people but a total lack of intuition in this respect. He has no friends and adheres to a set of daily rituals. The failure to perform one of these rituals (for instance, while travelling) makes him extremely tense and he cannot sleep. Even under ordinary circumstances he has a sleeping problem. He always takes notes when he is listening to other people 'in case something might be missed'. The father's brother also has many traits reminiscent of Asperger syndrome. The boy's mother is a warm, sensible woman, whom it has taken about twelve years to realise that her husband has a social handicap. The boy's eleven-year-old brother is normal but has suffered from recurrent depression since the age of seven. Both paternal grandparents suffered from severe recurrent depressions. A paternal aunt suffers from 'paranoia', according to psychiatric hospital records.

The boy's psychosocial circumstances are the best possible and the family is well-to-do. His mother took very good care of him at home during his first three years of life. Before the work-up in connection with diagnosing Asperger syndrome, he had been admitted to hospital once for a two-day period at the age of three. Apart from this and half a dozen middle-ear infections, he has so far been physically well.

From the neurobiological point of view, there are several interesting features in this case. The family history is one of Asperger syndrome, depression and 'paranoia' on the paternal side of the family. There are signs of brainstem dysfunction on the ABR, and the CSF mono amine balance is similar to that encountered in autism.

Clinically, this case is interesting in that it shows many similarities with autism. Also of particular importance is that this boy seemed at first to be very severely handicapped in the field of expressive language skills, an area in which after a few years' follow-up (into primary-school age) he excelled on formal testing. A diagnosis of mild mental retardation was suspected when he was four years old, but this is no longer so at the age of six when he scores above average in many areas. A particularly interesting point is that on formal testing with the Griffiths test his gross motor skills are average. Yet the clinical impression is one of considerable motor clumsiness.

In summary, this case illustrates clearly that autism and Asperger syndrome are sometimes not clearly separable diagnostic entities.

Family 5. The case of the mathematician

III: 1 is a nine-year-old boy with Asperger syndrome and at least normal intelligence. He was the first-born child to healthy, unrelated parents and he has a healthy sister. Pregnancy was uneventful. He was delivered by Caesarean section due to narrow pelvis. He was a quiet infant who had clear sucking and feeding difficulties. He developed hyperbilirubinemia with a maximum bilirubin value of 335 mg/ml. The mother was in training when III: 1 was born, and is now a clinical psychologist. She was interested in child development and thought very early on that something must be wrong. At seven weeks the boy was diagnosed as suffering from congenital hypothyroidism (due to thyroid aplasia), and appropriate medication with synthetic thyroid hormone was started. His feeding difficulties and icterus quickly disappeared. However, with regard to development of social and communicative skills, both parents agreed that he was slower than other children and from the point of view of motor development was more clumsy than his age-peers. He walked unaided only at eighteen months of age.

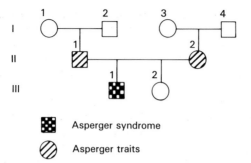

Fig. 4.5   Family 5

Typical from very early on were his obstinacy, impatience and 'lack of respect for other people's integrity' (mother's words). He needed little sleep (much less than his sister and his parents). He appeared to be restless, fixated on his own interest, 'not listening', hyperactive and his attention could rarely be gained. Around fourteen months of age he was placed in a day nursery where he remained until seven, the normal starting age for school. He never showed an interest in the other children. He was regarded by the pre-school teachers as 'domineering'.

From the age of three he showed an extreme interest in mathematics and before age four years he knew how to add, subtract, multiply and divide three-figure numbers.

At the age of seven, when I first saw him, he could instantly extract the square root of any number under 200. His only interest in life is mathematics and he turns everything into a mathematical problem. He solves the problem but is totally uninterested in any connecting aspects and fails to see similarities between problems which are not completely identical. His skills in the mathematical area at the age of seven corresponded to those of first-year university students in mathematics according to psychological testing and comparison with current university norms. The parents described him as totally disinterested in other children and minimally interested in members of his own family. He would treat people as objects, move them to suit his needs and bite them if they did not comply with his demands. He could not tolerate changes of routine, but if changes could be explained in terms of the solution to a mathematical problem, he reluctantly agreed to accept them. He incessantly asked the same set of questions and did not really care what the answers were. His gaze was very stiff and 'non-reciprocal'. He laughed when other people cried. He has always had great difficulties understanding human facial expressions. He was described as having had a very early development of speech (considerably earlier than the other children in the day nursery). From about the age of four he has often expressed himself by way of neologisms. Very often he has spoken only in sentences in which every word begins with the same letter. His voice has always (from the first month of life) been a little hoarse and his intonation flat.

His gross motor performance was very poor and he could not manage to hop on one foot more than two or three times. Diadochokinesis performance corresponded to that of a five-year-old (at the age of seven years nine months). His WISC score was 108 (performance 100 and verbal 188). His poorest performance was in coding (82) and his best in block design and arithmetic (138). On the ITPA his scores range from (visual memory) to auditory reception (118) and visual analogy (125).

His mother is very matter-of-fact, highly obsessional and always takes notes even when conversing with acquaintances. Both parents have traits reminiscent of Asperger syndrome, and the mother in particular is formal, pedantic and shows circumscribed interests. However, she is deeply devoted to her son's progress and has always tried to care for him in the best possible way. She has suffered two episodes of major depression.

The boy now attends a special class for bright children with autism and autistic-like conditions. He started school in normal class but his dislike of the other children and theirs of him made it impossible for him to continue there.

It is likely that the hypothyroidism which remained untreated for the first seven weeks of the boy's life has played some part in the pathogenetic chain of events in this case. It is equally likely that hereditary factors have played some part. The hypothyroidism may well have acted by way of producing hyperbilirubinemia (which the boy had), which in turn could perhaps have made Asperger-sensitive brain areas dysfunctional.

Family 6. The case of the little professor

III:2 at twelve years of age had classical Asperger syndrome. According to the WISC he was found to have a full scale IQ 150 with low results on the comprehension and picture arrangement and superior results on the other subtests. He was considered to have 'a lot of locked-up aggression and tension', according to projective tests (draw-a-man, children's apperception test). He was referred to me by the school doctor because the situation in his classroom had become intolerable and he had recently tried to jump out of a window on the third floor (smiling).

I had met him in the school setting several times before his father brought him for consultation at the clinic. As usual, on meeting me (or any adult), he started chatting away about various kinds of gunpowder for which he had amassed a multitude of prescriptions. He told me he would start to try them out in the school-yard. He then interrupted himself, stared intensely but briefly at me and said: 'I say, you do look a lot like Christopher Gillberg!' I asked him if he could guess the reason for my looking so much like Christopher Gillberg. 'How am I to know. You just happen to look like a copy of him, that's all!' I then said: 'Well, you see, I am Christopher Gillberg.' He looked up briefly and exclaimed 'What an extraordinary coincidence!' and then made his way into my secretary's office, stumbling on the threshold. I started to say 'This is my

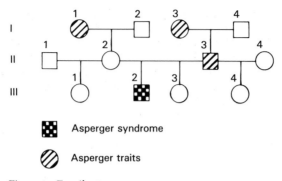

Fig. 4.6   Family 6

secretary . . .', but he did not seem to listen and, instead, immediately asked, 'How many letters per second can you type?' My secretary said: 'Well, it used to be 1100 in three minutes.' He then proceeded to her desk, made a quick computation and shouted: 'Six point one one one one one one in all eternity one one one.' My secretary looked astounded and said: 'Is that so?' He then pointed at me and stared into thin air and said: 'He does look like Christopher Gillberg! What a coincidence!'

He then entered my office and started picking out various books and papers from one of the shelves. Quite by chance he found a Swedish leaflet for parents on Asperger syndrome. He said: 'This is something I've never heard anybody say a word about before. I think I'll call it AS for short.' On reading the text aloud he soon remarked, as though in passing: 'It seems I have AS! By golly, I do have AS. Wait till my father hears about this!' He went on reading and soon decided: 'My parents just might have AS too, you know, my father in particular, he too has all-absorbing interests and . . .' He did not seem to react emotionally to what he read. 'Now I can tell my classmates the reason why I pace the school-yard briskly ten times up and down each break all the year round is I have AS. And it will get my teacher off my back. If you have a "handicap condition" they have to tolerate you.'

III:2 was the firstborn child to healthy unrelated parents of superior intelligence who both show mild – but clear – traits of Asperger syndrome (the father in particular). A little sister, seven years of age, also has Asperger-type traits but nothing near as severe as those of her elder brother. There are reports of extreme Asperger traits in both the maternal and the paternal grandmothers. Pregnancy and delivery were uneventful. III:2 was a little slow to start walking (fifteen months) and spoke very little before two and a half years but then started 'conversing with adult strangers' almost at once. He showed virtually no interest in age-peers other than as short-cuts to computers, his favourite pastime. His way of talking was very fast and formal, 'like a professor'. When very young he showed a number of stereotyped hand movements and grimaced in stereotyped ways. He soon started to amass facts about chemistry and at the age of eleven was judged by a professor of chemistry at a polytechnic to fulfil the requirements for a university degree. He is very clumsy in gross motor domains and does not want to take part in PE. He demands constant attention in the classroom. When ignored he threatens (and tries) to jump out of the window. The school psychologist thought he was depressed and was trying to commit suicide, but he replied: 'No! I just wanted to jump out of the window, that's all.'

A full neurobiological work-up (including chromosomal culture in a folic-acid depleted medium, CT scan of the brain, EEG and ear and eye examinations) has shown him to have a pathological bilateral prolongation of brainstem transmission time on the ABR.

Discussion

These six case histories of Asperger syndrome were chosen to illustrate various clinical and neurobiological issues which might be relevant for a discussion concerning the delineation of the syndrome *vis-à-vis* autism, the changing manifestations over time and possible aetiological pathogenetic mechanisms. They do not constitute a representative sample of children with Asperger syndrome but are fairly typical of the series of twenty-three patients seen in my own practice (Gillberg, 1989). The last three cases in particular are extraordinarily similar to the cases described by Asperger. The first three show the developmental course to adulthood of some relatively mild cases and there is the case of a girl with Asperger syndrome whose clinical picture is also rather mild. In the absence of population-based studies of Asperger syndrome these cases will have to serve as a reasonable clinical sample for formulating hypotheses which can be put to the test in future epidemiological studies.

From the diagnostic point of view, two of the cases (from families 3 and 4) fulfilled *DSM-III-R* criteria for autistic disorder in early childhood but later better fitted the prototype of Asperger syndrome. This is similar to what Wing (1981) reported in her series of thirty-four patients, some of whom had been autistic in the pre-school years but who later appeared to be classic cases of Asperger syndrome.

The main question that demands discussion is *the relationship of Asperger syndrome to autism*. It is clear that Asperger syndrome overlaps with autism in several key aspects, perhaps most notably with regard to some of the core symptoms, the persistence of handicap for many, many years and certain associated neurobiological markers.

Let us look at the core symptoms first. It is striking that all six cases described here show a *reduced capacity for conceiving of other people as creatures who think and feel*. This symptom has recently been proposed as a core deficit that underlies all autistic spectrum disorders, and this proposal is presented in detail in chapter 1. In particular, it is argued that this deficit very precisely accounts for the quality of the social impairment of autistic people.

We turn next to the symptom of *language problems*. All six cases had language problems, in particular with respect to semantics, pragmatics and comprehension. These same problems are also always encountered in autism. However, unlike individuals with autism all had good or very good expressive language skills at a level which far exceeds that usually found in autism. Furthermore, they all had developed a near-normal level of speech by the age of five.

It is often surmised that *stereotypies* are particularly typical of autism with mental retardation. Indeed severe motor stereotypies, such as excessive hand-flapping and rocking, are probably more often encountered when autism and mental retardation coincide. Nevertheless, it is clear that stereotypic motor behaviours occur in Asperger syndrome too. All six cases described showed pronounced behaviour of this kind in early childhood (hand-flapping, head-banging and tiptoeing in one case each). However, they later learnt how to hide these behaviours and perform them only in socially acceptable settings. Nevertheless, some still exhibited clear-cut repetitive finger or hand stereotypies or stereotyped facial grimacing (in one case each). Obviously, even though stereotypies of this kind in adult age are less conspicuous (and perhaps (?) less frequent) in Asperger syndrome than in typical autism cases, they cannot be used as a differentiating criterion.

Perhaps the most striking feature of Asperger cases is their *odd all-absorbing interests*. It may be thanks to their normal intelligence that they have turned those interests into areas of expertise in which they shine. Clearly, comparison with less able autistic individuals would be unfair in this respect. Nevertheless, autistic people too, even some who are totally mute and aloof, can develop rare circumscribed interests and skills, such as drawing. While the present symptom itself does not discriminate autism from Asperger syndrome, the attempts to impose the interest (or any special routines) on others in everyday life appears to be particularly pronounced in Asperger cases. However, the nature of this symptom is as yet too little understood for specific claims to be made.

Finally, with regard to possible distinguishing features in clinical diagnosis, the issue of *gross and fine motor skills* needs to be discussed. Unequivocal cases of classical Kanner autism usually exhibit *relatively* excellent skills in the motor domains, relative that is to their overall severe deficits in so many other fields. Asperger syndrome cases, on the other hand, are often described as showing clumsiness, a lack of co-ordination of movements and a stiff, awkward gait. In a recent comparison of twenty-three Asperger syndrome cases and twenty-three sex- and age-matched Kanner syndrome cases, motor clumsiness did indeed appear to be a hallmark of the former and not of the latter (Gillberg, 1989). Motor clumsiness had not been included as a necessary criterion for diagnosing Asperger syndrome in that study, but it was found that nineteen of the twenty-three cases showed motor skills to be more than fifteen points below the child's overall IQ. This held in only five of the twenty-three cases with Kanner autism. All the six cases described in this chapter had moderate problems in the field of motor control. One could argue that children with autism are so handicapped that they never get to show enough motor skills to make it apparent that they too have co-ordination problems and that the only reason for children with Asperger syndrome showing such problems so often is their generally higher IQ and hence their broader range of skills. However, such an explanation seems unlikely, considering that children with autism often perform *better* than brighter children with Asperger syndrome on tasks involving balance and fine motor manipulations (Gillberg and Gillberg, in progress).

On balance, therefore, the available evidence suggests that autism and Asperger syndrome are closely related clinical entities. The possible distinguishing quality of motor clumsiness, which cannot be accounted for by higher IQ, may imply that continuities may not exist across syndromes (Asperger syndrome representing but mild autism or autism in children with high IQ), but rather that there is important but not complete overlap with regard to the neural circuitries which are involved (Asperger syndrome engaging core 'autism centres' in the brain plus centres – or connections with centres – regulating motor but not expressive language skills). One way of testing part of this hypothesis would be to study the motor skills in those cases of autism which appear in families in which Asperger syndrome and autism cluster. In such families it seems plausible that there is a genetic basis for Asperger syndrome and that in cases with autism, brain damage has been added. It would be difficult to account for cases with autism and *good* motor skills in such families. Therefore, in such families one would expect motor clumsiness to appear in both autism and Asperger syndrome cases. In the two families described in this chapter where there were members with autism and members with Asperger syndrome, this certainly held.

In this connection one must not forget that most cases with autism do not show motor skills *above* the norms of age-peers and many do indeed perform *below* level (DeMyer, 1979).

Asperger syndrome manifests itself in varying ways according to the child's age and developmental level. In some cases there is clinical continuity across syndromes with autism as in two of the present cases who actually fulfilled *DSM-III-R* criteria for autistic disorder in early childhood but went on to develop a clinical picture which better fitted that described by Asperger. Further, it is obvious that even though some children with Asperger syndrome never fit the criteria for infantile autism or autistic disorder, quite a number of cases with autistic disorder would also fit in with the general criteria for Asperger syndrome outlined at the beginning of this chapter.

However, children with Asperger syndrome do not come all in one shape with regard to early symptoms and this is well illustrated by the six cases. Some present with a suspicion of autism, but others do not cause major worry or concern until well into their school years. This is not to say that such cases do not have Asperger-type problems from very early in their development, but there must exist relatively wide inter-individual variation with regard to severity of problems.

Szatmari, Bartolucci and Bremner (1989) have made claims for a distinction of autism vis-à-vis Asperger syndrome on the basis of well-developed early attachment behaviour and absence of severe language problems in the latter. In all the six cases described here – and in a majority of the clinical series of twenty-three referred to previously (Gillberg, 1989) – according to interview with the mother, early attachment behaviours were not quite normal, and neither was the child's language development. I do not think that at present we have a firm enough basis for subdividing cases with 'autism spectrum' or 'autism associated' disorders according to early attachment behaviour and language development. Again, it appears that, at least with regard to disturbed attachment behaviour, which can be seen as one aspect of overall social impairment, quantitative rather than qualitative differences between autism and Asperger syndrome prevail.

In respect of language development, there are certainly considerable differences with regard to the level of skills between cases with classic Kanner type autism and classical Asperger syndrome when examined in later childhood, but differences may be less pronounced in early childhood (perhaps in particular with regard to language comprehension) at an age when laymen do not yet react strongly to what they perceive as subtle problems. Many authors, including Hans Asperger, stress the excellent verbal skills of children with Asperger syndrome to such an extent that all the major problems (major, that is, in relation to overall IQ and other skills) in the field of semantics, pragmatics and comprehension in general are obscured. Seventeen of the twenty-three children with Asperger syndrome seen in my clinic over the last ten years (Gillberg, 1989) were slow to start talking, according to parental report. Once they started talking, however, their speech and language soon turned adult-type and formalistic. This perfect quality of their speech has tended to detract from the proneness of many of them to concrete misinterpretations.

One boy of fifteen reacted to his mother's statement 'She's on the way to getting better' by asking 'Whereabouts is that?' He then put a number of questions which showed that he believed that 'the way to getting better' was a street address. This boy had a full scale WISC IQ at the age of fourteen of 132. Many more examples of concrete misinterpretation are given in chapter 7.

Four of the six children showed late speech development and the fifth had echolalia. All the cases had problems with regard to prosody and language comprehension. Other speech-language characteristics included whispering echolalia (cases 2 and 4) repetitive questioning (all six cases) and galloping speech (case 6). Thus if one accepts the diagnosis of Asperger syndrome in these six cases, one would also have to accept that it is impossible to subdivide cases of Asperger syndrome and autism according to absence or presence of language problems, which seems to be what Szatmari and his group (Nagy and Szatmari, 1987) suggest.

The careful *neurobiological analysis* of the six cases described here (table 4.5) does not yield a consistent picture except in so far as Asperger-type problems heredity is concerned. All six cases had a close relative with Asperger syndrome (this was true for three of the cases) or Asperger-type traits (which was true for the other three). Two even had close relatives with autism. It is relatively uncommon for parents of children with classical autism to be themselves autistic-like or Asperger type. Four out of five examined cases showed signs of brainstem pathology according to auditory brainstem response examination. One case was probably triggered by the effects of congenital hypothyroidism and hyperbilirubinemia in the first seven weeks of life. The neurobiological problems encountered in these six cases are similar to, but not as pronounced as those seen in children of near-normal or normal IQ who have been diagnosed as suffering from autism. In the study of twenty-three Asperger syndrome and twenty-three children with autism referred to above, major indications of brain damage/dysfunction were found in 61 per cent of the former and 78 per cent of the later group.

One hypothesis which could account for most of the findings in the field so far is that we are dealing with three groups in this connection: (1) Kanner autism which is usually the result of environmentally determined brain damage or specific hereditary factors causing brain dysfunction; (2) Asperger syndrome which is usually caused by polygenic hereditary influences; and (3) a clinically less specific group with traits of both conditions, a developmental course during which both diagnoses are considered and a background of both hereditary Asperger-type problems and laboratory indications of brain damage.

The early histories of at least four of these cases seemed to indicate attentional problems early in life. All six cases had some motor-control or motor-perceptual problems. Courchesne (1987) has suggested that autistic-type disorders could arise as a consequence of disruption of normal development of attentional processes early in life, followed by development only of some higher brain centres which have been spared from the effects of stimulus deprivation due to the attentional deficits. Brainstem pathology was common in the present material and could mirror damage to crucial 'neural attentional circuitry'.

Table 4.5. *Characteristics of six children with Asperger syndrome*

Case	Age at examination (years)	Sex	IQ-V	IQ-P	First or second degree relative with Asperger syndrome (AS) or Asperger traits (AT)	First degree relative with autism	Recurrent depressions in first and second degree relatives	Late speech development	EEG pathology	Brainstem dysfunction	CT-scan pathology	Medical diagnosis	Other comment
1	12–33	M	?[b]	?[b]	AS mother AS brother	Brother Nephew	no	no (but echo)	—[c]	—[c]	—[c]	no	Familial clustering of AS and autism
2	0–14	F	127	110 WISC	AS paternal grandfather	Paternal aunt	no	yes	—[c]	+ABR[a]	no	no	Paternal granduncle Alzheimer's disease Familial clustering of AS and autism
3[d]	12–18	M	130	108 WISC	AT father	no	no	no (but echo)	no	no	no	no	Brother with mild mental retardation
4[d]	4–6	M	95 Leiter		AS father	no	yes	yes	no	+ABR[a]	no	no	—
5	7–9	M	118	100 WISC	AT both parents	no	yes	yes	yes (moderate increase of low frequency activity)	+ABR[a]	no	Hypothyroidism (congenital) – treated from age 7 weeks	Neonatal hyperbilirubinemia
6	12	M	>150	>150 WISC	AT both parents (mild in mother)	no	(yes)[e]	yes	no	+ABR[a]	no	no	—

[a] ABR = auditory brainstem response examination (+ = pathology).
[b] IQ exceeds 130 according to clinical judgement.
[c] — indicates 'not performed'.
[d] Fulfilled *DSM-III-R* criteria for autistic disorder in early childhood.
[e] Severe recurrent depression in several paternal relatives according to maternal report.

It has been suggested that there may exist a spectrum of autistic disorders (Wing, 1989). The disorders range from severe specific social impairment in conjunction with severe mental handicap, through Kanner's syndrome (autistic disorder), with moderate mental retardation and Asperger syndrome, in cases with low to normal or normal intelligence, to even more subtle social deficits seen in children with so-called DAMP (deficits in attention, motor control and perception) – often referred to as 'MBD-type problems' (minimal brain dysfunction) (Gillberg and Gillberg, 1989). The overlap both with autism and DAMP seen in several of the present cases could be seen as supportive of such a continuum.

Nevertheless, no firm conclusions can be drawn on the basis of the data presented here except that there is a great need for continued epidemiological clinical and neurobiological research in the field of autism spectrum disorders. The nature of the social deficits and attentional problems encountered in individuals, either from within or outside the autistic spectrum, warrants systematic study now.

References

American Psychiatric Association. (1980). *Diagnostic and statistical manual of mental disorders.* 3rd edn. Washington: APA.

Asperger, H. (1944). Die 'Autistichen Psychopathen' im Kindesalter. *Archiv für Psychiatrie und Nervenkrankheiten*, 117, 76–136.

Bowman, E.P. (1988). Asperger's syndrome and autism: the case for a connection. *British Journal of Psychiatry*, 152, 377–82.

Courchesne, E. (1987). A neurophysiological view of autism. In E. Schopler & G.B. Mesibov (eds.), *Neurobiological issues in autism.* New York: Plenum.

DeMyer, M.K. (1979). *Parents and children in autism.* Washington: Winston.

Gillberg, C. (1989). Asperger syndrome in 23 Swedish children. *Developmental Medicine and Child Neurology*, 31, 520–31.

Gillberg, C. & Svennerholm, L. (1987). CSF-monoamines in autistic syndrome and other pervasive developmental disorders of early childhood. *British Journal of Psychiatry*, 151, 89–94.

Gillberg, I.C. & Gillberg, C. (1989). Asperger syndrome – some epidemiological considerations: a research note. *Journal of Child Psychology and Psychiatry*, 30, 631–8.

Kanner, L. (1943). Autistic disturbances of affective contact. *Nervous Child*, 2, 217–50.

Nagy, J. & Szatmari, P.A. (1986). A chart review of schizotypal personality disorders in children. *Jorunal of Autism and Developmental Disorders*, 16, 351–67.

Schopler, E. (1985). Convergence of learning disability, higher-level autism, and Asperger's syndrome. (Editorial.) *Journal of Autism and Developmental Disorders*, 15, 359.

Szatmari, P., Bartolucci, G. & Bremner, R. (1989). Asperger's syndrome and autism:

comparison of early history and outcome. *Developmental Medicine and Child Neurology*, 31, 709–20.

Van Krevelen, D.A. (1971). Early infantile autism and autistic psychopathy. *Journal of Autism and Childhood Schizophrenia*, 1, 82–6.

Wing, L. (1981). Asperger's syndrome: a clinical account. *Psychological Medicine*, 11, 115–29.

Wing, L. (1983). Social and interpersonal needs. In E. Schopler & G.B. Mesibov (eds.), *Autism in adolescents and adults*. New York: Plenum.

5

Asperger syndrome in adulthood

DIGBY TANTAM

It's only by logic and lack of emotions that I get through. Hiding feelings
came after I became the victim. All emotions are a sign of weakness. I'm
about as flexible as a thick bar of metal in a barrel of nitrogen . . . I shall
turn out a mechanical, inflexible person who [sic] nobody likes, nobody
loves and who everyone will be glad about when I'm in my grave. I'd only
be concerned with money . . . It's a vicious circle. 1. I get teased 2. I make
myself miserable and cynical 3. I get teased again . . . The best school
would be one where I spent my time working with machines – remove the
human factor. If the people were very nice I could probably do very well.
What I find difficult about learning, as well as the teasing, is that there's a
massive great group of us and they're all unruly . . . I can break out of the
vicious circle, but I can't take down the barriers. The clay has set – I've
moulded my personality. The wall's there for good. I'm no good at
changing. My flexibility was one of the first things I lost – lost completely.

So wrote a twelve-year-old boy with Asperger syndrome to his mother to
explain his quite unprecedented emotional distress when the family cat died.
The teasing that he suffers, his inflexibility, his lack of emotional understanding and his other current difficulties are no different from the
experience of other children with Asperger syndrome, although his superior
verbal skills (his verbal IQ was measured at 152) give his expression of them
unusual articulacy. Alistair's major concern is also that of many parents –
what will happen to him as an adult.

In the introduction to a book on autism in adolescence and adulthood
Mesibov, one of the editors, writes: 'despite the tremendous increase in
research [into autism in childhood] there remains a large gap in our
understanding of autistic people as they become adolescents and adults'
(Mesibov, 1983). This applies *a fortiori* to Asperger syndrome which is only
just now entering the official taxonomy with its inclusion in the tenth

revision of the *International classification of diseases* (World Health Organization, 1990).

Diagnosis of Asperger syndrome in adulthood

Asperger syndrome is a developmental disorder with its origins in infancy, but it may cause the greatest disablement in adolescence and young adulthood, when successful social relationships are the key to almost every achievement. Abnormalities that are mild enough to be disregarded in childhood may become much more conspicuous in adolescence, leading to a specialist opinion being sought for the first time. Diagnosis may therefore have to be made after childhood, and should be suspected in anyone with abnormalities of reciprocal social interaction, non-verbal communication and imaginative activity (Wing and Gould, 1979; Wing, 1987; American Psychiatric Association, 1987).

Although there has been controversy about the relationship of Asperger syndrome to autism (see, for example, Rutter and Schopler, 1987; Volkmar, Paul and Cohen, 1985; Volkmar *et al.*, 1988; Bowman, 1988), there are good reasons (Tantam, 1988a) for considering that Asperger syndrome is one of a group of autistic disorders (called pervasive developmental disorders in the revised third edition of the American Psychiatric Association's *Diagnostic and statistical manual of mental disorders – DSM-III-R*) that all share features described as the 'triad of social impairments' by Wing and Gould (1979).

A definitive diagnosis of pervasive developmental disorder in adulthood can be made when a careful history shows that the triad of social impairments stretches back to early childhood and is not therefore attributable to a later deterioration after an episode of psychosis. Unfortunately, developmental information may not always be available to the general psychiatrist seeing an adult for the first time, but an attempt should always be made to obtain it.

The social impairments to be found in adults with Asperger syndrome are shown in table 5.1 and form, with clumsiness, its characteristic diagnostic features. People with Asperger syndrome give a strong impression of individuality. They have an interest in other people and the environment although this may be confined to details or characteristics that other people find peculiar. Their use of language is highly developed. They usually lack the marked stereotypies and unusual sensory preoccupations of more handicapped autistic people and, also unlike them, are generally not overly concerned with mere repetition although change usually upsets them and they often cleave to routine.

The adult with Asperger syndrome may have had similar handicaps in childhood or may have had more severe symptoms, including those that would have led to a diagnosis of early childhood autism. It has been

Table 5.1. *Diagnostic criteria of Asperger syndrome in adults*

In adulthood

Lack of non-verbal expressiveness, associated either with 1. idiosyncratic facial expressions, gestures, voice prosody or posture; or 2. an inability to recognise socially important cues; or 3. both.

Unusual 'special' interests which are narrow and private. The special interest may be idiosyncratic or pursued obsessively, or both. Special interests often involve collecting objects or memorising facts.

Difficulty in behaving according to socially accepted conventions, particularly when these conventions are normally implicit.

Pragmatic abnormalities of speech.

Lack of close peer relationships often but not always, as a result of social advances being rebuffed by peers.

Impression of clumsiness.

In childhood

Symptoms as above, or symptoms of autism.

If childhood history unavailable, symptoms cannot be attributed to psychosis occurring after early childhood.

---

suggested that the diagnosis of Asperger syndrome should be restricted to the former. This may be useful for research purposes, but what matters clinically is the level of current function. Asperger syndrome in this chapter will therefore be used descriptively to refer to anyone who currently meets Asperger criteria irrespective of the type of autistic disorder from which they previously suffered.

Studies of Asperger syndrome in adulthood

Only two large descriptive studies have been carried out. Newson, Dawson and Everard, based at the University of Nottingham, recruited ninety-three 'able autistic people' from non-clinical sources, notably the membership of the United Kingdom National Autistic Society (Newson, Dawson and Everard, 1982; Dawson, 1983). They based their diagnosis on Wing and Gould's (1979) triad of impairments, and included only people who were judged by a researcher to have normal or near-normal intelligence. Most, but not all, of their subjects meet the criteria of Asperger syndrome used in this chapter.

In the second study, carried out under the auspices of the Medical Research Council, I interviewed sixty adults already known to other psychiatrists who had identified them as eccentric and socially isolated (see also Tantam, 1986, 1988b, 1988c). Forty-six met criteria for an autistic disorder of the Asperger type, having had either the triad of social impairments in childhood or, if a thorough childhood history could not be obtained, problems of social development in childhood coupled with the

Table 5.2. *Nottingham and MRC samples compared*
(Newson, Dawson and Everard, 1982; Tantam, 1986)

	Nottingham (N = 93)	MRC (N = 46)
Mean age (years)	23	24.4
Male to female ratio	10:1	6:1
Professional or skilled parents (%)	70	62
Abnormal development of:		
Language (%)	96	45
Non-verbal communication (%)	97	74
Interest in people (%)	53	79
Play (%)	56	82
Autism already diagnosed (%)	>90	20
First professional contact younger than age 11 (%)	87	55

Asperger triad described above. Patients who were unable to give a clear account of themselves and their families were excluded from the study so that only able autistic people were included, as in the Nottingham study; 67 per cent of them were currently socially impaired (see below for details), 91 per cent had marked abnormalities of non-verbal expression currently, and 95 per cent had unusually restricted or asocial 'special' interests currently. Corresponding figures for the remaining fourteen, non-autistic, subjects were: 14 per cent, 38 per cent and 43 per cent. Ninety per cent of the autistic subjects had both abnormal non-verbal expression and special interests currently, compared to only 8 per cent of the non-autistic group with this combination.

The Nottingham and MRC samples were collected at the same time, but only one case is known to have been included in both. Comparison of the two samples (table 5.2) shows the expected preponderance of men, but the ratio of approximately six men to one woman in the MRC study is lower than that reported in Nottingham and by others (for example, Gillberg, 1989). There were more parents with professional or managerial occupations than in the general population in both samples, but this may be an effect of selection bias (see Wing (1980) for a general discussion). Newson, Dawson and Everard's subjects were more likely to have been previously diagnosed as autistic, to have had special schooling (usually in schools specialising in autism) and to have had language impairments in infancy. The age at which their child's problems were first acknowledged by parents was also lower.

Other findings quoted in this chapter are from the MRC study unless an alternative citation is given.

Robert: a clinical example of lifelong Asperger syndrome

Robert is a nineteen-year-old man who is enrolled in an employment training scheme and attends a self-advocacy group for mentally handicapped people. He attended an ordinary school, in a remedial form. His intelligence when he left school was assessed as 79 (verbal) and 80 (performance). The diagnosis of Asperger syndrome was only recently suspected.

Robert was delayed in his use, but not in his understanding, of speech, and in physical co-ordination. Although he is said to have enjoyed playing with other children, he played in parallel, without interaction. He has never had a close mutual friend. When he refers to friends it is to people to whom he has attached himself, and who act towards him more as carers than as friends. He has always disliked physical contact but has never seemed unusually passive. His parents occasionally had difficulty in interpreting his facial expressions, and this lack of facial expressiveness, coupled with occasional facial grimaces, persists. His voice is also monotonous and he does not use expressive gesture. His gaze is roving, rarely resting on one's eyes when one talks to him, but there is no obvious avoidance. As an infant, he sometimes repeated words parrot fashion and may have occasionally used stock phrases, but his language was not otherwise abnormal. Nowadays he is articulate, but uses the word 'whatever' in stock fashion and repeats some phrases several times.

His parents could remember no stereotyped movements or abnormal sensory behaviour, but he was occasionally fascinated by certain sounds and became distressed if he heard the nursery song 'London Bridge is falling down'. He did not resist change and his parents did not think he had special routines, although these are currently a prominent feature of his life. He has always had special, engrossing interests. As a child these were, at different times, pots and pans, watches and clocks, and street-lamps which he noticed, to his parents' surprise, were individually numbered.

Since his family moved to a new house and his mother told him that he could be responsible for emptying the rubbish, the interests have largely centred on rubbish disposal. He spends much of his money on black rubbish bags and monopolises the disposal of the household rubbish. He often throws useful articles away in the interest of making a large rubbish pile and has several times requested more dustbins from the local council.

In the past he has hoarded rubbish in his bedroom. He has also collected newspaper cuttings about disasters, and has entered into correspondence with a local undertaker about funeral arrangements: he is very concerned that he should be buried and not cremated. Since befriending the undertaker, he has started to cut out the notices of funerals for which his friend has made the arrangements. His favourite television programme is one which reports on crimes.

Robert is clumsy and has an unusual head shape. He does not

appear immature, but a childlike impression is given by his assumption that an interviewer already knows a great deal about him. His parents think that he is becoming increasingly self-conscious and were recently surprised by how upset he became over the death of an aunt. He unexpectedly told his friend that he was thinking of killing himself although he was not depressed or otherwise ill at the time. He has no interest in girls, but has asked his father to blow up balloons and 'burst them with his naked bum' which his father interpreted as serving a sexual interest. He has passed his driving test, and drives to local cities. He lives with his parents, but has been away from home to conferences of advocacy groups which he has addressed. Currently he is working full-time in a kitchen and doing well.

The non-autistic subjects in the MRC study were themselves an unusual and interesting group. Their social isolation arose from a failure to make relationships rather than from an abnormality of social interaction. Most met diagnostic criteria of either schizoid, schizotypal or borderline personality disorder, but often the features were very mixed, as in the following case example.

Dennis: NOT a case of Asperger syndrome

Dennis's birth was induced because of his mother's pre-eclampsia. He was blue at birth but responded to oxygen. Subsequently he was noted to be a sickly baby who had frequent ear infections and was a poor feeder. He was slow to walk (at two years) and talk (first words at two years and six months), and was not fully continent until the age of four. His mother had been depressed following his birth, having lost her one-year-old daughter during her pregnancy.

From the age of three he had frequent nightmares and spent nights in his parents' bed. He clung to his mother when he was due to go to school and, in fact, missed his first six weeks. At school he mixed little and was easily upset. From the age of five his mother noticed that he masturbated every night. At seven he was referred to a child psychiatrist for assessment of social withdrawal, anxiety and obsessional behaviour, he was noted to prefer dolls and doll's houses to other toys, and this interest continued until he was thirteen. He was reluctant to open his bowels in a strange toilet and would sometimes soil himself rather than do this. He said that he was frightened of the hole in the toilet.

His mother answered yes to almost every question about developmental anomaly, but close questioning did not disclose stereotypies, unusual sensory interests, anomalies in speech or non-verbal communication development. She did think him lost in his own world, however, and also distressed by change.

At the time of the study Dennis had been confined by anxiety to his home for two years and was described as withdrawn and apathetic. He spent much of each day checking that there was no one at the front door, that the tablets in the bathroom cabinet were as he had left them and that the bath was not full of water. He was perturbed by intrusive thoughts that he might kill someone or that he had already done so without realising it. He sometimes thought that he was telepathic. He never made eye contact at interview, but his mutual gaze when talking to peers was normal. His major interest was in pop groups, about which he was knowledgeable, football and television. He collected miniature liqueur bottles and stamps.

Detailed description of the diagnostic characteristics of Asperger syndrome in adulthood

Impaired social interaction

Appropriate social conduct is regulated by conventions shared with other social actors. People with Asperger syndrome act as if they are unaware of these conventions, or of their underlying ordering principles, which enable social actors to generalise rules to new situations. One father, for example, described to me how upsetting it was that his son who had Asperger syndrome, would sit with him and his wife in the same room but his chair would never be in the same group as theirs so that they never felt he was with them. Another instance of his son failing to follow the 'rules' was shown when he terminated an interview with the headmaster of a private school to which he had applied by asking the headmaster's age. In this he transgressed social conventions relating to intimacy versus formality, and age conventions.

Sociolinguistic versus psycholinguistic abnormality   Social conventions are particularly closely applied to that class of social actions known as speech acts. Speech and language impairment are prominent features of autism and have in the past overshadowed the social impairments in clinical descriptions. Asperger (1979) considered that the children he had described had relatively normal language development, and that this was a contrast to the children described by Kanner, although he did recognise that some of them had abnormalities of speech development which, he implied, were predominantly social rather than linguistic in origin.

Distinguishing between verbal and non-verbal aspects of speech, and between syntactic, semantic and pragmatic abnormalities of word-use, may go some way towards clarifying the distinction that Asperger was making. In the MRC study, speech prosody – pitch, stress and rhythm of speech – was considered separately from the use of words in speech. The latter was rated according to three criteria, namely, the occurrence of syntactic abnormalities, defined as the occurrence of ill-formed or meaningless phrases in which meaning could not be restored by the substitution of a single word; of semantic abnormalities, defined as meaningless phrases in which the substitution of a word would restore meaning; and of pragmatic abnormalities.

Examples of syntactic abnormalities were phrases like 'They bring that into three pages with each other, that small detail' or 'It took him too shortly later'. Semantic abnormalities, with the meanings suggested by their context, included neologisms such as 'tammer' (get involved?), 'fonding' (affection), 'missage' (defined by the subject as 'going to sleep when your favourite person goes away for a long time'), 'begrudgement' (being made to bear a grudge?) and 'pretendly' (insincerely?). Syntactic errors were, in fact, rare and always occurred in association with semantic errors. They were shown by fourteen (30.4 per cent) of the subjects, but were conspicuous in only six. I later consider evidence that syntactic and semantic abnormalities occur in only some adults with Asperger syndrome; in other words, they are not part of the essential autistic handicap but are expressions of a distinct language handicap.

Pragmatic abnormalities of speech have affinities with non-verbal communication rather than with the purely linguistic abnormalities mentioned above. Van Dijk (1977) defines the pragmatic dimension of speech as follows: 'an utterance should not only be characterized in terms of its internal structure and the meaning assigned to it but also in terms of the act accomplished by producing such an utterance. This *pragmatic* level of description provides crucial conditions for reconstructing part of the conventions that make utterances acceptable, viz. their *appropriateness* with respect to the communicative context'. Non-verbal expression, for example prosody, may determine what sort of illocutionary act is encoded in the utterance: the difference between a question, a command or a statement may reside, for example, only in the tone of voice in which it is uttered. There is thus a considerable overlap between a pragmatic description of an utterance and the description of the non-verbal expressions that accompany conversation.

Pragmatic considerations, which are discussed in detail by Happé in chapter 7, include the wishes, intentions and goals of both speaker and hearer as well as a grasp of the relationship between discourse type and social conventions, such as role and hierarchy. Features of pragmatic competence include the distinction between presupposition and introduction of facts, objects or persons; focus; and the ability to convey a point of view (Van Dijk, 1977).

The pragmatics of the discourse of autistic children have recently been studied intensively (Tager-Flusberg, 1985; Tager-Flusberg *et al.*, 1990) and a preliminary attempt to assess pragmatic errors was made in the MRC study. Abnormal pragmatic perspective, in this case a failure to respond to social convention, was apparent in a subject's over-familiarity with the

Table 5.3. *Asperger and non-Asperger subjects in MRC study*
(Tantam, 1986) compared

	Asperger % affected	Non-Asperger % affected
Circumscribed, unusual interests	95	43
Impaired non-verbal expression	91	38
Pragmatic abnormalities	67	14
Semantic or syntactic abnormalities	30	7
Clumsiness	91	36
Autistic disorder in childhood (where history available)	100	0

interviewer, for example hailing the doctor, at a first meeting and across a crowded room, by his first name. Another abnormality of perspective was a lack of the guardedness which would have been appropriate to the beginning of an interview with a stranger and a lack of curiosity about the purpose and consequences of the interview. Abnormal choice of topic was rated as 'idiosyncrasy' or 'fanaticism', depending on how forcefully the topic was imposed on the conversation and how odd it was. Ratings were also made of the assumption by the subject of knowledge which the interviewer could not be expected to have, an example of the failure to use the illocutionary act of 'introduction', and of gaucheness, a residual category of pragmatic abnormality.

Pragmatic abnormalities of the type described occurred in the speech of two-thirds of the Asperger group (table 5.3) and were significantly more common in the subjects with lower verbal IQ scores and clumsiness. Semantic and syntactic abnormalities tended to be more common in subjects with lower verbal IQ, but were not associated with clumsiness. Nor was there a tendency for semantic and pragmatic abnormalities to occur more frequently together.

Semantic abnormalities were associated in the MRC study with deviant language development, lower verbal than non-verbal IQ, and presence of Rutter's (1978) criteria for autism in early childhood, but not with abnormality of non-verbal expression (table 5.4). These associations can be interpreted as indications that the syntactic and semantic abnormalities are a language handicap which is distinct from the handicaps associated with pragmatic errors.

The severity of language handicap was significantly (p<.05) associated with an excessive use of routines in childhood and an early age of recognition of abnormality, these associations probably contributing to a highly significant (p<.01) association with a history of Kanner syndrome.

On a principal components analysis of ratings on the various standard-ised assessments used in the study (table 5.5), 60 per cent of the variance of the scores of the combined ratings of the subjects in the MRC study was

Table 5.4. *Association between linguistic impairment, abnormal language development and early childhood autism, contrasted with the lack of association with measures of non-verbal impairment (Tantam, 1986)*

| | Semantic errors currently | |
	Present	Absent
Deviant language development (%)	70	37.0
Meet Rutter's criteria of childhood autism (%)	60	23.3
Mean verbal IQ	84	95
Mean non-verbal IQ	85	88
Mean severity of abnormality of non-verbal expression	6.8	6.0

accounted for by the first three factors. Low intelligence, pragmatic abnormality and clumsiness had the highest loadings on the first factor with impaired non-verbal expression having a smaller loading. Syntactic, semantic errors and abnormal sentence sequencing (thought disorder) had the highest loadings on factor II. Impaired non-verbal expression, schizoid personality severity and restrictiveness of interests had the highest loadings on the final factor.

These findings are further evidence that the symptoms of Asperger syndrome are the result of several handicaps. Factor I may be interpreted to be a general mental handicap factor and the loadings on this factor of clumsiness and pragmatic errors suggest that there are non-specific findings indicative of generalised rather than specifically autistic impairment. Factor II corresponds to the language handicap. The final factor has the best claim to be the fundamental handicap. Interestingly, schizoid personality characteristics have almost as large a loading on this factor as impaired non-verbal expression.

Abnormal non-verbal communication

Expressive abnormalities   Asperger's own account contains constant references to expressive abnormalities. A brief experiment demonstrates how readily such abnormalities are picked up in a social interaction, and that special expertise is not needed to detect them, although it may be needed to identify them consciously. Video-recordings were made under standardised conditions of adults with Asperger syndrome talking to normal volunteers. Five of these recordings were shown to five autistic experts and three to a general professional audience of forty-one. On each occasion, the viewers were asked to rate whether or not each of the interactants was 'odd'. The experts were shown two minutes of interaction, first with the sound turned off and then with the sound on. In the second experiment, only one minute of recording was shown, without sound.

There was little difference between experts, between the one-minute and

Table 5.5. *Principal components analysis of abnormalities (Tantam, 1986)*

| | Factor loadings after varimax rotation | | |
	I	II	III
IQ	−0.64	−0.19	0.19
Pragmatic errors	0.65	0.01	0.23
Clumsiness	0.75	0.07	0.15
Psycholinguistic errors	0.08	0.93	0.08
Sequencing errors in speech	0.14	0.91	0.14
Impaired non-verbal expression	0.44	0.04	0.75
Schizoid personality severity	−0.42	0.20	0.70
Special interests	−0.01	−0.07	0.55

the two-minute exposure, and between viewing with and without sound. The rating of oddness was, however, almost completely restricted to the Asperger subjects, about whom it was common: 89 per cent of the general professional audience, for example, rated the Asperger subjects as odd, whereas only 3 per cent gave this rating to any of the control subjects. What conveyed the impression of oddness? Raters gave the following reasons: odd posture, lack of expressiveness, unusual clothes and, in the case of the sound playback, unusual speech patterns.

When the assessments of the forty-six subjects with Asperger syndrome were compared to the fourteen isolated and eccentric subjects without a developmental disorder, a similar pattern of expressive abnormality emerged (see table 5.3). Abnormal non-verbal expression is common among Asperger subjects, and co-occurs with clumsiness. It is also more common than speech abnormality, but less specific.

Non-verbal expressive abnormalities were rated in the MRC study using a specially designed rating instrument (the *express* scale). This scale differed from otherwise similar rating scales for negative symptoms in schizophrenia (for example, Andreasen, 1989) in differentiating abnormal expressions from an abnormal lack of expression. Abnormalities of speech prosody, facial expression, gaze and gesture made the largest contribution to the rating of abnormal non-verbal expression. More detailed analysis of video-recorded interviews has shown that the frequency of expressive movements, including other-directed gaze, does not differentiate Asperger and non-Asperger subjects, nor are there forms of expression that are restricted to Asperger syndrome subjects (Tantam, Holmes and Cordes, in press). Our analysis suggests that the impression of abnormality results, in fact, from a lack of integration of expression, speech and gaze. This can have the effect of making an ordinary gesture seem incongruous or inexplicable. We postulate at the moment that the lack of integration results from a failure to orientate, by gaze or change of expression, to actions by another person: the apparent lack of expression is, actually, a lack of expression at the expected time.

Interpretation of emotion   Parents of children with Asperger syndrome sometimes comment on their child's insensitivity to their facial expressions. Occasionally, parents also say that their children are unable to identify family or people that they know well from photographs. The ability to recognise people and their emotional states correctly is one facet of order in the social environment that most people take for granted, and its impairment in Asperger syndrome would be further evidence of the disordered nature of the subjective world of the Asperger sufferer.

There is growing evidence that autistic children have difficulty with facial (Hobson, 1986a, 1986b; Tantam *et al.*, 1989) or other expressions of emotion (Hobson, Ouston and Lee, 1988) and with the recognition of identical faces (Langdell, 1978; Tantam *et al.*, 1989). Several studies have produced results suggestive of similar problems also occurring in Asperger syndrome.

Wolff and Barlow (1979) gave tests to 'schizoid' children, a group that they consider includes children with Asperger syndrome, and found that they showed abnormalities. Scott (1985) gave ten in-patients with Asperger syndrome or Asperger-like characteristics tests of vocal and facial recognition, as well as vocal and facial expression. Their performance was compared to those of ten staff members and ten patients who showed few or no characteristics of Asperger syndrome. The Asperger patients were significantly worse than the other patients in selecting the correct label for photographs or prints of facial expressions, and significantly worse than the staff at labelling video-recordings of posed emotional expressions.

The patient groups were matched for age and intelligence, although no information is given about whether the latter was a verbal, non-verbal or full-scale score. No other cognitive tests were included in the actual study, and so it is uncertain whether Scott's findings could reflect only non-specific differences in attention or motivation between the groups.

In the MRC study, sixteen adults with Asperger syndrome and seven eccentric and socially isolated individuals without Asperger syndrome were given photographs of faces of trained actors, one male and one female, posing six 'basic emotions' from a standard book on facial expression (Ekman and Friesen, 1975) or no emotion. There were fourteen photographs in all which subjects had to (1) pair according to emotion, (2) label with cue cards showing emotion words, and (3) rank according to mouth width. The latter was used as a test of attention and comprehension. The groups were matched on age, male-to-female ratio but not on intelligence: the control subjects had significantly greater verbal and highly significantly greater non-verbal IQs. In a second experiment, seven of the sixteen Asperger subjects were compared with the seven controls on their ability to match cue cards with video-recordings of posed actions, meaningless postures, emotional behaviours, facial expressions of emotion, figures drawn in the air and verbal labels, and with sound-recordings of action sounds and emotion sounds. The cue cards showed schematic drawings of actions or emotional expressions which the subjects had previously been taught to identify.

In the event, the subjects with Asperger syndrome were highly significantly ($p<.01$) worse at interpreting still photographs of posed emotions on both of the tests of this, but no worse at the control task using the photographs. They were also worse on all the tests using the video-recordings except for the identification of shapes drawn in the air and significantly worse at the tests involving faces or sounds alone, or requiring labelling. It was expected that the subjects with Asperger syndrome would do less well at the tasks involving emotions, but not at the others which were included as control tasks. Emotionally neutral actions, such as sneezing or halloing, were included in the latter group, but contrary to expectation, the autistic subjects also made errors in labelling these or in matching them with their appropriate sounds.

The results in both of these tests may be the consequence of the poor matching of the experimental and control groups, but they are in line with Scott's findings, and both studies together suggest that Asperger syndrome may be associated with an impairment in the interpretation of non-verbal expression as well as its production.

Special interests

These self-selected leisure activities are both unusually narrow and unusually engrossing. They are pursued privately and with no eye to their social implications. They often involve an element of systemisation or repetition. The simplest interests, usually found in the least intellectually able, involve either routines or collections. Examples of routines are arranging a particular toy car-track in a certain configuration and putting every object in the sitting-room into a particular place every day. The collections of some of the people with Asperger syndrome I have met have included toy mobile cranes, records and photographs of cats, pictures and books about cathedrals, *TV Times* issues, maps, pictures of trains and of car washes. More complex interests involve memorising facts, producing stereotyped drawings or lists or pursuing a detailed line of abstract study. Examples of facts memorised by people with Asperger syndrome include carrot varieties, rose varieties, boxing records, heights of tallest buildings, dates of historical events, the Dewey Decimal Classification, names of jockeys, bus routes, addresses of courts and the livery of Great Western trains.

The following case history contains an example of a special interest.

> Rosalind, the daughter of a music teacher, had a particular interest in
> singing. She said that she would like to sing in a choir but became upset on

one occasion singing in public. She developed the habit of practising with her mother and would have a temper tantrum if her mother refused or if the practice was shorter than half an hour. On occasions she had literally dragged her mother away from guests to another room so that she could practice. Her mother complained that she did not put any expression into her singing. She liked to sing the same songs over and over again and refused to practise alone. Her mother found these demands difficult, and so often left it uncertain whether there would be a practice session until the last minute, and sometimes cut practices short.

Rosalind's interest had an obvious relation to her parents' life, but it was pursued in an unusually solitary way and was rather narrow in that she showed little interest in other branches of music than singing and disliked religious music particularly.

The choice of a special interest may be determined by one, presumably emotionally charged, moment in a relationship. Robert's special interest in rubbish has already been mentioned. His mother dates this behaviour to their moving into a new house when she told him 'You can be responsible for clearing up'. Robert, like most people with Asperger syndrome, has few social roles that he occupies and none in which people rely on him except this.

James has given his own description of this. As a child he was lively and intelligent, spending a considerable amount of his time writing. Nowadays he is withdrawn and his main interests are children's radio, a particular record and asking strangers the question: 'What would you do if a tall man with yellow hair came and swung you up on to his shoulders?' This is a longer account, written when James was younger, of what this man meant to him (I am grateful to Professor David Taylor for making this available to me):

This wicked witch thought it would be great fun to make someone suffer for all absolute endless eternity. So one night, after I started school, the wicked witch came to my house and crept upstairs to my bedroom. Then the wicked witch put a spell into my mouth and gave me a drink of water to swallow the spell so that it would work. The magic spell was to make me fall in love with that man who was nine feet tall with long straight light yellow hair down to his elbows, who was wearing a dark brown three-piece suit . . .

And then one day, when I had been at that school for six or seven years, this man at my school who looked so fine to me and made me feel so great decided to leave school and go to live somewhere else millions and millions of miles away. When I came back to school on the first day of the following term, I looked all round and about the playground for this man who looked so fine to me and made me feel great, but I couldn't find him anywhere. So I asked the teachers, 'Where is that man who is nine feet tall and thin with long straight yellow hair down to his elbows, who wears a dark brown three-piece suit, because I love him with all my heart, and he looks so fine to me that he makes me feel great?'

When the teachers at my school said that I wouldn't be seeing him any more, I was so upset I just didn't want to live any more. So I asked the people in the Real World to take away all the interesting things which I liked to see or do, so that I completely forgot about them, and to put me to sleep in a dark, underground cave which no daylight could get into . . .

But so far he has never come to see me again so there I am still fast asleep in that dark, underground cave.

James's account shows some imaginative ability which is even more apparent in a short story he wrote when he was eight (see Tantam, 1986).

Wing (1981) has described the lack of imagination typical of the play of children with Asperger syndrome, but this description needs some modification to account for James and other people with Asperger syndrome who make up stories, imaginary worlds or imaginary play companions. My experience has been that the crucial element lacking in the play of more able children with Asperger syndrome, and its later development into interests and hobbies, has been an ability to role-play, to switch into a different persona. Children with Asperger syndrome, in my experience, do not spontaneously dress up or play cowboys and Indians or cops and robbers. Adults do not have the ability deliberately to charm, seduce or disguise and are often unable to detect this sort of behaviour in others. When they act a part on stage, they have difficulty in infusing it with a character other than their own.

The hypothesis needs testing, but some substantiation is offered by a further case example.

Elspeth is the elder of two daughters who has been markedly delayed in her social and motor development since birth, although her language was neither delayed nor anomalous. She attended a normal school but was socially isolated at the time. Her play was stereotyped. She lacked normal facial expressiveness, her speech was delayed and she had many other features of autism. However, one feature of my home assessment that did not fit in was that Elspeth dressed up as a fairy and came back to show me her costume.

On review a year later she had rapidly progressed in her social relationships and was playing normally with age-peers. Her parents thought that she had lost most of the autistic features that had previously concerned them.

Elspeth may have suffered from Asperger syndrome transiently or had a different, though related, disorder with a better prognosis. Whichever of these is so, her use of role-play was the only clinical indication when I first saw her that her social development was going to proceed well.

Abnormal attention can explain much of the idiosyncrasy of people with Asperger syndrome. Dele, when asked about his family, mentioned each of their names and then their waist measurements. Robert, whose history was described earlier, had noticed that lampposts had numbers. Reg, noting the effect of rapid cutting in television advertisements asked 'Why life in advertisements goes faster than in real life'. To remark on how plump someone is becoming is not in itself odd, but in some circumstances it is inappropriate and hence socially unacceptable. To be interested in the numbers on trains is not odd either, because many people are. But because hardly anyone notices the numbers on lampposts, to be interested in them would be considered odd. The attention structure of autistic individuals such as Dele and Robert is unique rather than shared. In some circumstances, therefore, it would be expected that autistic people are more attentive than non-autistic people to certain stimuli and there is, indeed, some evidence for this (Shah and Frith, 1983).

Although the obsessive nature of many special interests is often their most salient feature, it is also a feature of normal interests in which it is, however, 'forgiven' because it is socially expected. Thus the fisherman who spends every weekend watching a float or the nineteen-year-old who scatters bits of engine throughout the house are not seen as having pathological interests, but the boy with Asperger syndrome who stares at electricity pylons or the girl who makes lists of 'nonsense' which she leaves everywhere, is.

Abnormal attentional strategies may account for the apparently sudden shifts in the topic of special interest which sometimes occur. Idiosyncratic attention structure may also explain why even common interests are interesting in unexpected ways to the person with Asperger syndrome, why, for example, Roger who had a particular interest in chess problems, never discussed them with others and had no idea who was playing in the world chess championship which was then taking place.

Special interests are often tangentially related to social relationships but are not products of them:

> John was in hospital for behavioural treatment after an indecent assault on a girl. He had been attracted to her but had not known how to approach her. In hospital, he studied 'non-verbal communication' by staring at girls and writing down any movement they made. John lacked a workable theory of how boys meet and get on with girls, since normal social interaction and imitation were closed to him. He was, instead, resorting to trying to learn what to do by finding out the rules.

Clumsiness

Children and adults with Asperger syndrome typically give an impression of clumsiness, which is borne out by delayed motor development and a lack of aptitude for all ball games. Yet they can be surprisingly dextrous in pursuing their interests, for example, building toy engines or drawing objects which fascinate them.

Ninety-one per cent of the forty-six Asperger subjects studied in detail were judged to be clumsy, and a number of tests were devised to investigate this further. Clumsiness was assessed by means of two tests developed to assess right and left hemisphere brain damage (Kimura and Archibald, 1974; Kimura and Vanderwolf, 1970), a catching test and a test of balance on the right and left legs. The scores on all these tests were significantly inter-correlated and the first factor in principal components analysis, accounting for 50 per cent of the total variance, had factor loadings on all of the tests. Gesture-copying, catching and leg-balancing were all significantly more impaired in the Asperger subjects, with the most errors relative to the non-Asperger subjects being made in the catching test.

Many parents described the abnormal routes used by their children to acquire motor skills, although this was not confined to the autistic children in the MRC study. Walking 'just happened' without prior crawling or shuffling, and talking could be acquired after reading. On the other hand, if a motor skill was not 'invented' in this way by the child, it proved very difficult to acquire. Demonstration, the normal means of teaching motor skills, is of limited help to autistic children or adults. Poor performance on the tests described above may therefore also have reflected this difficulty in copying movements that another person is making. It is consistent with this that copying simple designs was performed by the Asperger group as well as the non-Asperger controls, although unusual strategies were also in evidence here. For example, some subjects drew the Necker cube by superimposing two diamonds and then joining them up.

The most typical Asperger syndrome patients, who were usually the least neurologically impaired, were often the most clumsy. If it is in learning movement, rather than in producing it, that the abnormality lies, then it would be expected that movements which require little learning would be dextrous while those that require considerable learning, such as socially determined behaviours, would be poorly learnt and therefore poorly performed. This may be one explanation of why people with Asperger syndrome, who are less handicapped than people with classical autism, are more clumsy: their behaviour contains a much higher proportion of attempts to imitate the behaviour of others and since these are the source of the clumsiness, the appearance of clumsiness preponderates.

Clumsiness may not be entirely attributable to motor abnormality. It is, for example, a feature of the self-consciousness of adolescents who are striving to adopt new and more socially acceptable motor schemata. Movement patterns are subject to social structuring: certain postures are condemned or emulated, for example. Children may be instructed in the use of gaze – 'Look in my eyes', they may be told, or 'Look at the ball and not the thrower'. Such instruction focuses on the importance of integrating gaze with motor sequences. Many people with Asperger syndrome seem to have particular difficulty with this. One who liked to play table-tennis was said to do so without ever seeming to look at the ball. Another had difficulty sighting down a telescope.

The problem of co-ordinating gaze and movement seems to be one aspect of a general problem of integrating individual movements into actions which may have its basis in a brain lesion, but may also reflect the autistic person's inability to model behaviour on that of others and thus to acquire socially transmitted motor schemata. Gaze is discussed in greater detail in a later section.

Subclassification of Asperger syndrome

Some people with Asperger syndrome – Robert is an example – are conspicuously clumsy and gauche, use language fluently but idiosyncratically and have marked abnormalities of facial expression, tone of voice and gesture, but despite these are able to convey feeling, and often have a degree of empathy for others.

Others, by contrast, do not show obvious non-verbal abnormalities, although they use emotional expressions less frequently, but are more passive in their social interactions. They are less clumsy and give an impression not so much of adolescent-type gaucheness as of a less self-conscious social immaturity. Their intelligence tends to be lower than that of the first group. They are generally less empathic and this group contains a higher proportion of the callous individuals first described by Asperger, which needs further testing. A possible explanation is that they are more impaired in the recognition of non-verbal cues than in their expression, whereas the opposite is true of the first group.

Diagnostic stability of the triad of social impairments

The unchanging nature of social impairments in Asperger syndrome has been noted before (Howells and Guirguis, 1984). In the MRC study, all the elements of the triad of social impairments showed considerable stability over time. There was 81 per cent agreement in the rating of non-verbal expression in childhood made retrospectively by the parents and non-verbal expression in adulthood made independently by me. Agreement on special interests was also high: 74 per cent. When the frequencies of developmental abnormalities reported by parents was considered (figure 5.1), abnormally restricted play, lack of facial expression and lack of vocal expression were the three most common abnormalities. Restricted play and apparent deafness were specific to Asperger syndrome, never being reported of the non-autistic subjects.

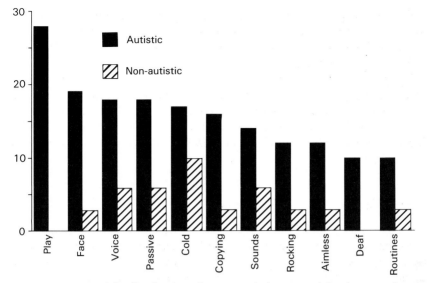

Fig. 5.1   The distribution of retrospectively reported developmental anomalies in a sample of fifty eccentric psychiatric patients: numbers affected

Play – play narrow, restricted
Face – facial expression difficult for parents to interpret
Voice – voice flat, monotonous, mechanical
Passive – no initiation of social contact
Cold – avoidance of cuddling, dislike of touch
Copying – difficulty in copying actions
Sounds – inexplicable aversion to certain sounds
Rocking – rocking in a stereotyped manner
Aimless – movements sometimes aimless or purposeless
Deaf – suspicion of deafness
Routines – routines for everyday life

Aetiology

Cases of Asperger syndrome have been reported in association with Tourette syndrome (Kerbeshian and Burd, 1986), aminoaciduria (Miles and Capelle, 1987) and ligamentous laxity (Tantam, Evered and Hersov, 1990). Gillberg (1989) found a variety of neurological abnormalities in 60 per cent of twenty-three people with Asperger syndrome that he examined. Some of the organic handicaps associated with Asperger syndrome in the MRC study are shown in table 5.6. A history of epilepsy could be reliably ascertained only in a proportion, and only a proportion had had a thorough physical examination or neurological investigations. The frequencies of abnormalities may therefore be overestimated, but it is clear that organic brain disease is over-represented.

Table 5.6. *Neuropsychiatric*
abnormalities in Asperger syndrome
(Tantam, 1986)

Epileptic fit ever (% of 39)	20.5
EEG or CT scan abnormalities (% of 31)	41.9
Neurological soft signs (% of 30)	26.7
Full-scale IQ 50–69 (% of 42)	9.5
40–49 (% of 42)	2.4

Other aetiological factors that have been implicated in autism include biological factors such as birth injury or heredity and socio-psychological factors, such as having foreign-born parents or being the first-born. The presence or absence of these factors in the Asperger group and the non-autistic group were compared in the MRC study (table 5.7), and there was limited evidence for the importance of heredity and of some biological factors, but no support for socio-psychological explanations of autism (table 5.8).

Heredity

Two twin pairs were included in the Asperger group in the MRC study. One pair, whose uniovularity had been confirmed by blood grouping, were concordant for Asperger syndrome. The second pair, who were identical but in whom uniovularity had not been confirmed, were concordant for many features of Asperger syndrome, but one was less severely impaired than the other. The father of this latter pair also had some features of Asperger syndrome.

The numbers are too small to draw any conclusions but the findings are consistent with the model of Burgoine and Wing (1983) that the severity of the expression of the Asperger/autism genotype can be influenced by other factors, so that the same genotype can result in severe autism or milder Asperger syndrome.

Birth injury

Perinatal complications were retrospectively reported in 51 per cent, but this figure was lower, although not significantly so, than the 62 per cent of non-autistic subjects in whom perinatal complications were reported. This finding contrasts with previous findings in autism (for example, Finegan and Quarrington, 1979) in which a normal control group was used which showed a lower rate of perinatal complications than the non-autistic control group in this study. This could be explained if birth injury is actually linked to a non-specific feature, such as coming to medical attention, rather than to Asperger syndrome. One possible non-specific link might be the increased

Table 5.7. *Factors of possible aetiological importance compared in people with and without Asperger syndrome (Tantam, 1986)*

Only occur in Asperger syndrome	Family history of autism (in 3/44)
	Epilepsy (in 8/39)
Significantly commoner in Asperger syndrome	Brain abnormality on EEG or CT scan
	Clumsiness
As common in Asperger syndrome	Parents aloof or antisocial
	Parents born abroad
	Early separation from parents
	Family history of psychiatric disorder
	Birth injury
	Report of post-partum anoxia
	Body build
	Neurological signs
	First-born child
Significantly less common in Asperger syndrome	Parents divorced
	Older parents

Table 5.8. *Measures on which individuals with and without Asperger syndrome did* not *differ*

Age	Male-to-female ratio
Class	Per cent time employed
Birth order	Sibship size
Accommodation	Contact with child psychiatrist
Involuntary admission	Per cent committing offence
Teasing at school	Sexual relationships

likelihood that mothers will remember birth problems if their children are impaired in any way.

Brain lesions

It has been suggested that Asperger syndrome is the behavioural expression of a lesion of the right cerebral hemisphere on the basis of the similarity of the communicative abnormalities of Asperger syndrome to the aprosodia described in adults (Weintraub and Mesulam, 1983) and children (Voeller, 1986) with acquired right hemisphere lesions. Such a view does not take into account the plasticity of cerebral development when lesions occur sufficiently early in life, although the extent of the compensation possible as the result of the development of other structures is, admittedly, not known. If the suggestion is correct, an excess of right hemisphere structural and functional abnormalities would be expected in Asperger syndrome. There was some evidence for this from the MRC study in which the Asperger subjects had an excess of right hemisphere lesions in the CT scans or EEG

Table 5.9. *Lateralisation of CT scan and EEG abnormalities (Tantam, 1986)*

	Nil	Right-sided %	Left-sided %
Asperger syndrome	17 (54.4%)	13[a] (41.9)	8[a] (25.8)
Non-autistic	7 (70.0%)	2[b] (20.0)	2[b] (20.0)

[a] Seven subjects with bilateral lesions included.
[b] One subject with bilateral lesion included.

(see table 5.9). Unfortunately, not every subject was fully investigated by this means, and selection bias cannot therefore be ruled out. Furthermore, EEG abnormalities may be an unreliable means of lateralising dysfunction. In some cases (one of which is reported in detail on Tantam, Evered and Hersov, 1990), the apparent focus changed from being right- to left-sided over a period of years. Balancing on the left leg was slightly worse than balancing on the right leg in the Asperger group, but this also fell short of significance and may, anyway, have been an effect of right leg dominance.

Although the mean verbal IQ was 92.2 and non-verbal IQ was 86.7, there was a considerable scatter of scores between subjects, with one subject having a verbal IQ of 65 and a performance IQ of 104 and another having a verbal IQ of 94 and a performance IQ of 65. The IQ distribution was skewed towards a lower than average score. Five out of forty-two subjects were mentally handicapped 'overall' but rather more were handicapped either verbally or non-verbally. Asperger syndrome does not have an association with mental handicap but, as others have reported (Burgoine and Wing, 1983; Gillberg *et al.*, 1986), does not exclude it.

Van Krevelen (1971) has made the suggestion that autism results from a, possibly heritable, handicap in association with brain damage. When there is no brain damage, Asperger syndrome results. This suggestion is partly supported by some of the findings of the MRC study. Many of the patients in the study had been physically examined and had had EEGs or CT scans performed. When the results of these are compared to the results of one of the balancing tests, it is apparent that the clumsier the subjects the more likely they are to have EEG or CT scan abnormalities and to have soft neurological signs. They are also more likely to have had a fit at some time in their lives, to make syntactic or semantic speech errors, to have lower verbal IQs, and they are also more likely to have met Rutter's criteria for early childhood autism (table 5.10).

These findings are evidence for an association of psycholinguistic abnormalities, brain damage and Kanner syndrome, and are consistent with Van Krevelen's hypothesis that brain damage may lead to Kanner syndrome. However, even the least clumsy subjects and the subjects without evidence of semantic or syntactic problems have an increased risk of EEG or CT scan

Table 5.10. *Association of neurological abnormalities and motor, linguistic and intellectual impairments (Tantam, 1986)*

| Balancing on right leg (seconds) | Mean IQ | | Percent with | | | |
	Verbal	Performance	Soft signs	Psycholinguistic abnormalities	History of fit	EEG or CT abnormal
>10	102.8	91.4	15.3	25.0	12.5	16.7
5–10	87.8	84.6	20.0	30.0	25.0	33.3
<5	82.6	85.2	44.4	50.0	36.4	66.7

Table 5.11. *Frequency of psychiatric disorder in eighty-five adults with Asperger syndrome examined by the author*

	Number affected
Mania only	4
Mania alternating with depression	4
Depressive psychosis only	2
Schizophrenia	3
Epileptic psychosis	1
Hallucinosis	4
All psychosis	18 (21%)
Depression only	5
Depression and anxiety	2
Anxiety only	4
Obsessive-compulsive disorder	2
All psychiatric disorder other than autism	30[a] (35%)

[a] One man who experiences hallucinations and has obsessional symptoms counted only once in final total.

abnormalities as well as epilepsy, suggesting that the distinction between Asperger syndrome and autism is not whether or not brain damage occurs but its severity and extent; the greater the extent, the more likely other symptoms secondary to brain abnormality become conspicuous. These may include epilepsy, aphasia and apraxia.

Complications of Asperger syndrome

Mental illness

Thirty (35 per cent) of eighty-five adults with Asperger syndrome examined by me met criteria for a psychiatric disorder other than a developmental disorder (criteria taken from the Ninth Revision of the *International classification of diseases*, World Health Organization, 1978). This proportion is likely to be higher than that to be found in an unselected community sample, as psychiatric disorder is one factor leading to psychiatric referral. As recently reported by others (Gillberg, 1985; Clarke *et al.*, 1989), there is a higher than expected risk of psychosis, with mania (occurring in 9 per cent) being commoner than schizophrenia (3.5 per cent) (table 5.11). The single most common disorder is depression, occurring in 15 per cent. Anxiety disorder is also common, reaching clinically significant severity in 7 per cent, and is often associated with depression.

Richard: a case of bipolar affective psychosis complicating Asperger syndrome

Richard has attended a psychiatric day hospital for the last three years, since he was aged eighteen. He is the younger of two sons. His mother's previous pregnancy had ended in a miscarriage. His birth was induced because of pre-eclampsia, and he was a small baby. He would not settle away from home, sometimes could not be soothed when he was upset and was slow to gain weight. He walked at fifteen months and first talked at two. He was investigated for small stature at the age of four, when temper tantrums were noted but no physical abnormality was found. It was at this age that his parents first thought there was something wrong with him. He would not tolerate any change of position of any articles in the house, would never sleep without all his windows closed and later developed a routine of checking that the doors too were closed.

He was placed in a day nursery while his parents went out to work, but was never happy there. His mother thinks that he made friends and played with other children, but this is doubtful in view of the fact that he subsequently only made one friend and this seems to have been a relationship in which he was regularly humiliated, for example, by being made to drink coffee into which his friend had spat.

He occasionally used stock phrases, and his speech has always been monotonous and shown a lack of spontaneity. He has always avoided mutual gaze. His play and interests have always been restricted and privately pursued. As a young child his main interest was in dismantling electrical appliances. Later he became interested in computer games. Now he seems to have few interests. He occasionally flicked things repetitively, and became absorbed in staring at objects. He has always been fascinated by tapping noises and sometimes liked to spin round and round.

At primary school he quickly learnt to read, and at seven his reading age was eleven. However, he had difficulty in learning to write and developed an idiosyncratic script. Arithmetic was also a problem. He has always had great difficulty in catching or hitting balls, and his inability to participate in organized games became a problem at this time. His parents had already noted that he had difficulty in copying movements or actions, and also thought that his memory was not as it should be. He was again investigated for his small stature, without any abnormality being found. At the age of eight he was referred to a child psychiatrist because of behaviour problems. His IQ was found to be 96 at that time. At nine his checking of the doors and windows before bedtime was taking up so much time that he was not going to bed until 1 or 2 am. He would also worry that he was not getting the right thing if sent on an errand for his mother, and would return three or four times to check.

Richard went to a private school at the age of eleven but there were many problems there with his idiosyncratic behaviour, which included the habit of repeating aloud what was said to him. His parents took him to a private psychologist and also to acupuncturists and hypnotists. He was often teased and was nearly expelled. With the help of private tutors in mathematics and English, he was able to pass the simplest public examination in three subjects. After leaving school at seventeen, he had difficulty finding work or going on to further education, but did manage some placements in various firms on a training basis. He was admitted to an adolescent unit at the age of eighteen because of increasingly disturbed behaviour at home. Richard had been slamming doors so hard in temper that they had broken, and had also made several apparently unprovoked attacks on his mother. He has not been in paid work since.

Family therapy was tried without success, and Richard was referred to a general psychiatrist whom he told that he had occasionally heard voices when there was no one there, that people spied on him and that his father could take thoughts out of his mind and put thoughts in. These ideas seem to have developed over the period when Richard had changed from his previous affectionate over-trustful manner to being irritable, suspicious and cold. Over the ensuing years of day hospital treatment, which also included several hospital in-patient admissions, cycles of over-activity and disinhibited behaviour, and episodes of low mood associated with suicidal thoughts, became apparent. The combination of lithium and a depot neuroleptic was found to minimise these, and also to reduce Richard's suspiciousness and ideas that his father was interfering with his thoughts. The situation became worse when either of the medications was omitted. Violent outbursts at home became rare, although Richard continued to take his meals alone in his bedroom where he also spent most of the evening watching his television and listening to the radio simultaneously.

Psychometric testing showed Richard to have a full-scale IQ of 98, with a verbal score of 106 and a performance score of 89. He did best on the comprehension, similarities and vocabulary subtests of the Wechsler Adult Intelligence Scale and worst on the arithmetic, picture arrangement and digit symbol subtests. His score on a simple memory test (paired associate learning) was above average, but on the logical memory test he scored more than two standard deviations below the average. No specific abnormality has been found on neurobiological examinations, and two CT scans have been normal.

Richard began to attend classes in computing and a day centre. He had many sessions of social skill training but these resulted in little improvement: Richard could not refrain from monopolizing the group leader's attention or, otherwise, withdrawing. He managed better with his own carer whom he met once a week, but there was no change in his social avoidance or his lack of sensitivity to social cues. He did, however, became more able to tolerate change.

Several of the cases of depression were severe and associated with biological symptoms and suicidal ideas. Five were associated with delusions and one with stupor. The biological symptoms in these cases were typical of depression but the content of the illness was coloured by previous, autistic preoccupations such as in the man who threw himself into the Thames because the Government refused to abolish British Summer Time. He believed that watches were damaged by being altered twice a year when the switch to or from GMT occurred. People with Asperger syndrome who become depressed may also not seek help and, because of their impairment in non-verbal expression, may not have a depressed appearance. The diagnosis may therefore be missed. Similar problems may be presented by mania, although sleep disturbance is as reliable a diagnostic feature in Asperger syndrome as it is in non-autistic people. In less able autistic people, this may not be so as their sleep may normally be disturbed. Lithium was effective in reducing the frequency of mood disorders in several patients.

The excess of affective disorder over schizophrenia is a further point against Asperger syndrome being genetically related to schizophrenia as has been suggested by some workers (Wolff and Chick, 1980). It is not possible to say whether there is an excess of affective disorder compared to the general population from the present sample because of selection bias but it seems likely. Leff, Fischer and Bertelsen (1976) have estimated the incidence of mania to be 2.6 per 100,000 per year in Camberwell. For the risk period from which most of the present subjects were drawn, aged fourteen to thirty, this gives a likely prevalence of 44 per 100,000. On that basis, the eight cases in the present study would have been drawn from a notional population of 55,250. Since eighty-six cases of Asperger syndrome were also drawn from this population, the absence of any particular association between mania and Asperger syndrome leads to a prevalence estimate of detected Asperger syndrome of 1.6 per 1,000. This is higher than many estimates but lower than one (Gillberg, 1988).

Only unequivocal cases of mania have been considered as such: the remaining cases are difficult to classify. A fairly confident diagnosis of schizophrenia can be made in the presence of a clear episode of increased disturbance associated with new first-rank symptoms but even these may be misleading when they are described by an autistic person whose experiences, self-image and vocabulary may all be idiosyncratic (see Clarke et al. (1989) for an example). None of the people with schizophrenia experienced a clearly deteriorating course, although one had become a hospital resident.

A diagnosis of schizophrenia, often simple schizophrenia, was made in a majority of the group that I studied in detail, and most had received neuroleptics (major tranquillisers) at one time or another before entry into the study. Neuroleptic medication can be helpful, especially in a crisis, but was associated in the study with significantly greater facial inexpressiveness and may therefore have worsened the impairment in non-verbal expression and thus contributed to chronic social difficulties (Rifkin, Quitkin and Klein, 1975).

Asperger syndrome and personality disorder

Asperger used the term 'autistic psychopathy' (which could also be translated as 'autistic personality disorder') for the syndrome that he was describing in the knowledge that autism was considered at one time by Bleuler to be a fundamental symptom of schizophrenia and of what would now be called the schizophrenia spectrum. The other personality disorder associated with schizophrenia was known for many years as schizoid personality disorder, but has more recently been renamed schizotypal personality disorder on axis II of *DSM-III-R*. Schizoid personality disorder can be diagnosed in childhood, and several workers, notably Wolff and her colleagues, have assumed that childhood schizoid personality disorder and Asperger syndrome were alternative descriptions of the same condition (Wolff and Cull, 1986).

I have argued elsewhere (Tantam, 1988c) that the autistic-like abnormalities of social interaction characteristic of Asperger syndrome are of a different kind to schizoid abnormalities of social relationship, evinced by emotional detachment, introversion and over-sensitivity. Because abnormal social interaction is likely to lead to some impairment in social relationships, some contingent association between them might be expected but this would be a less strong association than would be expected if they were a part of the same syndrome. The MRC study of Asperger syndrome in adulthood enabled a test of the strength of the association since the severity of schizoid personality traits could be compared with the frequency and severity of abnormalities of the development of social interaction and the presence in childhood of autistic-like behaviours. In the event there was no association between developmental problems and either schizoid severity or a diagnosis of schizotypal personality disorder.

There was an association of personality and the severity of current communicative abnormalities, but non-autistic subjects who were without communicative abnormalities sometimes had as severe schizoid personalities as autistic subjects (see figure 5.2). Comparison of more with less schizoid subjects suggests that the special response to the communicative problems posed by Asperger syndrome may be one factor that determines whether or not a schizoid 'defence' develops.

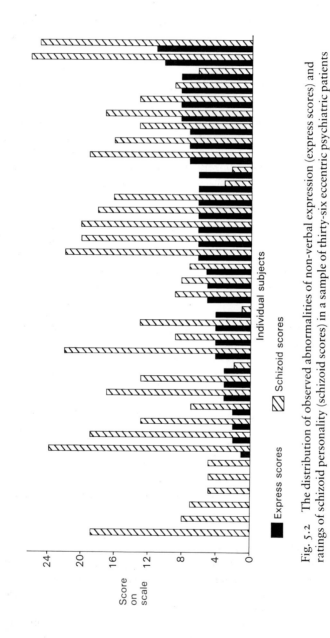

Fig. 5.2   The distribution of observed abnormalities of non-verbal expression (express scores) and ratings of schizoid personality (schizoid scores) in a sample of thirty-six eccentric psychiatric patients

Peter: an example of a person with schizoid personality traits and Asperger syndrome

Peter was born during the war while his father was overseas with the armed forces. His father first saw him when he was three, and shortly after that his mother left him in the care of her mother-in-law in order to set up house with another man. He had intermittent contact with his father for the next two years and spent one year in a residential nursery before returning to his elderly grandmother's care.

In adult life he was estranged from his family, contacting them only when he was short of money. He had fallen out with his father because he day-dreamed instead of working on the family farm (he himself attributed this to lack of energy). Furthermore, when he was living with his family, he had become a laughing-stock in the local village as a result of his behaviour when intoxicated with alcohol or illicitly obtained paraldehyde – a frequent occurrence at that time.

He drifted from one temporary accommodation to another. He would move on if he felt that too much interest was being taken in him by medical services. He also disliked changes in his routine and had become aggressive to landlords who had, for example, confronted him about some aspect of his accommodation. Often these incidents resulted in the police being called by Peter. He was continuously carrying on litigation with various authorities over slights that he felt he had received from them. He had many unusual beliefs, for example, that a man with red hair had attempted to assassinate him with an umbrella (this after a similar incident involving a Bulgarian *émigré*).

He has always been a loner and was described as being 'detached and unaware of other people' and by the staff of a psychiatric hospital as 'like a machine' and 'metallic'. Notwithstanding this, he did well working out from the ward, in a laboratory, during the later part of this admission. At the time of the study, he was working at night, packing. He found it more congenial to work then because there were fewer people. Most of his interests were solitary but he did attend evening classes in karate and had enrolled in, but infrequently attended, a Russian evening class.

Simon: An example of a person with Asperger syndrome but few schizoid traits

Simon was the elder son of a couple who had married late in life. His mother had been a nurse, and his father had a successful career in a bank. Both grandparents lived locally and provided considerable support to the mother during Simon's upbringing. His parents and grandparents were fond of Simon and had a good relationship with him. There had been no periods of parental separation.

In adult life, Simon described as friends the many people whom he met through his very active involvement with an evangelical church. He also considered himself to be a well-respected resident at the working men's hostel where he lived. He liked most of the other residents and the warden.

He worked full-time in a stores department and enjoyed this. Very few of the people he described as friends would have regarded themselves as such. Simon often treated near-strangers in an intimate way and liked to make long and frequent telephone calls to many of these acquaintances, a practice which sometimes resulted in the termination of the relationship. Despite this he managed to maintain an active social life and a considerable trust in the good-will of others. Possibly his open, innocent manner, coupled with his eccentricity, protected him.

He was on good terms with his family whom he often visited, was punctilious and was never rash, even if he sometimes acted oddly.

Antisocial behaviour

Many adults with Asperger syndrome have rather strict, law-abiding attitudes, but in a minority these may coexist with a lack of empathy that can result in unpredictable violence towards others. My own clinical experience suggests that this may be more common in those innocent-looking autistic people who seem to have particular impairment in their ability to interpret non-verbal expressions.

Lack of empathy may result in inappropriate emotional reactions, for example, some would laugh when others were hurt, and some would respond to domestic crises caused by sudden illness by complaining of a disrupted meal or television-viewing. Lack of empathy may also have been linked to the serious, unheralded violence to vulnerable individuals that occurred in a few cases, examples of this included attacks on younger siblings, on younger, unrelated children, on young animals and on mothers. These attacks were rarely understandable. Frustration often seemed to have been involved, although the target of the aggression was often not responsible, often being chosen, it seemed, for their vulnerability or proximity.

The attacks were occasionally serious. Four people with Asperger syndrome known to me set fire to a building while there were people in it, and one started a forest fire. Another killed a school-mate, probably as an experiment, and has subsequently been detained in a special hospital.

Violence as a result of one person dominating another – in a fight, in an explosion of rage or in sexual excitement – is rarely shown by people with Asperger syndrome. Sexual offending is generally rare, although indecent exposure may sometimes occur. Property offences are also rare except when they are side-effects of the pursuit of a special interest.

Unconcern for others is not a universal characteristic of people with Asperger syndrome. Many of those showing it had experienced separation from one or both parents for a significant period of their childhood, but further study is needed to find out whether this is a contributory factor.

Table 5.12. *Social adjustment of adults with Asperger syndrome in Nottingham and MRC studies (Newson, Dawson and Everard, 1982; Tantam, 1986)*

	Nottingham %	MRC %
Higher education	11	4
Employed currently	22	9
In residential care	16	53
Living independently	7	3
Living with parents	71	41
Interest in sexual relations	76	76
Heterosexual relations ever	15	1
Married	1	2

Outcome

The social adjustment of the Nottingham (Newson, Dawson and Everard, 1982) and the MRC subjects are shown in table 5.12. The latter were a more socially handicapped group than the Nottingham subjects. Only two (4 per cent) had had any education after school, compared to ten (11 per cent) in the Nottingham sample, and only four (9 per cent) were working compared to twenty (22 per cent) in that sample. The number attending a social group regularly was probably also greater in the Nottingham sample, but the proportion who had had a regular girl-friend (defined as dating for longer than one month) was the same. Information about the IQs of the Nottingham sample is lacking, but the pattern of their developmental handicaps (see table 5.12) suggests that it is unlikely that they had a higher than normal intelligence. Their better social adjustment is thus likely to be due to some other factor. Fewer of them had seen a psychiatrist and more of them were living with parents, perhaps indicating that they were less disabled.

My clinical experience strongly suggests that, while the fundamental handicap of Asperger syndrome is *not* produced by emotional factors, its long-term effects may be altered by them. Of course, it is not possible to be sure about this because of the complicating effect of other associated physical handicaps and the difficulty of measuring severity. However, there is a marked variation in adult adjustment, especially in sociability and adaptability, which is most readily explained by the differences in upbringing, including the strategies that parents have used to deal with autistic traits and the differences in the emotional environment of the family.

The provision and receipt of help or support was one of the measures used to assess the strength of social networks in the present study. It is consistent with the greater dependence of the autistic people in the present study that only one of thirty-seven questioned (3 per cent) considered that they were able to help others in exchange for the help that they received, while thirty-seven (40 per cent) of the Nottingham sample thought that they did.

Eight (22 per cent) of the present subjects in whom a confident rating could be made were thought to be close to those at home: usually this rating was given only to those in hostels or living with their parents. A similar proportion, 20 per cent, of the Nottingham sample was reported to be close to their mothers. Many of the parents in the Nottingham study reported concern about their child in the future. In the MRC study, parents of twenty-eight subjects, out of the twenty-nine subjects who had parents who could be questioned, reported that their child was a source of concern to them. The commonest worry, troubling 55 per cent of parents, was the fate of the child after the parents' death. This was the main worry of rather fewer, 21 per cent, of the parents interviewed in the Nottingham study. The parents of only three subjects (10 per cent) complained of the burden imposed by their child. However, the home situation of many people with Asperger syndrome was not satisfactory: 39 per cent reported regular conflict which in half had led to violence.

Only one parent reported guilt about their child's condition. Most had been told at some stage that they were over-reacting or that their child's disorder was an emotional reaction with the implication of some fault in their upbringing, and reassurance that this was not so was requested at some time during almost every interview with parents.

The parents could be reassured that Asperger syndrome is not a consequence of child-rearing practice, but it was noticeable that only some of the Asperger subjects presented conduct or emotional problems. These tended to be more common when there was familial stress or separation of parents early in the child's development. The latter may itself be due to the considerable difficulties posed by the upbringing of a child with autism, and more evidence would be needed before it could be assumed that these familial factors led to the emotional disturbance.

Asperger considered that the prognosis for the syndrome he described was good and, indeed, my own clinical experience has shown that able people with autism can sometimes have childhood histories indicating much more severe impairment. Recent follow-up studies (Fombonne et al., 1989; Szatmari et al., 1989) have also tended to confirm Asperger's view, although the characteristics that predict a good outcome are still unclear.

The general trend towards amelioration of the symptoms must, however, be balanced against the often poor social outcome. A minority of subjects in both the Nottingham and MRC studies were working (see table 5.12), fewer than 10 per cent were living independently, and very few had established any sort of intimate relationship outside the family. Asperger syndrome, despite being a milder form of autism in terms of the apparent severity of its symptoms, is, clearly, still a highly socially disabling condition.

Asperger thought that special education played an important part in improvement. Relatives, on the other hand, have often reported to me that improvement was due to active socialisation, with limits on time spent in withdrawal into special interests, inactivity or stereotypy. Their own efforts, encouragement from younger siblings and particular schools were all credited with putting this into effect.

Adolescence, with all its social upheavals, is a particularly trying time and previous gains may be temporarily lost. Once over these troubled waters, many people with Asperger syndrome seem to go on improving on their social abilities well into their twenties and thirties.

Conclusions

Wing and Gould's (1979) triad of social impairment persists throughout the vicissitudes of autistic development as the cardinal feature that distinguishes autism from other developmental disorders. My own study of Asperger syndrome in adulthood quoted here provides further evidence for this, at the same time suggesting some slight modifications to Wing and Gould's formulation of the triad as it is expressed in Asperger syndrome.

Two variants of the triad can be usefully distinguished: passivity in social interaction coupled with reduced, but not obviously unusual, non-verbal expression and, I have previously hypothesised, particular impairment in the recognition of facial and other non-verbal expression; and, corresponding to Wing and Gould's (1979) category of 'active, but odd', a greater degree of social initiation, odd and idiosyncratic non-verbal expression and, according to my hypothesis, less impairment of the interpretation of non-verbal cues than the first group. My clinical impression is that the former group tend to contain disproportionately more of the minority of callous individuals, to be more immature in person and manner and to be less intelligent. Those in the latter group are not always deficient in imagination, as Wing (1981) suggests, but may lack the ability to role-play.

The more evidence of brain damage there is – in the form of soft neurological signs, abnormalities on CT scan or EEG, epilepsy or low IQ – the more likely the affected person is to be clumsy or to have a language problem affecting semantic and syntactic competence, or both.

One interpretation of this is that the core neurological defect producing the trait often coexists with more severe neurological abnormalities which may affect speech areas or motor cortex, or both. This would provide an explanation of the greater likelihood of mental handicap in Kanner syndrome compared to Asperger syndrome: that the greater language impairment in the former results from neurological involvement of the speech areas. This core defect may correspond to a specific anatomical lesion or, as seems more likely, to a specific loss of function equivalent to a specific sensory loss such as colour blindness (see Tantam, 1988d) or to a specific expressive abnormality, such as aphasia.

My own hypothesis discussed in detail elsewhere (Tantam, in press) is that Asperger syndrome results from a failure of congenital gaze reflexes, which ensure that the normal infant attends to social signals preferentially and locks the normal infant into the ebb and flow of social interaction. The normal child, it is hypothesised, learns to anticipate how much gaze they and others merit, and this leads to the development of an 'attention structure' which is shared with other people. It is from this, I argue, that social theories evolve.

According to this hypothesis, the lack of inbuilt gaze responses results in the person with Asperger syndrome being unable to acquire the fundamentals of social competence. Many of the features of Asperger syndrome could be derived from the failure of the first developmental step, the gaze reflex, but supportive experimental evidence still needs to be obtained. Until then the hypothesis, and its implications, remain speculative.

This hypothesis, like others that have recently been applied to autism, emphasises the importance of abnormalities of social competence in Asperger syndrome. These are not speculative. Quite the contrary, they and their ramifications have been the focus of a growing body of experimental evidence. This is exciting because it brings closer the identification of the fundamental handicap of Asperger syndrome. Once that happens there is likely to be a dramatic improvement in the diagnosis of Asperger syndrome even when it is mild and even when, as is not uncommonly the case, it first becomes a problem in adolescence or adulthood. From that it will be a much shorter step to the discovery of the neurological cause or causes of the handicap, very early diagnosis and the possibility of remedial programmes being instituted early enough for social development to be put back on the right track.

References

American Psychiatric Association. (1987). *Diagnostic and statistical manual of mental disorders*. 3rd edn, revised. Washington: APA.

Andreasen, N. C. (1989). The scale for the assessment of negative symptoms (SANS): conceptual and historical foundations. *British Journal of Psychiatry*, 155, supplement 7, 59–62.

Asperger, H. (1979). Problems of infantile autism. *Communication*, 13, 45–52.

Bowman, E. P. (1988). Asperger's syndrome and autism: the case for a connection. *British Journal of Psychiatry*, 152, 377–82.

Burgoine, E. & Wing, L. (1983). Identical triplets with Asperger's syndrome. *British Journal of Psychiatry*, 143, 261–5.

Clarke, D. J., Littlejohns, C. S., Corbett, J. A. & Joseph, S. (1989). Pervasive developmental disorders and psychoses in adult life. *British Journal of Psychiatry*, 155, 692–9.

Dawson, M. (1983). The natural history of autistic people with normal or near-normal intelligence: their management and functioning in social context. Unpublished Ph. D. thesis, University of Nottingham.

Ekman, P. & Friesen, W. (1975). *Unmasking the face.* Englewood Cliffs, N.J.: Prentice-Hall.

Finegan, J. & Quarrington, B. (1979). Pre-, peri- and neo-natal factors and infantile autism. *Journal of Child Psychology and Psychiatry,* 20, 119–28.

Gillberg, C. (1985). Asperger's syndrome and recurrent psychosis – a case study. *Journal of Autism and Developmental Disorders,* 15, 389–98.

Gillberg, C. (1988). Epidemiology of Asperger's syndrome. Paper presented at seminar on Asperger's syndrome, King's Fund, London.

Gillberg, C. (1989). Asperger syndrome in 23 Swedish children. *Developmental Medicine and Child Neurology,* 31, 520–31.

Gillberg, C., Persson, E., Grufman, M. & Themner, U. (1986). Psychiatric disorders in mildly and severely mentally retarded urban children and adolescents: epidemiological aspects. *British Journal of Psychiatry,* 149, 68–74.

Hobson, P. (1986a). The autistic child's concept of people. *Communication,* 20, 12–17.

Hobson, R. P. (1986b). The autistic child's appraisal of expressions of emotion. *Journal of Child Psychology and Psychiatry,* 27, 321–42.

Hobson, R. P., Ouston, J. & Lee, A. (1988). What's in a face? The case of autism. *British Journal of Psychology,* 79, 441–53.

Howells, J. G. & Guirguis, W. R. (1984). Childhood schizophrenia 20 years later. *Archives of General Psychiatry,* 41, 123–8.

Kerbeshian, J. & Burd, L. (1986). Asperger's syndrome and Tourette syndrome. *British Journal of Psychiatry,* 148, 731–5.

Kimura, D. & Archibald, Y. (1974). Motor functions of the left hemisphere. *Brain,* 97, 337–50.

Kimura, D. & Vanderwolf, C. H. (1970). The relation between hand preference and the performance of individual finger movements by left and right hands. *Brain,* 93, 769–74.

Langdell, T. (1978). Recognition of faces: an approach to the study of autism. *Journal of Child Psychology and Psychiatry,* 19, 255–68.

Leff, J. P., Fischer, M. & Bertelsen, A. (1976). A cross-national epidemiological study of mania. *British Journal of Psychiatry,* 129, 428–42.

Mesibov, G. (1983). Current perspectives and issues in autism and adolescence. In E. Schopler & G. B. Mesibov (eds.), *Autism in adolescents and adults.* New York: Plenum.

Miles, S. W. & Capelle, P. (1987). Asperger's syndrome and aminoaciduria: a case example. *British Journal of Psychiatry,* 150, 397–400.

Newson, E., Dawson, M. & Everard, P. (1982). The natural history of able autistic people: their management and functioning in a social context. Unpublished report to the Department of Health and Social Security, London. Summary published in 4 parts in *Communication,* 19–22 (1984–5).

Rifkin, A., Quitkin, F. M. & Klein, D. (1975). Akinesia: a poorly recognised drug-induced extrapyramidal disorder. *Archives of General Psychiatry,* 32, 672–4.

Rutter, M. (1978). Diagnosis and definition of childhood autism. *Journal of Autism and Childhood Schizophrenia*, 8, 139–61.

Rutter, M. & Schopler, E. (1987). Autism and pervasive developmental disorders. *Journal of Autism and Developmental Disorders*, 17, 159–86.

Scott, D. W. (1985). Asperger's syndrome and non-verbal communication: a pilot study. *Psychological Medicine*, 15, 683–8.

Shah, A. & Frith, U. (1983). An islet of ability in autistic children: a research note. *Journal of Child Psychology and Psychiatry*, 24, 613–30.

Szatmari, P., Bartolucci, G., Bremner, R., Bond, S. & Rich, S. (1989). A follow-up study of high-functioning autistic children. *Journal of Autism and Developmental Disorders*, 19, 213–25.

Tager-Flusberg, H. (1985). Psycholinguistic approaches to language and communication in autism. In E. Schopler & G. B. Mesibov (eds.), *Communication problems in autism*. New York: Plenum.

Tager-Flusberg, H., Calkins, S., Nolin, T., Baumberger, T., Anderson, M. & Chadwick-Dias, A. (1990). A longitudinal study of language acquisition in autistic and Down syndrome children. *Journal of Autism and Developmental Disorders*, 20, 1–21.

Tantam, D. (1986). Eccentricity and autism. Unpublished Ph.D. thesis, University of London.

Tantam, D. (1988a). Annotation: Asperger's syndrome. *Journal of Child Psychology and Psychiatry*, 29, 836–40.

Tantam, D. (1988b). Lifelong eccentricity and social isolation: I. Psychiatric, social, and forensic aspects. *British Journal of Psychiatry*, 153, 777–82.

Tantam, D. (1988c). Lifelong eccentricity and social isolation: II. Asperger's syndrome or schizoid personality disorder? *British Journal of Psychiatry*, 153, 783–91.

Tantam, D. (1988d). Asperger's syndrome or autistic personality disorder. *Communication*, 22, 37–9.

Tantam, D. (in press). Characterising the fundamental social handicap of autism. *Acta Paedopsychiatrica*.

Tantam, D., Evered, C. & Hersov, L. (1990). Asperger's syndrome and ligamentous laxity. *Journal of the American Academy of Child and Adolescent Psychiatry*, 93, 769–74.

Tantam, D., Holmes, D. & Cordess, C. (in press). Non-verbal expression in autism of Asperger type. *Journal of Autism and Developmental Disorders*.

Tantam, D., Monaghan, L., Nicholson, H. & Stirling, J. (1989). Autistic children's ability to interpret faces: a research note. *Journal of Child Psychology and Psychiatry*, 30, 623–30.

Van Dijk, T. A. (1977). *Text and context: explorations in the semantics and pragmatics of discourse*. London: Longman.

Van Krevelen, D. A. (1971). Early infantile autism and autistic psychopathy. *Journal of Autism and Childhood Schizophrenia*, 1, 82–6.

Voeller, K. K. S. (1986). Right-hemisphere deficit syndrome in children. *American Journal of Psychiatry*, 143, 1004–9.

Volkmar, F. R., Cohen, D. J., Hoshino, Y., Rende, R. D. & Paul, R. (1988). Phenomenology and classification of the childhood psychoses. *Psychological Medicine*, 18, 191–201.

Volkmar, F. R., Paul, R. & Cohen, D. J (1985). The use of 'Asperger's syndrome'. *Journal of Autism and Developmental Disorders*, 15, 437–9.

Weintraub, S. & Mesulam, M. M. (1983). Developmental learning disabilities and the right hemisphere: emotional, interpersonal and cognitive components. *Archives of Neurology*, 40, 463–8.

Wing, L. (1980). Childhood autism and social class: a question of selection. *British Journal of Psychiatry*, 137, 410–17.

Wing, L. (1981). Sex ratios in early childhood autism and related conditions. *Psychiatry Research*, 5, 129–37.

Wing, L. (1987). The continuum of autistic characteristics. In E. Schopler & G. B. Mesibov (eds.), *Diagnosis and assessment of autism*. New York: Plenum.

Wing, L. & Gould, J. (1979). Severe impairments of social interaction and associated abnormalities in children: epidemiology and classification. *Journal of Autism and Developmental Disorders*, 9, 11–29.

Wolff, S. & Barlow, A. (1979). Schizoid personality in childhood: a comparative study. *Journal of Child Psychology and Psychiatry*, 20, 29–46.

Wolff, S. & Chick, J. (1980). Schizoid personality disorder in childhood: a follow-up study. *Psychological Medicine*, 10, 85–100.

Wolff, S. & Cull, A. (1986). Schizoid personality and antisocial conduct: a retrospective case note study. *Psychological Medicine*, 16, 677–87.

World Health Organization. (1978). *International classification of diseases: ninth revision*. Geneva: WHO.

World Health Organization. (1990). *International classification of diseases: tenth revision*. Chapter V. Mental and behavioural disorders (including disorders of psychological development). Diagnostic criteria for research (May 1990 draft for field trials). Geneva: WHO (unpublished).

6

Living with Asperger's syndrome

MARGARET DEWEY

An informal test of social know-how and its uses

Challenged to write about problems which face adults with Asperger's syndrome, I would like to begin by challenging readers to a simple test. The aim of the test will become clear later. For the moment, think of it as a test of your knowledge of human relations. I have offered the stories to my autistic friends with the following explanation and reassurance: 'I am interested in your opinions so that I can compare them with others. There are no precise right or wrong answers to this test, so you cannot fail it.'

The test was composed in 1974 for some young men whose parents were members of the American National Society for Autistic Children. It was my first attempt at trying to understand the frustrations of adolescents who no longer fitted the stereotype of younger autistic children. After constructing stories involving some ordinary social interactions mingled with unusual interactions, I presented them first to a class of normal college students. They compared their answers and challenged me to a lively debate. After a few revisions, I was satisfied that the stories were understood consistently by normal students, and that unconventional answers might help pin-point problems in my autistic subjects.

The autistic subjects were most co-operative, taking a lot of trouble and risking humiliation in order to be helpful to people like themselves, that is, high-functioning autistic individuals who might also be classified under the term Asperger's syndrome. Later, I will discuss their responses, but for now you can go and find a pencil.

Test instructions

In the following stories some parts are in *italics*. Immediately following there is a pair of brackets ( ). Rate the behaviour which is illustrated by the portion in italics according to how you think most people would judge that behaviour if they witnessed it. Use this scale.

Fairly normal behaviour in that situation	(A)
Rather strange behaviour in that situation	(B)
Very eccentric behaviour in that situation	(C)
Shocking behaviour in that situation	(D)

Story no. 1. In the supermarket

The market where Robert always shopped had a small sign in the door which read BARE FEET PROHIBITED IN THIS STORE BY STATE LAW. One summer day Robert saw a pretty girl enter the store without shoes. She seemed about his age, twenty, with long hair and an old-fashioned dress reaching to her ankles. Robert wanted to warn her about the sign but he was afraid to speak to her. Unpleasant things happened if he tried to talk to strange girls. Finally he decided he might be able to shield her feet from being seen by the manager. *He pushed his cart close behind hers down aisle after aisle.* ( ) Once or twice the girl looked back at him with a cross expression. *Suddenly she wheeled into the quick-check lane with twelve items in her basket although the sign said* FOR TEN OR FEWER ITEMS. ( ) Robert was more upset than ever. He thought this pretty girl was tempting fate by breaking another rule. When the check-out clerk let her through without comment, Robert finally relaxed. *Just then, the barefoot girl turned and said to him, 'I don't know why you are following me, but buzz off or I'll call the police!'* ( )

Story no. 2. In the elevator

Charlie, twenty-three, had been out of work for several months. On this day his hopes were high because he was on his way to apply for a job which seemed just right for him. As Charlie rode the elevator to his interview *a stranger said pleasantly, 'Nice day, isn't it?'* ( ) Just then, Charlie happened to see his reflection in a mirror by the elevator buttons. His hair was sticking up in a peculiar way and he had no comb with him. *He turned to the friendly stranger and asked, 'Do you have a comb I could borrow for a minute, please?'* ( )

Story no. 3. In the park

Keith, age twenty-five, was a file clerk who worked in an office in the city. At noon he took his lunch to a small park and sat on a sunny bench to eat. *Often he tore part of a sandwich into bits, scattering it on the ground for pigeons.* ( ) One day when he came to his favourite bench a baby carriage was parked beside it. Keith noticed that a young woman was swinging an older child nearby. The baby in the carriage began to cry but the mother did not hear this because the swing was squeaking. Now, Keith had learnt that when his baby nephew screamed, sometimes this meant that a pin in his diaper had opened. *Rather than bother the mother in the park, Keith quickly checked the baby's clothing to see whether he could feel an open pin.* (🔲)

Story no. 4. The forgotten name

Paul, twenty-three, had a little shop where he renovated old furniture. Sometimes a customer would ask to have some work done in her home. On one such occasion an elderly lady called him to stain a scratch on her desk. *Unfortunately, Paul forgot to jot down her name when he wrote the address.* (   ) The lady greeted him warmly at her door, saying 'Come right in, Paul. I have heard that your work is good.' Ashamed because he had forgotten her name, *Paul waited until she left the room and peeked into a drawer.* (   ) Sure enough, he found some letters addressed to Mrs Isabel DeWitt, and this jogged his memory. Satisfied, Paul shut the drawer without disturbing anything and soon had the scratch nicely refinished. When the lady of the house saw it she said, 'That's perfect! How much do I owe you, Paul?' *He replied, 'It did not take very long, so ten dollars will be fine, Isabel.'* (   )

Story no. 5. In the airplane

Emily, age nineteen, overslept on the morning of her airplane trip. When she woke up, there was just enough time to dress and get to the airport, *so she skipped her breakfast.* (   ) At noon, the stewardess came around with lunch, but Emily was so hungry by then that one portion did not satisfy her. She watched a little girl across the aisle toy with her food, complaining, 'I can't eat it.' Apparently, the father didn't want any more, because he told the child to just leave it. *Emily leant across the aisle and said, 'If your little girl doesn't want her tray, can you pass it over for me?'* (   )

Story no. 6. The dinner invitation

Roger, twenty-two, lived in a rented room alone. He was quite a nervous person, but it seemed to him he felt better if he ate every two hours and limited his diet to certain foods. One day a lady called and invited him to dinner explaining that she was a friend of his parents. Roger gladly accepted. *However, he warned his hostess that he ate no meat and would like his vegetables served unsalted.* (   ) When Roger arrived at the appointed time he recalled that he had not eaten for two hours. *Without wasting any time, even before the introductions, he asked the hostess when dinner would be served.* (   ) She replied that it would be about an hour before the meal would be ready. *Hearing this, Roger opened his briefcase, removed an apple and some nuts and promptly ate them.* (   ) After that, he was introduced to the family and they sat around talking for an hour. Just before dinner, the hostess showed him an attractive platter of fruits and vegetables, asking whether it looked like enough. *'It looks fine, thank you,'*

Roger said, 'but if you don't mind I will wait another hour to eat. I just had some food an hour ago.'

Story no. 7. Forbidden foods

Elizabeth had been diabetic most of her life. Doctors told her that careful attention to diet was necessary to avoid serious complications. When she was invited to someone's home for a meal, she explained her problem in advance. *But at large gatherings she handled the matter herself by avoiding forbidden foods or leaving them untouched on her plate.* ( ) On such occasions she did not mention her medical condition unless somebody urged forbidden food on her, in which case she said, 'No thanks, I'm diabetic.' At some parties there was not much she could eat, and *in such situations she enjoyed the conversation and companionship, waiting until she returned home to eat the food she was allowed to eat.* ( )

Story no. 8. The lunch-time nap

Frank found employment at the age of nineteen with a company that cared for people's yards. He carried his lunch with him in a box. *At noon, Frank washed his hands under the hose and sat in a shady part of the yard to eat.* ( ) Since he was allowed an hour for lunch, *he sometimes snatched a quick nap by curling up behind a bush.* ( ) One day it began to rain at noon. Frank knocked on the door and asked permission to eat inside. The lady said he could come in, and since she was busy with her children he decided not to bother her further. *He located the bathroom by himself and washed his hands.* ( ) *Then he found the dining room by himself and ate his lunch.* ( ) *He cleaned his crumbs from the table and looked around the house for a place to rest.* ( ) The living room carpet was thick, *so he decided to curl up for his nap behind a large chair.* ( )

If you responded to these stories like my student controls, four categories were not enough. For example, some behaviours were decidedly abnormal, yet more laughable than shocking. Other underlined behaviours seemed so bland and ordinary that they hardly deserved to be rated at all. That was deliberate. I wanted to find out whether autistic people misjudge in one direction as well as the other, that is, do they sometimes perceive normal behaviour as strange in addition to rating some odd behaviours as normal? The answer is yes, but before further discussion of responses let me summarise the purpose of the test stories:

> They serve as examples of common social situations which can create problems for autistic people.

> They reveal the idiosyncratic thinking which is a clue to the nature of the handicap.

> They challenge teachers to provide more flexible guidelines for social behaviour than rigidly applied rules.

They provide an opportunity for non-autistic people to reflect on their automatic but perhaps misguided reactions to the blunders of autistic individuals.

In individual cases, they illuminate aspects of social behaviour which can benefit from further discussion.

They offer a tactful way to engage autistic people in discussions about social behaviour without the pain of direct personal confrontation.

Some informative responses

The seven autistic young men who took this test in 1974 rated the behaviours in idiosyncratic ways. They plainly failed to understand the stories in a conventional way. Their judgements appeared to be influenced by their own experiences or behavioural rules they had learnt and applied rigidly. These differed from person to person, so they did not have predictable answers as a group, yet they were similar in failing to attach the usual significance to social interactions. More instructive than A-B-C-D ratings are the comments which parents passed on to me. All the quotations, printed in italics, are by autistic subjects, followed by my comments.

Story no. 1. In the supermarket

You shouldn't follow people closely. It makes them nervous. This is an example of a learnt rule, well applied.

I do not think it is normal to go out a check-out lane with more items than a sign says because that is not obeying the rules. All autistic subjects were critical of this behaviour, some to the point of being shocked.

It is shocking for the girl to say she would call the police because she should only call the police if the guy hit her or touched her or threatened her. This guy never even touched her! This remark was typical of autistic reactions, whereas the normal controls readily understood the girl's reaction to being followed by a strange man.

Story no. 2. In the elevator

I never saw an elevator with a mirror in it. This is a typical pedantic, irrelevant remark.

It was eccentric for the stranger to say, 'Nice day isn't it', because you can't see the weather in an elevator. This is a typical literal analysis which misses the point that comments on the weather are common pleasantries between strangers.

Borrowing the comb is normal behaviour for him because he has to look nice for the interview. This is the most important thing because he needs very badly to get this job. Most controls rated the comb incident as quite shocking. Other autistic subjects varied, as some may have learnt rules about sharing combs.

Story no. 3. In the park

That's eccentric to waste good food by throwing it on the ground for birds. Other autistic subjects rated this as strange without saying why. By contrast, all controls recognised that feeding pigeons is a common recreation for people relaxing in a park.

   Babies should be left to the care of their own mothers. A learnt rule well applied, contrasts with another autistic subject's reason for rating the baby incident as rather strange: *I wouldn't know how to handle diapers.* It is interesting that several autistic subjects put the diaper incident in the same league as feeding pigeons, whereas the controls rated touching a strange baby as shocking and bird-feeding as perfectly normal.

Story no. 4. The forgotten name

I wouldn't have forgotten her name. It is too important that you remember. Other autistic subjects thought it was shocking that Paul forgot his customer's name, whereas the controls recognised that it was fairly normal behaviour, though deplorable.

   You shouldn't look through personal papers. This was apparently a good rule which the autistic subject had learnt. Other autistic subjects and the student controls responded in variable ways to this incident. Some students thought it would be a logical way to recall a forgotten name, and that many people would do it if they felt certain they would not be observed. Therefore they rated it as fairly normal.

   All of the autistic subjects overlooked the oddness of Paul addressing his customer by her first name. Instead they focused on the way the price was set: *That's normal. It's up to the two of them to decide on a price.* The student controls laughed at the name incident, considering it either eccentric or strange.

Story no. 5. In the airplane

That's the most important meal, said one autistic subject who rated skipping breakfast as shocking. Other autistic subjects thought it abnormal to skip the meal even when late for a flight. They rated this behaviour more severely than asking another passenger for leftover food. In fact, two subjects thought the latter was normal behaviour for the situation, or at least a good idea, *I would be tempted to do that. The food would go to waste, otherwise.* My student controls were in agreement about the normalcy of skipping breakfast on occasion. They had mixed reactions to Emily's polite request for the child's uneaten food. Some thought it would be acceptable if she had established contact with the child's family already through exchange of smiles. If she explained, 'I had no breakfast and am still quite hungry,' her request would be within the range of normal.

Story no. 6. The dinner invitation

On the whole, my autistic subjects rated Roger's behaviour as normal and appropriate because he was a nervous person. Their comments reflected admiration for Roger in that he had found a way to control his nervousness. One subject did consider it eccentric not to eat meat, however, because he himself is very fond of meat. The student controls recognised vegetarianism as fairly normal. As for Roger's behaviour at the dinner party, student controls rated it in the range of eccentric–shocking because it violated custom and seemed insensitive to the feelings of others.

Story no. 7. Forbidden foods

Autistic subjects varied in their reactions to this story, being generally dissatisfied with the way Elizabeth handled her problem because she went to a party and had to go home hungry. They viewed this as strange or eccentric, certainly not normal. I had hoped to provoke comments about her enjoyment of the conversation and companionship, but the low ratings suggested that autistic subjects did not think such pleasures could override the deplorable situation of being unable to eat the party food. The student controls rated Elizabeth's behaviour as normal, being aware of the seriousness of diabetes and more significantly, the fact that it is widely recognised, thus socially acceptable, as a valid reason for avoiding certain foods.

Story no. 8. The lunch-time nap

Both the student controls and the autistic subjects were tolerant of Frank's behaviour outdoors. The reaction to Frank's indoor behaviour was markedly different, however. On the whole, the autistic subjects graded it as normal behaviour except for the nap. One autistic man thought that napping behind a chair was acceptable because some carpets are thick and soft. I am left wondering whether the others graded the nap as strange because they thought it would have been more suitable for Frank to rest in his customer's bedroom! The student controls were amused at Frank's indoor behaviour, which they regarded as mainly eccentric, not shocking.

Some general characteristics of the responses

Parents reported that their autistic sons pondered the stories for a long time before they felt ready to answer. They carefully weighed the merits of segments of behaviour with little regard for the social context or social convention. There was almost no consideration of how the targeted behaviours might be interpreted by other characters in the stories.

In contrast, student controls rated the behaviours in question quickly and intuitively. When the stories were first read aloud to the class, they frequently laughed in unison. Such laughter signifies an unexpected turn of events, the recognition of an incongruent element or a shift to an uncommon viewpoint. The spontaneity of their laughter revealed that the students shared a common social perspective, although their ratings showed minor variations. They argued some points because they were bright young adults who enjoy challenging convention. The autistic subjects showed little awareness of convention except in a few situations where they saw a chance to apply a learnt rule for social behaviour. A few older intelligent autistic subjects have taken the test since 1974. With more social experience, they show an improvement in awareness of social conventions. Nevertheless their judgements seem to be based on rules rather than intuition.

Uses of the test stories as catalysts for informal training

Even though the eight story situations do not come close to covering all the social errors that a person with Asperger's syndrome might commit, they give an idea of how aware any individual is of situational nuances. Most of the parents in the original group were amazed at the extent of social handicap the test revealed in their own sons. A young adult may already know the proper behaviour for all situations he shares with his parents, having been observed and corrected by them. Appropriate behaviour at home is not likely to fit other situations, however.

Teachers or parents may want to use the test to insert one or two new stories which fit the needs of a specific subject. For effective disguise, the name, age and setting should obviously be changed and totally new circumstances invented. The underlying behaviour should be similar but not identical to the target problem behaviour. Two of the stories in my test were, in fact, created to help two different subjects with personal idiosyncrasies. Neither subject recognised that the story had been based on his own behaviour.

An autistic person is not likely to feel manipulated by this ruse, though he may be sensitive to certain subjects and resist altering his viewpoint at the time of the discussion. An interesting phenomenon many parents report is belated acceptance of new viewpoints. At some time, perhaps months later, the autistic person may reopen an argument which had seemed lost. He shows a new comprehension of what his helper was trying to convey, presenting it as his own idea. My advice is, 'For goodness sake, give him credit!' It took a lot of pondering to come to full understanding. For all practical purposes, his new viewpoint really *is* a product of his own thinking. The worst thing the helper can say is, 'Well, it's about time. That's what I have been trying to tell you all along.'

Common misunderstandings of behaviour in intelligent autistic individuals

Astute as Asperger was at recognising traits which are common in the syndrome he identified, he was sometimes tripped up by his own intact system for social analysis. That is, he attributed certain motives to behaviours which might be associated with such motives in normal children. Occasionally he did concede that his patients seemed unaware of their effect on others. But elsewhere he labelled behaviours as spiteful, hostile, malicious, cruel or sadistic. These terms imply awareness of the feelings of other people and an intention to influence them. This is clearly an over-interpretation.

What causes such misunderstanding of autistic behaviour? Autistic children would have to possess a genius for getting into the minds of others in order unfailingly to pick the worst possible time to create a disturbance, as Asperger reported. More likely that impression is the cumulative effect of listening to parents and teachers attempt to explain their exasperation. It is still difficult to put one's finger on precisely what is wrong.

The tales that are remembered and repeated are precisely those that are most shocking. It is also true that certain tense situations invite action, without any malice or premeditation on the part of the child. Consider, for example, the hush that falls just before the most significant moment of a solemn ceremony. Rather than observing the ceremony, an autistic child may be listening to other noises in the room such as coughs, shuffles, whispers and rustles. Suddenly, a complete silence falls. The child notices and is tempted to fill it with his favourite silly noise. The worst time? Yes, but not because that autistic child spitefully plotted to ruin the occasion.

Now consider one of Asperger's examples which could be based on a similar misinterpretation. Here are the reported words and behaviours of a seven-year-old boy who was viewed as sadistic:

> 'Mummy, I shall take a knife one day and push it in your heart, then blood will spurt out and this will cause a great stir.' 'It would be nice if I were a wolf. Then I could rip apart sheep and people, and then blood would flow.' Once, when the mother cut her finger, 'Why isn't there more blood? The blood should run!' When he injured himself on one occasion, he was said to have been utterly thrilled, so that the doctor who tended the wound remarked on the child's state as extremely odd.

I do not see in this account a sadistic child, but one who is obsessively interested in the way blood is forcefully pumped through the body. Even his own injury is viewed as an exciting occasion to observe the phenomenon. The first remark is shocking because it appears to be a threat to his mother. But autistic children are socially far younger than their actual age. Many young children resort to exaggerated threats to show displeasure. I know a four-year-old who became so upset with his father that he shouted, 'I'll make you drive 100 miles without your seat belt fastened!' At four, a normal child is unaware of amusing or shocking nuances in his utterances. Autistic children remain socially unaware much longer.

It is also possible that child-rearing practices in Austria in the decade before 1944 contributed to the hostility Asperger observed in some patients. That was a turbulent period in history. Asperger spoke with admiration of the dextrous fighting of normal children. One can imagine the chagrin of parents at the sissyish behaviour of autistic children, averting their eyes and avoiding physical contact whenever possible. By punishment and exhortation the parents might have changed the natural inclination of frightened children to flee, causing them to defend ourselves with excessive force. Let me give an example.

Once I intervened just in time to stop a litle boy from hitting a playmate with a segment of iron pipe. Stuart was not autistic but he was puny. He was no match for others his age, yet if he ran home in tears he was punished. His father scolded him for acting like a baby and sent him back to fight his own battles. Having no chance of winning in fair combat, Stuart was about to make his point with an iron pipe.

One other factor may have contributed to an excess of violence in Asperger's sample. Perhaps the main reason for their referral was their tendency to fight. Asperger's willingness to work with 'violent' children could have resulted in a reputation for knowing how to deal with just such problems. In that case, the teachers and therapists in guidance clinics would selectively refer their most aggressive autistic patients to Asperger. Others who posed no threat to their classmates might have been counselled in clinics near home, muddling through school as very odd fellows. The wonder is not that an astute observer like Asperger would make some false assumptions, but that he identified so many traits that are correctly associated with the cognitive handicap we call autism.

Overcoming misunderstandings

Smoothing the way with interpretation

The idea of an interpreter for such verbally articulate children as Asperger describes may seem odd at first, but I am not concerned with interpreting their discourses. Sometimes their strange behaviour must be interpreted for a teacher, fellow students, shopkeeper, banker or employer. Just as often, the puzzling words or actions of other people have to be interpreted for autistic individuals.

Asperger accepted as natural the behaviour of normal children, rejecting and tormenting the autistic ones whose behaviour 'cries out to be ridiculed'.

Perhaps this is the natural reaction of *uninformed* children to incomprehensible oddness. It does not need to be accepted as inevitable, however.

In many American and British schools, handicapped children are now integrated into regular activities from which they can benefit. The entire school staff is briefed in preparation for dealing with them. Selected students may be chosen to interact with the handicapped pupils on a one-to-one basis. This is recognised as an honour, often accompanied by fringe benefits such as being excused from some tedious drill. During periods when the special students are absent from the classroom for individual tutoring, the teachers sometimes present material on the nature of the handicaps, using the occasion to praise the normal students for their help and compassion.

Similar programs of interpretation have been used to ease qualified autistic youths into jobs. In this instance, the job placement team has two aims: to help the autistic person learn the work routine and to ensure that fellow workers are sympathetic supporters of the effort rather than disrupters.

The fact that some autistic workers are warmly accepted by co-workers who understand them belies the unpleasant generalisms Asperger made about personality. This is not to say I have never met an autistic person who seems indiscriminately hostile. I know one, and I know a few others who risk exploitation by being indiscriminately trusting. It is the lack of appropriate discrimination which typifies autism. Asperger's candid portrayal of disagreeable traits can serve as a warning, however. A child who is often rejected and tormented may well develop hostile defences. The need for interpretation is therefore greater when an autistic child has Asperger's syndrome than when he is non-verbal and sheltered as a matter of course.

Beyond providing a compassionate environment, parents can decrease hostility by the way they interpret other people's behaviour. This presents a dilemma. They want to send their naive child out into the world prepared to recognise evil in all its disguises. Yet they risk warping the child's outlook if they put much stress on ways others deceive and exploit him. The only solution seems to be a kind of benign supervision through an ongoing support system. That is a tall order with many ramifications. The support system merits attention as a new topic in itself.

Some insights on management

When Jack, the third of our four children, was born in 1947, the few doctors who had heard of autism tended to blame it on defective mothering. We were lucky, therefore, that his first diagnosis was mild retardation. After a brief period of shock we could accept that Jack would learn more slowly than our other children. Yet we took hope from glimmers of talent and kept faith in our parenting abilities, which were sorely needed to help Jack by trial and error. That may still be the best way to handle some unique problems of autistic individuals. Eventually, one comes to recognise what kinds of intervention work for each child and what kinds are counter-productive.

Today Jack is a reasonably contented middle-aged man, gainfully employed as a piano tuner and living in his own small house. Younger parents sometimes ask 'How did you do it?' Actually, *he* did it by dint of sustained effort as well as ability. My insights stem from a forty-year perspective and fortuitous contacts. Certainly, I cannot write as an infallible parent.

Asperger's paper is a convenient reference point from which to discuss the problems of high-functioning autistic people. Obviously, they are capable of more independence than those who are severely handicapped. But that does not necessarily ensure that life will be easier for them. Each step towards greater independence is accompanied by new pitfalls. Asperger dwelt on one such transition, the start of school. He observes, 'Parents can often cope with the oddities of small autistic children, but at school they cannot be handled in the ordinary way.'

The phrase 'in the ordinary way' is rich with meaning. It suggests that readers will know what everybody, even little children starting school, should know. There are expectations surrounding the school situation. Unfortunately, many of the most elementary things which everybody is assumed to know can elude an autistic child. (Don't ask for a list: it is too variable). An unspoken expectation is nothing but an idea in other people's minds, something which quite baffles an autistic person. Even when the message is put into words it is apt to be misinterpreted. The phrases most commonly used in everyday speech can seldom be taken literally. If 'Fold your hands!' seems like an impossible order, an autistic child does not look around to see what others are doing. He is more likely to look for a way out. The teacher is perplexed because this child leaves his seat for no apparent reason and wanders away. She is no more perplexed than he. The same comedy of errors will be repeated on the occasion of every drastic change in an autistic person's life.

The more capable an autistic person appears to be, the more likely it is that he will be expected to manage his own affairs without supervision. It would seem that he should be able to handle at least simple social interactions of the everyday variety. But that is not necessarily so. The oddness of an autistic person shows up most starkly in commonplace situations. He does not intuitively know what everybody is presumed to know, and he lacks the awareness of other minds which would enable him to get guidance from subtle cues on the spot. By contrast, in situations where almost everybody is baffled by expectations, autistic people are less obvious misfits. They may do well travelling abroad, for example, seeming just a bit more odd than other tourists.

I will not concern myself with how to teach autistic adults to be law-abiding citizens. They are generally quite good at that. Instead I want to address some of the eccentricities Asperger noticed. How can one protect an autistic person from scorn and its devastating effects on self-esteem? Can autistic people be guided to change long-standing habits and mannerisms that set them apart?

An interpretation of the belated acceptance phenomenon

Why do some autistic people belatedly convert other people's ideas into their own insights? I once viewed it as an unconscious ego defence. It seemed as though they had an exceptional need to give the appearance of being able to figure things out on their own. Therefore I assumed, they resisted immediate change in their stance even when it should have been obvious that they were mistaken. By waiting a while, they hoped the original discussion would be forgotten so that they could appear to reach the correct conclusion by themselves. This is an explanation anybody can understand. It is based on the emotional reactions of ordinary people, plus the awareness that an autistic person suffers more than his share of social humiliation.

Now I have revised the above interpretation. After reading *Autism: explaining the enigma* by Uta Frith,[1] I realise that autistic people cannot easily assume a viewpoint other than their own. They have the greatest difficulty *simultaneously* perceiving two different interpretations of one situation. If the notion is correct that autistic people lack a theory of mind, then they may not realise that they changed a belief or why they changed it. They have beliefs, they *can* change them but it is another question whether they actually know how beliefs come about. As far as they are concerned, insights just happen like the light that flashes over a cartoon character.

A highly motivated person may mull over advice in private. If he tests it in a social situation and finds it to be helpful, he begins to change his previous position. Then, in all sincerity, he may return to the person who implanted the idea for change and announce, 'I decided not to make phone calls after 9 pm because some people like to go to bed early.' An appropriate response would be, 'That's very smart! Some of them have to get up early to commute to their jobs', and let it go at that, without reference to his previous habits or the origin of the suggestion.

The ultimate tool for change

Probably nothing is as effective in guiding an autistic person as positive reinforcement. I do not mean bribery in the form of a reward offered for

[1] Oxford: Blackwell, 1989

changing behaviour. That sometimes works, but if the reward is valued, the cost of failure is also dear. The autistic person becomes so anxious that one slip can provoke a catastrophic emotional reaction.

I have in mind continuous positive reinforcement by favourable notice and well-timed approval. It is selectively directed at any sign of desired change up to the point of victory and well beyond that.

Consider the child's game, Hot and Cold. One child is kept in the dark about the location of a hidden prize. (This may be compared to the way an autistic person may be in the dark about appropriate social behaviour.) The player starts out blindly, counting on others to direct him. If he moves away from the prize, they chant words like 'You're cool–cooler–cold–freezing!' So he changes direction and continues to change until he hears 'You're warm–warmer–hot–burning!' Even the tone of the guiding voices heats up with excitement as the triumphant player closes in on his trophy. Ultimate success is assured with this step-by-step reinforcement. The cool signals are positive because they are not delivered as a punishment to deter him from his reward, but as an additional guide to help him win. (Remember this game. You can use it to explain to an autistic person why it is sometimes necessary to point out errors as a short-cut to success.)

In real life, the guidance game is often played quite differently. Correct behaviour is scarcely noticed because it is taken for granted. Every situation has implied rules, and every person is assumed to be marginally acquainted with them, at the least. The person who drives in the correct direction down a one-way street is not singled out for praise. But if you are aware that he frequently goes in the wrong direction you may take notice. (How you notice and what you say depends on the individual's personality. All the autistic adults I have known respond favourably to sincere compliments. Do not be afraid you will provoke misbehaviour by saying something nice.)

Here is an excerpt from a letter written by one mother about her autistic son:

> I have been trying positive reinforcement with surprising success. Deciding on what behavior I wish he would develop, I compliment him greatly when I see the slightest sign of it. It works like magic! He is so guileless he doesn't see through it as you or I might. He always monopolizes the dinner table conversation, so one day I waited for a pause as he was eating, and I said 'You know, Barry, you talk much less at the table than you used to.' (It was true, although he still talked far too much.) 'And sometimes you listen to what others say and follow the dinner conversation.' Well, this statement brought a marked change, so much so that his sisters noticed when they came home.

In the above example, the family should repeat the compliment often to encourage him to keep on trying to control his compulsion to spill out all the ideas he has been mulling over. The follow-up compliments would be even more appropriate, and should be phrased in different ways. When an autistic person has made a concentrated effort to overcome some habit it doesn't hurt to mention the improvement at intervals to prevent backsliding. This is true even when the original impetus is something else, as in the following example.

Years ago, a parent wrote to the newsletter of NSAC[2] asking for help in dealing with annoying little problems like the way her son never took his trousers out of his socks after he had tucked them in to ride his bike. I laughed, because our Jack did the same thing. He would go around tucked in all day because he didn't see how he looked and was too preoccupied to pull his pants out after dismounting his bike. At the time, I resorted to frequent reminders. Recently, he happened to mention that he was about to sing a solo in front of his church congregation when the organist whispered to pull his pants out of his socks. 'Oh, Jack!' I blurted out. 'Not *again*! All those times we reminded you, and you still forget? Isn't there some way you can jog your memory by putting a note on your bike lock, or something?' (He always locks his bike.) Stung by my reaction, Jack went home to ponder the challenge. I do not dare to criticise him often, and he has learnt not to explode when I do, yet he always dislikes it. The next day he triumphantly brought his bike lock to show me. On it, he had painted what looked like an electric plug with a diagonal line across it. 'That's an international signal that means "unplug your pants",' he explained. Never since then have I seen Jack with his trousers tucked into his socks except when he is about to mount his bicycle. We still compliment him on this victory before we challenge him to try to solve another problem.

Compromises: learning when well-enough will do

On a scale of one-to-ten, plugged-in trousers certainly rank low in importance. (It is a good idea to introduce such a scale to autistic people, otherwise they tend to view criticism as hostility, judging their errors as equally significant.) Yet appearance does play a part in social acceptance: it is hard to maintain a tolerable degree of self-esteem without cleanliness, for example. Asperger believed that autistic children do not show the proper attitude to their bodies, noting that even as adults some walk about unkempt and unwashed. I believe that the peculiar grooming habits of some autistic adults result not from poor attitude but from poor understanding of what is appropriate, combined with their inability to sense how they appear to others. Many are overly formal rather than unkempt.

Today, we all know normal individuals who have a casual attitude to grooming. Some young people, in particular, vie with each other in adopting outrageous new styles of dress and hair. No doubt all of this makes it easier for the occasional odd autistic person to go his way unnoticed. Yet there is

---

[2] National Society for Autistic Children. It is now called ASA for Autistic Society of America.

conformity even in non-conformity. Each season has its 'look' which the autistic person is unaware of.

Asperger made many references to family conflicts which arise from the difficulty of teaching autistic children the practical chores of daily life. This tense situation may be eased when one understands that the basic difficulty is not wilful obstruction but a need for precise and patient instruction. Autistic people can be guided to develop grooming habits which help them look (and smell) acceptable in most situations. The trick is to keep it as simple as possible with a minimum of contingencies. For example, a man wearing corduroy slacks and a clean shirt will pass at a picnic or a funeral, even though jeans are more suitable for the former occasion and a dark suit is traditional for the latter. Habits of cleanliness should be the basic ones, without too many daily rituals.

Under pressure of time, an autistic person will not intuitively know which details of grooming to eliminate. Tooth-brushing, nail-trimming, deodorant use, shampoo, underwear-changing, body-washing, hair-cutting, sock-changing, clothes-cleaning and many more common details of grooming need to be put in perspective for an autistic person. The best tactic is to set up a schedule – and keep instructions basic. Interestingly, Asperger himself made the suggestion of a timetable for everyday practical necessities. Beyond that, a degree of discrimination can be taught by use of a one-to-ten scale applied just to grooming. Other common activities also have scales and the activities themselves fit somewhere in an overall scale of importance for survival.

Normal people compromise with their own schedules more than they are willing to admit when they give advice to others. There is no way to cram one day with all of the proper procedures for care of one's self and possessions. Each gadget and each garment comes with rules for care and dire warnings for failing to heed them. This can quite overwhelm an autistic person who cannot discriminate the essential from the trivial.

The more sheltered the individual the less he has to worry about. Those who venture out on their own deserve candid advice which includes short-cuts and acceptable omissions. Sirens do not sound for failing to floss one's teeth!

Helping an autistic person identify a support system

By support I mean tactful counsel and intercession when it is needed. In a sheltered setting, there would be such support as a matter of course. Yet autistic adults who live independently are no less in need of support, their greater skills being offset by greater risk from a wider sphere of activity.

Human beings are normally born with a desire to form social relation-ships. Their natural social awareness provides a support system consisting of associates such as family, friends and co-workers. In almost any situation, they intuitively know where to turn for a helpful suggestion. In fact, normal people seek advice before taking a significant step, knowing that two minds are better than one. Asperger commented on the unusual degree of mental independence in his young patients, noting the way they tended to pursue their own interests single-mindedly. With the benefit of present-day knowledge he might have said they are not aware that other minds have entirely different perceptions.

By adolescence, autistic people of normal intelligence must realise that other people's minds can have knowledge they lack, such as factual informa-tion. Yet they still tend to assume that others should know what is on their minds without being told. Conversely, they sometimes feel accountable for knowledge which nobody would expect them to have. (This is not surprising, in view of their common experience of being blamed for not knowing something which would be obvious to anybody else.) One of the functions of the support system is to help them sort out confusing situations, to relieve them of worry or help them make amends. Here is a very recent example.

Yesterday, Jack made a telephone call in response to a request left on his answering machine by a lady customer. Her husband answered the phone and said he would take the message. Now, Jack's explanations can be rather wordy because he wants to be sure he is understood. After a while the man said he would tell his wife about the call, but he himself had to leave. 'Are you late for work?' Jack asked in some alarm. 'A little,' the man replied. Jack ended the conversation with profuse apologies and called us, dis-traught over his mistake. Would he lose his customer-friend because of this? Would the man lose his job for being late and might he then blame Jack? If so, could the husband sue? (I think he deliberately exaggerates the possible complications to ensure that our reassurances will be emphatic. Therefore, I now mix reassurances with reminders.) In this case, we talked about keeping messages short and ending a conversation graciously at any hint of inconvenience. I also told him that he had no way of knowing that the husband was about to leave for work until the man told him so. Jack would not be held accountable, just as he must not hold other people accountable if they unwittingly call him at a bad time.

The best sources of support are family, friends and co-workers because these are the people who are most understanding of the individual. But, in time, family members are less able to help. An autistic person seldom has close friends. Co-workers are even more scarce, given the limited opportuni-ties for employment of the autistic. Without the kind of support system other people take for granted, autistic people may turn to various agencies. Sometimes they do so in preference to confiding in family members. But if the agencies are not familiar with the cognitive disorder of autism, they may react in a punitive way which discourages autistic people from seeking help again. This was Jack's experience when he visited various agencies on his own, as a young adult:

I need help to know whether a problem is serious enough so that I ought to see a lawyer, call the police, go to a doctor or something. I thought a crisis clinic would give me that kind of advice. But now I would not want to go there because I am afraid of getting the wrong reaction.

The 'wrong reactions' he feared are:

Ridicule: being laughed at or treated with contempt for being so naive.
Anger: being scolded for bothering them about a trifle or for not having enough 'common sense' to seek help at the 'proper place' immediately.
Fear: Being denied help because the volunteer worker is afraid of 'crazy' people and does not want to get involved. In this case, instead of offering an honest evaluation of the problem, the person insists that the matter should be handled by a psychiatrist even when the problem is not serious enough to warrant that.

Mental comprehension is often expressed by the word *see*. ('Do you see what I mean?' 'Yes, I see.') In this sense, an autistic person can be blind to the meaning of a situation. No helper of the blind would react with ridicule, anger or fear to a request for visual help! The autistic handicap is in need of wider understanding.

The amount of support autistic people need is an individual matter, but all of them should be taught to keep in touch with people who understand them. Needing other people is entirely normal and acceptance of this is praiseworthy. Parents must ponder the need and arrange things as best they can.

Two insider viewpoints

On a cool October evening in 1988, we find Anne Carpenter and Jack Dewey on easy chairs beside the fireplace. I have pulled up a seat between them. The tape recorder picks up the crackling sound of burning wood as we relax a moment, watching the flames. Then our discussion begins.

Margaret: Would you introduce yourselves and tell your ages?
Anne: My name is Anne Carpenter and I am thirty-one and a half years old.
Jack: My name is Jack Dewey and I am forty-one.
Anne: Jack, you're the same age as my sister! She's forty-one too.
[Many autistic individuals seem to delight in coincidences involving names and birth dates. Perhaps this is because human relationships are generally based on subtleties which are not readily pin-pointed.]
Margaret: We are relaxing by the fire now, but I am curious to know why both of you told me that you often feel anxious. Is it because you are afraid that something unexpected may happen –
Anne and Jack: (almost in unison) Yes!
Margaret: – and you can't handle unexpected things easily, so you lose control of what happens to you?

Jack: Yes, I have that feeling a lot.

Anne: I relate to that.

> **Margaret**: Or are you afraid you may say or do the wrong thing for the situation?

Anne and Jack: (even more emphatic) Definitely! That is absolutely the feeling!

> **Margaret**: Are you also afraid of losing ground after all you have worked for?

Anne and Jack: (their affirmation reaching a crescendo) YES! YES!

Jack: I am pathologically over-sensitive to criticism, I fear that people are not going to be pleased with me. I am afraid that if I do the wrong thing or say the wrong thing I will undo all the progress I have made so far. It could happen as the result of doing something by accident.

Anne: I think I am capable of doing good work and of being a loving wife. But I may never be able to participate fully in society. I may never be able to find somebody or be able to have a full-time job and support myself. There may be just this barrier and society will not *let* me. I worry about that. I don't want to live on social security the rest of my life.

[It is appropriate to mention here that both Jack and Anne have gone far in overcoming obstacles raised by their handicap. They each live independently, Jack in a small house and Anne in a rented apartment. By dint of great determination, Jack took two years of music composition at the university before training as a piano technician. Anne obtained a master's degree in library science. Against a background of autism from early childhood, their accomplishments are impressive.]

> **Margaret**: I am sorry that my questions reminded you of your worries. What I intended was that you would tell how you deal with such anxieties, because I am impressed by how well adjusted you both seem on the surface. Other autistic people might benefit from your insights. For example, do you have a philosophy for dealing with people who do not understand you?

Anne: A lot of people ask me, 'What's the matter with your eyes?' [She attributes her lack of visual control to autism.] I've been very honest and open. It seems to work. People accept that. But sometimes they say, 'Oh no, you couldn't be because autistic people don't talk and they're retarded.' Then I explain that I'm high-functioning. My doctor, Dr Andrew Maltz, says Asperger's syndrome is the same as high-functioning autism.

Jack: I have problems with people who accuse me of not listening if I don't understand what they're trying to tell me. Sometimes I say I'm autistic and say 'Please be patient'.

> **Margaret**: I know that tuning takes concentration, and you don't like to be rushed when you work. Anne, do you have this experience, too?

Anne: I had one temporary job where I didn't know what was expected of me. I went real slowly and carefully, but it turned out they had wanted me to whip through it. Nobody explained that, and they were displeased. Generally, I need to to think things through. That's one reason I don't want to drive a car. You have to react real fast.

Jack: I certainly identify with you 100 per cent, Anne. I didn't want to learn to drive, and even after I took driver's education I refused to drive for a long time. I would rather take the bus, I would rather ride my bike or walk. But finally my boss said he couldn't drive me to jobs any more, so I bought a car. It was a long slow process gradually getting used to driving. I was very cautious, planning my routes ahead. I had to automate my driving skills one by one. The way I handle the hurry-up pressure on the job is choosing who I work for. I now refuse to do concert tunings because I know there is a deadline to finish the piano. I don't like to have the artist saying, 'Hurry up! Get that done so I can practise!'

> Margaret: Do you have a philosophy for dealing with your reaction to people who seem disappointed in you or angry with you?

Anne: I think, 'That person might be upset about something in his or her own life. Maybe I can gain something from this experience.'

Jack: (after a moment of silence) I am very impressed with Anne's philosophy for facing people who are disappointed in her. It has always been one of the worst traumas for me to feel I have displeased somebody. I tend to remember it years afterwards. It hurts more than I can bear, practically. One thing I do is daydream about how I can be reconciled with people I have displeased and change their opinion of me.

> Margaret: Do you have a philosophy for dealing with feelings of failure?

Anne: I think, 'Maybe this wasn't meant to happen right now. Maybe this wasn't meant to work out, but something else will.' I believe strongly in God and often it works out that if I say, 'This wasn't meant to be', it does turn out to be for the best. I believe that there is a good and benevolent force beyond us. If I say, 'I am going to leave everything up to God' after I have done my best, things seem to work out eventually.

Jack: My most profound feelings of failure are as far as music composition is concerned. My musical compositions have had virtually no impact on the professional music world. The philosophy I have for dealing with that is like the fox and sour grapes story. I say, 'If I *were* successful I might get some very caustic reviews and I would be crushed because of the way I feel about criticism.' Also, the way to lose all of your private life is to become famous. You can't reverse that, and I like my privacy.

> Margaret: Does either of you suffer from loneliness?

Anne: I don't feel as though I have enough friends but I've been feeling a lot better lately because of all the things I've been doing. I work part-time organising the library for the Autistic Society. And I do some part-time work with the Developmental Disability group. Right now I am a volunteer with the Dukakis campaign. There are some benefits from being alone, too, I can think things through and be more ready to go out again. I often feel lonely for a man. I would really like to have somebody but I am glad that I haven't gotten attached yet so I make further progress and be more acceptable.

Jack: Actually, I don't suffer from loneliness. If I have to relate to people too much I become nervous and uncomfortable. As I said before, it is important to me to please people. Once I have pleased people it is not that important that I see them often. I seem to crave a lot of privacy. I am practically an after-work recluse. Since I am pathologically sensitive to criticism if I were married, quite frankly, I'd feel sorry for my wife. All she'd need to do is criticise me and I might have such a fit it would ruin our marriage. It would be a bad thing for her.

> Margaret: Couldn't you learn to control your reaction to criticism?

Jack: No! In fact, so much not that I actually plan my life in such a way that I make sure it doesn't happen. For example, the only customers I accept for my tuning work are the two 're's', referrals and repeats. I never have trouble with those people.

> Margaret: Have you thought about controlling your reactions rather than trying so hard to control the circumstances?

Jack: Of course, I've been conditioned not to scream when I am criticised, but the feeling is there inside me just the same. It's like being poisoned.

> Margaret: Now, here is a question for both of you. Do you have trouble letting go of ideas?

Anne: Yep – I sometimes drive my mother up the wall by talking too much about the same subject. I do have fixations.

Jack: Oh, yes, I have quite a number of things I talk about and can't let go of. But since you've conditioned me not to bore people, I talk to myself incessantly.

Anne: Oh, I talk to myself all the time, too!

> Margaret: I have heard of this happening in so many cases that it must serve some useful purpose for you.

Anne: I think it does. You know, I like the sound of my own voice because it keeps me from feeling lonely. I think there is also a little fear that if I don't talk a lot I may lose my voice. I didn't talk until I was almost five, you know. Before I started talking I noticed a lot of things, and now when I tell my mother she is amazed I remember them. I remember that the world was really scary and everything was over-stimulating.

Jack: Talking to myself helps me figure out and practise how to express ideas well. [On other occasions Jack had mentioned many reasons he feels compelled to talk to himself, though he avoids doing so in public places. Apparently it organises his thoughts and serves as a memory aid. Like Anne, he enjoys the companionship of his own voice.]

> Margaret: Can you say a few words about your reaction to being called autistic?

Anne: The autism diagnosis was like a great big weight being lifted from my chest! [She celebrates the anniversary of that diagnosis as a special day.]

Jack: Me too! I was relieved to know that it was a real thing and it wasn't just my fault for not trying hard enough.

> Margaret: You had other diagnoses before autism. Why didn't those explanations work for you?

Anne: People thought I was mainly visually impaired at first. My lenses were removed when I was a baby because of cataracts. I didn't talk or indicate to people that I saw things, so they thought I was practically blind. I was started in a blind class in school. When I started to read instead of learning braille, they realised I could see. I didn't even need large print. Then they called me hyperactive with minimal brain dysfunction and tried various things for that. For a while, I thought my problems were all psychological and I had psychotherapist after psychotherapist. I won't say some of them didn't help a little bit, but they weren't able to make the autistic behaviours go away. It was a relief when Dr Maltz identified my problem as autism, and suggested the behavioural approach.

Jack: First they thought I was retarded, then brain-damaged. I was often accused of not paying attention or not listening even though I was trying my best. The way I knew when I did the right thing was when people were pleased, not because it was clear to me or obvious. [Maybe this is why Jack is so senstive to criticism and eager to please people.]

Anne: I still have to work on my problems caused by autism. I even get new ones. Recently I've developed obsessive-compulsive behaviours. I go to bed and wonder, 'Did I turn off the stove and slide the dead bolt?' I get so anxious I have to get up and check again.

Jack: I know what you mean. The same thing happens to me. I always have to make sure! I am not comfortable until I have checked certain things.

Here we end our discussion. It seems we have come full circle to the topic of anxiety once again. Autistic people are likely to feel anxious about safeguarding their achievements after their tremendous effort to attain independence. Is it all worth it, then? Jack and Anne obviously think so. In some follow-up conversations they talked eagerly about the things that give them joy. There are many small daily pleasures as well as weekly events and special occasions which are anticipated for months.

Jack has always been involved with music for pleasure as well as work, both creating and listening. As a baby, he walked around beaming with joy and singing songs long before he could talk. Now he gets excited about using a sampling keyboard at a recording studio. He says he loves to orchestrate musical sounds in ways that have never been done before. I believe his claim that the combinations are unique because he never forgets a sound-combination. His ability to recognise and identify classical music seems limitless. It is as if all the music he has ever heard – and he is a prodigious listener – has been forever recorded in his mind for instant recall.

Anne seems attracted to people by nature. She enjoys occasions which give her a chance to mingle with people in small groups. (Large gatherings can be confusing, she admits.) On a typical Sunday recently she rose early, joined a friend for a festive breakfast and walked a considerable distance to the little church she attends. After the formal meetings she remained at church for a pot-luck dinner. Planning her contribution and seeing it appreciated was another pleasure of that day.

Both Anne and Jack enjoy watching nature documentaries on television. Travel films are favourites too. Jack is drawn to documentaries about science while Anne confesses to favouring those about people. Both have been avidly following a recent series about the mind. In fact, they were thrilled because the first program included a segment about a young man who is autistic. They easily recognised symptoms they share with him, although his interests are different.

Jack sometimes relaxes at home by playing the organ or piano. He bought a large used organ which the movers were able to fit into his bedroom by removing the door frame. A grand piano from his grandmother dominates the living room. Just as Jack enjoys expressing himself on all sorts of musical keyboards, Anne finds pleasure exploring ways to use her personal computer. She is looking forward to adding components from time to time.

When asked what she enjoys doing with free time, to relax, Anne said she loves to read. She likes to write too, poetry, prose and letters. In fact, she belongs to a correspondence club of single book-lovers. Through this group she acquired some pen-pals, and mail-time became something to look forward to. Jack admits that reading is a slow process for him, yet he ranks reading in bed as one of his pleasures. He has explored many scientific subjects, enjoying astronomy in particular. He also reads biographies of composers, finding comfort in the fact that not all of them achieved recognition early in life or even within their lifetimes.

Anne does volunteer work. Jack sings in a church choir. The list of activities which enrich their lives goes on and on, as it should. When we concentrate on the grim task of solving the problems of autistic individuals it is easy to overlook the importance of pleasure. Yet without joy in living, all else is pointless.

7

The autobiographical writings of three Asperger syndrome adults: problems of interpretation and implications for theory

FRANCESCA G. E. HAPPÉ

'How far can autistic children go in matters of social adaptation?' This question formed the title of a paper by Kanner in 1973. It is a question still asked by parents and professionals, and in a sense it is the question we ask when we look at the writings of the more able autistic or Asperger syndrome[1] individual. Surely the self-expression of writing, and especially of writing about oneself, must put to the greatest test those social, imaginative and communicative skills thought to be crucially impaired in autism? There can be little doubt, then, that those autistic adults who manage to produce autobiographical works are among the most successful cases – in terms both of their degree of social adjustment and of their intellect.

Several questions then arise: just how able are these people, or rather perhaps just how handicapped? What can we point to in their writings that deserves the label 'autistic'? And what is it about even the most able patients that leads us to say autism is a handicap that one does not grow out of? These writings, then, present a challenge to our theories of autism in so far as they represent and bring home to us the very real and striking range of abilities shown within the group of people we call autistic. This range requires explanation, and a new theory of communication presented by Sperber and Wilson (1986) may hold the key to understanding the vast spectrum of autistic communication problems – as well as giving us an insight into the special qualities of the autobiographical works presented here. This theory will be discussed below, and the claim made that in its

---

[1] The terms 'Asperger syndrome' and 'able autistic' are used interchangeably throughout this chapter. While more precise criteria for Asperger syndrome are discussed in other chapters of this volume, the term is used here to apply to autistic individuals with fluent language and normal intelligence.

light the writings of these able autistic adults have much to tell us about autism in general and the nature of autistic communication in particular.

An impressionistic account of the writings

Temple Grandin: *Emergence labelled autistic* (with M. Scariano) and 'My experiences as an autistic child and review of selected literature'

Temple Grandin is a highly intelligent and articulate woman in her early forties. She works as a consultant designing livestock facilities, and has her own company. She also has a PhD in animal science and has published over 200 articles on her work and studies.

In many ways, the first impression of Temple's book, *Emergence labelled autistic*, is one of great normality. It begins with her receiving an invitation to her old (normal) school's reunion, and then as if in flashback proceeds chronologically through her life, from 'Early school days' to 'Working – coping – surviving'. Some of what she tells us about her childhood is unusual – such as her throwing her hat out of the car window while her mother was driving, and causing a crash (which she seems to have rather enjoyed). However, we are more struck by what we do not hear – for example, about her family life and the odd behaviour that she surely must have shown for her to have been referred to clinicians. In other words, what Temple tells us in her book is in some ways less informative than how she tells us and what she leaves unsaid.

An important point to note about this fascinating book is that it was edited by Margaret Scariano, a children's writer, who rewrote sections of the book, gave it its flashback format and generally structured it to make it easier to read. This obviously presents us with problems, casting doubt on exactly those passages which are most interesting and challenging to our ideas about autism. For example, there are accounts of friendships and imaginative games which are surprising, coming from an autistic child. These stand as a challenge to current theories of autism – which see a social handicap and the lack of pretence as key features of the disorder – but they are, sadly, undermined by the presence of a second, non-autistic author. At one point Temple recalls:

> Even in the games at school I tried to be creative. We used to play hide and seek. In order to confuse the goalkeeper so I could come in and touch 'free', I'd take off my coat and stuff it with leaves and then put it where the goalkeeper would see it. When he went to tag the stuffed coat, I'd run to the goal and win. I always tried to think of new ways of doing things (p. 40).

This is an extraordinary thing to be told of an autistic child doing, and it is very hard to know what to make of it. It does not sound a plausible scheme for playground games, but if true it shows a very good understanding of others' minds. Temple goes on to tell the story of wrecking her teacher's garden and then feigning sympathy and lying about who had done it to escape punishment. This shows a sophisticated understanding of how to manipulate another person's beliefs and emotions.[2] It is a great shame that we cannot be sure of the authenticity of these accounts or of the degree of rewriting by the co-author. It is clear from these instances, and from the overall difference in tone and pattern of Temple's co-written book, compared with her unedited article, that only the work of the autistic writer alone can give us a reliable insight into autism.

Temple's article 'My experiences as an autistic child', is all her own work. It includes a brief account of her childhood, a section on her tactile experiences, which Temple feels are of central importance in autistic development, and a description of her own creation – the squeeze machine. This machine is based on the cattle shutes used to hold cattle still during branding, and was made by Temple to provide firm but controlled pressure, which she finds soothing and believes is of therapeutic value. She goes on from her own experiences to a review of research on the physiology and effects of touch, and work on perceptual and attentional issues in autism. The following extract gives some idea of the style of her writing:

> As a child I wanted to feel the comfort of being held, but then I would shrink away for fear of losing control and being engulfed when people hugged me. At the age of 18 I built a squeeze machine. I could barely tolerate being touched and I would stiffen up, flinch, and jerk away. One day about twelve years ago, a Siamese cat's reaction to me changed after I had used the squeeze machine. This cat used to run from me, but after using the machine I learned to pet the cat more gently and he decided to stay with me. I had to be comforted myself before I could give comfort to the cat.
>
> I have found from my own experiences with the squeeze machine that I almost never feel aggressive after using it. In order to learn to relate to people better I first had to learn how to receive comfort from the soothing pressure of the squeeze machine. Twelve years ago I wrote, 'I realise that unless I can accept the squeeze machine I will never be able to bestow love on another human being', (Grandin, 1970, unpublished). When handling cattle, I often touch the animals because it helps me to be gentle with them. 'Touching the cattle is very important. If I never touch or stroke the animals, it would become easy to shove or kick them around' (Grandin, 1974, unpublished) (p. 151).

Although surprisingly well written, Temple's unghosted work is hard to follow in places, in ways that are perhaps significant, for example, there are

---

[2] Interestingly, Temple's account of this incident also shows a *lack* of understanding of her reader's probable reaction. She does not temper such candour with excuses or claims of guilt or regret.

changes of topic that do not run smoothly for the reader. An enlightening example is where she switches abruptly from talking about her squeeze machine to talking about how to handle cattle, in the passage quoted above. At this point in the article, the reader does not know the origins of the squeeze machine, and the topic change is puzzling and hard to follow. Knowing about this link, on the other hand, makes the change of topic appear smooth. It is as if she fails to appreciate that her reader does not share the important background information that she possesses. Similarly, after many references to the squeeze machine, Temple waits until page 152, after the passage quoted above, to describe the machine – thus giving information vital to understanding earlier references only *after* these references. On page 167, in the middle of a description of her nervous episodes, she introduces, with no further explanation: 'After I swam through the dip vat, the organophosphates greatly reduced the "nerves".' Again, it is as if she does not realise that the reader does not share her personal knowledge, or perhaps that, without further explanation, swimming through a dip vat will seem a pretty odd thing to do.

The dip vat episode also raises an interesting point about Temple's ability to empathise – not just in terms of understanding her reader's state of knowledge, but also in terms of emotion and feeling. Temple's motive for swimming through the dip vat, which is the vital piece of information for making her reader understand this strange action, is revealed only in the reference at the end of the article: 'Grandin, T. 1978. How stressful is dipping – I jumped in to find out. *Calf News* (November), pp. 6–46.' This, in turn, is interesting in two ways. Firstly, it suggests perhaps a lack of ability to empathise, since she felt it necessary to put herself through the same experience in order to feel the same feelings. When we empathise with another person we generally mean that we *feel with* them, despite the fact that we are not actually *suffering with* them. It might also be an inability to empathise to the normal extent that leads Temple to fail to distinguish what is unusual in her experience from what is universal. So, for example, she tells us that 'Even as an adult, I find that it is easier to learn something if I can actually do it instead of watching' (p. 164) – an almost universal experience, in much the same way as she tells us of her extraordinary early 'fixation on spinning objects, refusing to be touched . . . destructive behaviour . . . inability to speak . . . and intense interest in odours' (p. 144).

The second point of interest raised by the dip vat episode, is Temple's attitude to animals. She quotes animal research data throughout her article, much more than she quotes experiments with human subjects, and uses this data without any suggestion that some allowance might have to be made when reasoning from animal to human subjects. She does not seem to see the divide which, rightly or wrongly, most people feel the need to construct between animals and humans. This is evident in her creation of the squeeze machine, and it is interesting that while Temple is certainly aware that her teachers and family find the machine odd and disturbing, she herself does not feel this perhaps irrational, but none the less intuitive, unease. The photographs in her book capture this disregard for the usual barriers we construct between ourselves and other animals, and it must be in part due to this disregard that Temple has been so successful in her job designing livestock facilites in ranches and meat plants.

One explanation for Temple's merging of human and animal data may be that she ignores or discounts the importance of our affective or emotional life. Evidence for this comes mainly from a lack of reference to her own emotional life, the reader's potential emotional reactions or her family relationships in her account of her childhood. It is also revealed in what she does say, for example, in discussing the beneficial effects of the presence of younger 'therapist' monkeys on adult monkeys reared in isolation, she writes: 'The beneficial effect could possibly be due to a combination of tactual stimulation and increased motor activity' (p. 150). The social and affective effects of the presence of the therapist monkeys are not seen to be important.[3] Again in her description of her own anxiety attacks, it seems that Temple discounts the emotional significance of events in favour of a more physiological analysis of her reactions: 'An intermittent itch would be totally insignificant to most adults, but in me it created the same reaction as being chased by a mugger' (p. 167). Elsewhere she talks about her 'emotions' where most people would feel that stress or anxiety (in some sense, the physiology of emotion without the affective meaning) better describes her state: 'The only relapse I have had was during an extremely emotionally arousing event when some new equipment I designed was being started up at a meat packing plant' (p. 168). Such examples leave the reader with the feeling that Temple's emotional life is not like most people's.

This lack of interest in the affective and emotional significance of events is perhaps most striking where she talks about her view of the fundamental deficits in autism. She seems throughout to disregard the fact that most people would feel the social handicap to be the most striking aspect of autism. Instead she is more interested in the autistic person's differences in cognitive style, perceptual experiences and underlying nervous system. One example of this is where she talks about Genie, the girl who was found after spending her first thirteen years tied to a chair with almost no social contact. Temple writes: 'Genie . . . had many autistic behaviours. "Genie is an 'appositional' thinker, visually and tactually oriented, better at holistic than sequential analytic thinking" (Curtiss, 1977)' (p. 149). This seems an odd thing to say, since Genie was notably not autistic in terms of forming affectionate relationships with her nurses soon after being rescued – a feature which most people would feel was of more significance in any

---

[3] Even behaviourists, who make a point of not appealing to mental states, acknowledge the importance of affect and social factors.

comparison with autistic children than features of preferred cognitive style. We get an important insight into Temple's view of autism in the following passage: 'Geschwind (1983) states that people with delayed left hemisphere growth have talents. If autism and dyslexia were prevented maybe the price would be turning potentially talented individuals into ones with mediocre talents' (p. 147). Thus she seems to see autism not so much as a handicap but as an alternative cognitive style – and perhaps, if the social handicap is taken to be unimportant, this is a fair view. Interestingly, she begins the next paragraph, 'Research with artificial intelligence may provide some insights . . .', confirming her lack of interest in the social aspects of the autistic handicap.

It is important to stress, of course, that Temple's biological bias is one shared by many respected researchers and is in no sense given here as an indication of handicap. It is interesting, however, in conjunction with her evident lack of interest in her own and others' emotions – and it should perhaps serve as a warning to us that these autistic writers may not be interested in, or capable of writing on those subjects about which we should most like to hear their views. It is, of course, hard to tell whether a writer is not describing, say, emotions because she is incapable of doing so. In Temple's writing there are some indications that she lacks insight into the world of social relations and feelings, in addition perhaps to a natural lack of interest (maybe with its roots lying in a lack of comprehension). For example, at one point she seems to attribute people's reaction to her as due solely to her odd voice: 'I wish one of the psychologists would have told me about my speech problem instead of worrying about my id. I was aware that sometimes people didn't want to talk to me, but I didn't know why' (*Emergence*, p. 87). Later on, she feels that clothes might be an important factor in social acceptance, and reveals her lack of understanding in saying: 'I still had problems with social relationships. Some of the students called me "Buzzard Woman"! Even when I wore stylish clothes, many of the students didn't want to talk to me. I couldn't figure out what I was doing wrong' (p. 108).

Finally, Temple's writing shows two features which we may want to see as due to her autism. The first is a tendency to keep returning to the same topic – the squeeze machine. She also shows a degree of perseveration across her various articles. She tends to use precisely the same words and phrases to express the same point in different contexts: for example, in a recent article, 'An inside view of autism' (in press), she replicates the passage quoted in full above practically word for word – although almost six years separate the two pieces of writing. The second feature worth noting is that she tends to take metaphorical expressions rather literally. So, for example, in her book she recounts how upon hearing the passage, 'I am the door: by me if any man enter in, he shall be saved . . .' (John 10:9), she looked for an actual door through which to pass (p. 80). Again, she uses the phrase 'a pat on the back' in the sense of actual physical contact as praise (p. 144). This literal use of language, as we shall see, may be an important feature of autistic communication.

Overall, the writing is remarkable and an achievement of which almost anyone would be proud. There can be no doubt that Temple Grandin is a capable and intelligent woman and a success story to encourage parents, teachers and those who themselves receive a diagnosis of autism. Her success lies, perhaps, in her lack of interest in social matters, and hence her lack of distress at her relative isolation. It is interesting too, as a last thought, that she has succeeded in a field which requires some 'empathy' for farm animals – since this is an area in which we are all left guessing and using scientific facts to infer 'feelings'.

Barry: letters

Barry is a young man who was in his twenties when he wrote these letters. He lives in the United States and started writing to his correspondent – a middle-aged woman – after visiting her and her autistic son. The correspondence lasted for about a year, when it suddenly stopped as abruptly as it had begun. Barry wrote sometimes as frequently as three times a month letters which were often several pages long. These letters are exceptional in being totally self-motivated and without any external editing. The following is the first letter Barry wrote to his correspondent, and gives some impression of the style of the letters:

> Dear Mrs Jones,
> I'm glad you enjoyed our visit very much. I am eager to write to your son Tom, but I don't know his home address. Please give me his own home address.
> Also too I'd like for you to send me that old fashioned peanut butter if you would. That old fashioned peanut butter here is too expensive.
> Would you please send me a list of addresses of all the people I met at the meeting in Flint, Michigan when Christmas comes around, so that I can write them Christmas cards.
> Speaking of girls, I've met two girls, one named Darlene, age 20, the other Denise, age 17 and getting friendly with them. I began thinking that it would be better for now that I can have one or two more girlfriends for three years and find another one or two girlfriends or more for the next three years and so forth. Lots of guys do that. Here almost all of the girls are getting married, which are those of my age. They seem to be marrying very rapidly. When I think about girls of my age I think of the passenger railroad trains which are going off the tracks here in the USA.
> So write soon. My address is included in this letter.
> Yours truly, Barry

Barry's letters are quite different from Temple's published works. As one would expect from the less formal genre, the writing is less polished, less fluent, and the grammar is sometimes awkward. However, all of this might be expected of someone of similar intellect and education, without autism. Some aspects of his writing style, on the other hand, seem peculiar in a more significant way. Here we shall look at a number of these features, including his idiosyncratic use of language, his flitting between topics, his perseveration, parroting and social naivety about other minds.

One of the most striking aspects of Barry's writings is his use of idiosyncratic terms, which are not explained, and which the reader could not be expected to understand by normal conventions. For example, in the letter above, he writes, 'When I think about girls of my age I think of the passenger railroad trains which are going off the tracks here in the USA'. This rather opaque comparison appears several times in the letters, with no direct explanation as to what aspect of the girls reminds him of trains. The only clue is an aside in a letter over a year later, about passenger trains being cut in number: 'Now, we hardly have any passenger trains left anymore'. Presumably Barry, who is his twenties, feels that girls of his age are slowly disappearing as they get engaged and married to other men. Another example – which, interestingly, Barry seems to realise is idiosyncratic, although that does not lead him to explain why he employs it – is his use of the phrase 'student nurses' age group' for those aged seventeen to twenty-one.

This use of idiosyncratic terms is important and revealing. Kanner wrote about similar cases in 1946, referring to the autistic subjects' 'irrelevant and metaphorical language'. Kanner showed that apparently nonsensical phrases could often be traced back to a first occurrence, from which the child had derived his or her own meaning. He gave the example of J.S., a three-year-old autistic boy who referred to himself as 'Blum' whenever his veracity was questioned. This was explained when the boy, who read fluently, pointed out an advertisement claiming 'Blum tells the Truth!' Kanner pointed out that this association is just the same as that which we would recognise in our culture between, say, all lovers and Romeo, except that it is essentially a private rather than cultural and shared association. Hence, 'the basic difference consists of the autistic privacy and original uniqueness of the transfers' (Kanner, 1946). The important point is, perhaps, that even an autistic writer who is *trying* to communicate will use such private 'transfers' without explanation. Thus it seems that, like Temple, Barry does not recognise what knowledge is shared and what is personal. In accord with this explanation, he also fails to explain to his reader the meanings of several train abbreviations which, although conventional, are obscure to non-rail enthusiasts (such as his correspondent). That his own idiosyncratic terms are based on normal parallels and equivalences is shown in one letter where he coins and explains a new term: 'Steam locomotives have been the most expensive and the most painful locomotives ever to run on any railroad track. For this reason, I shall call steam locomotives girls.'

The lack of awareness of what is private, as opposed to general, knowledge may also account for the apparently random flitting from subject to subject in Barry's letters. For example, in the letter quoted in full above, he starts a new paragraph, 'Speaking of girls . . .', when as far as the reader is concerned he has simply been talking about the people he met in Michigan. Another example of an awkward change of subject follows the passage about calling steam locomotives girls, quoted above: ' . . . I shall call steam locomotives girls. I got a map of Cleveland for Christmas.' It is an interesting question whether Barry's association processes are different from other people's, or whether it is simply a literary convention that most of us recognise – that one does not simply write the first thing that comes into one's head but tries to lead smoothly from one topic to another. This is perhaps an instance where having appropriate control letters may help to shed some light on what is special about the writings of these able autistic individuals.

Two aspects of Barry's writing style that seem unusual, and possibly peculiar to autistic writers, are a tendency to perseverate and the use of what would appear to be parroted material. The perseveration appears in the form of repetitive openings, something of a fixation with transport (which is indulged rather than limited with a view to the reader's interests), and the same closing remark – 'So write soon' – at the end of every letter. Parroting seems probable in view of the style of some passages in the letters, on topics about which Barry is very likely to have read reports. For example, when talking about the decline of rail transport, Barry writes: 'Our passenger train service is dying rapidly . . . we are now the only first class country on earth without first class passenger train services.' The style of such parroted material contrasts strongly with the rest of the letters.

We see a degree of social naivety in Barry's letters, as in Temple's writing, the more noticeable as he, unlike Temple, is very interested in such things as finding a girl-friend. Indeed, it is when talking about girls that Barry appears most socially immature and odd, for example, he writes in one letter: 'If the girl does too much talking . . . I would let her get away with it only if she is saying just things that interest me.' Elsewhere, talking about the possibility of a girl he likes getting married, he says, 'my old friends can always get me another girl'. Barry's ignorance of many social dos and don'ts is obvious in much of what he writes, and in his open and childlike requests for his reader to send him peanut butter, cookies and so on. In one letter he talks at length about how women's hair-styles have changed. He says that he would not go out with a girl whose old-fashioned hair-style made her look 'even older than my mother', and goes on to say: 'I would be better to have a girlfriend with the popular hairdo that makes her at my age only look like a little first grade kid.' What is fascinating about this comment is that while society would frown on someone saying they wanted a girl-friend who looked like a schoolchild, it is certainly true that many fashions play on the attraction to men of baby-doll looks in women. Barry's observation and desires are normal here, he is different only in so far as he says what most people would be embarrassed to admit or too socially constrained to recognise. Similarly, he says of a pop singer whose record he has just bought: 'Melanie is a great singer, but her voice sounds whiny. She sounds like a little kid.' Again, his observation is perfectly accurate, but he does not recognise the negative overtones of the description 'whiny' and its contradiction with being a 'great singer'. It may be just this alternative perspective, free from cultural rules or conventions, that led Asperger (1944) to describe his autistic patients as unusually 'imaginative' or 'creative'.

Underlying Barry's lack of social awareness is, it seems from his writings, a more general inability to understand the independence of other minds. For example, he writes about a girl he likes – 'If something bad happens to Geraldine such as Geraldine getting married to somebody else . . .' – as if he does not recognise that his misfortune might be another person's happiness, or that the same event might make one person happy and another person, with different goals, unhappy. He does write at one point: 'You've said Tom got hit by a hoodlum when he was living in an urban apartment or motel or hotel? Well, I can imagine he was glad to move out of there.' This might be taken to show Barry's understanding of other minds, but it is important to recognise that Tom's reaction to the attack can be predicted by Barry referring to his own reactions – and indeed Barry says elsewhere that he too had problems living in rough neighbourhoods. What would indicate a full understanding of the independence of others' mental states is a recognition that someone else might be *glad* to be hit, say to get sympathy, make someone feel guilty and so on. A lack of insight into others' minds may also explain Barry's very simple moral reasoning in a letter where he writes: 'I am never going to kill anyone since I would hate to die in the electric chair or get life imprisonment.' This sort of crime and punishment moral reasoning may be a feature of mental age, but it also shows a lack of insight into others' feelings and one's own duties and responsibilities. Without a full and rich knowledge of how others feel in different situations, we would have little more than a fear of retribution to guide our actions.

Barry's letters, then, give us some insight into the workings of a mind with limited understanding of the independence of other people's minds in terms of knowledge states, feelings and desires.

David C. Miedzianik: *My autobiography*

David differs from the above writers in being English rather than American. He differs from Temple in that he is unemployed and shows no academic interests that might make an unemotional stance seem normal. He comes from a background with few privileges and lives at present with his grandmother and mother near Rotherham. He was about twenty-eight when he wrote this autobiography. His interests are primarily in the normal desires of life – getting a job, being liked, finding a girl-friend. This, plus his enthusiasm for writing, makes him a very open and potentially very informative subject. In view of all this, it is perhaps surprising that on reading the autobiography the most striking impression is of a man who is a little simple, but more importantly, is simply lonely, bored and depressed. Of course some social gaucheness shows through which in part accounts for his loneliness, but he shows a degree of social understanding not seen even in Temple's edited work. The question of parroting cannot, of course, be ruled out – but if David's remarks are his own they are surprising and challenging.

David wrote his autobiography as a sort of personal advertisement, in the hope that 'someone that can offer me some love and affection will get in touch' (p. 101). It follows a loose chronological order with diversions on various topics. It has not been edited except to correct spelling errors, add commas and split the text into more paragraphs than David himself used. The following extract is representative of the writing in this autobiography:

> I think religion helps some people but it doesn't help others. I think I'm one of those people that it doesn't help much. I've led a more or less pure life for so long that I'm sick of it. Mind you [Jane] smokes a lot and I don't think she minds drinking a bit too. She just turned up at our house last Sunday; perhaps if she'd have rung up it would have been an idea. She gave Peter her address and said I can bring Peter up to call on her sometime. I hope she doesn't go out with Peter. My mother told me that you needn't be afraid of him. She said girls like lads to look clean. My mother sees that I look clean. She's just brought me a new pair of shoes and I've put them on this morning. Sometimes new shoes are murder to wear. I wear the soles out on my shoes very quickly because I do an awful lot of walking. My mother seems to always have the washing machine on, it's on again this morning. I don't think my mother likes anything to go dirty and it's on most days, the washer. I think it's one of those washers with a programme so she just puts it on and leaves it. We've had this washer about 2 years. I think she wore the last washer out by using it too much, no doubt. Odd times during the winter the pipes on the washer get frozen up and water spills out of the washer then. This winter was that cold the water wouldn't run out of the bath one day because it was that cold. The water eventually went down the pipe; the hot bath water must have melted the ice after an hour or so being in the pipe (p. 90).

This passage illustrates David's tendency to roam from one subject to another, as he does throughout the book. However, it is interesting to note that unlike the two previous writers, David rarely introduces material to the reader without a proper explanation. For example, when he mentions a friend called Paul who has been described earlier in the book, he writes: 'Paul who I go and see up Thorpe Hesley, the one I've wrote about earlier on in the story' (p. 76); and both Jane and Peter who are mentioned in the passage above, have been fully introduced to the reader earlier. Such consideration for the reader's state of knowledge is not seen in Temple's or Barry's writing. This is only one example of David's apparently good understanding of others' minds, or – as it has come to be known – *theory of mind*. A rather different example is where he writes about going into a pub, with two badges pinned 'on a funny place on my chest, and a fellow in the pub was very amused and he said "you've got your badges stuck in the wrong place". I think he thought I was trying to imitate a woman because of the places I'd stuck those badges' (p. 72). Here David seems to show that he can appreciate another person's mistaken ideas about his intentions (thus understanding someone's ideas about his thoughts).

Understanding another person's false belief about a situation or mental state has been accepted as good evidence in the experimental literature (for example Baron-Cohen, Leslie and Frith, 1985) for the possession of a theory of mind. David clearly passes this test and, indeed, shows an appreciation of and interest in more subtle social interactions. He writes of his family, for example: 'My mother doesn't always get on well with my grandmother . . . I think my mother gets out of her way by going to French classes a lot . . . These classes help her take her mind off things' (p. 100). Understanding of jokes and deception is often thought to be a skill that even able autistic adults do not master, and Barry's and Temple's (unedited) works seem to bear this out. David, however, seems to have a grasp of these forms of communication: 'I also know a group called 3-D fiction,' he writes, 'I think they've got some of my poems . . . They said they might write some music to my poems but I think they might be joking' (p. 82). Later on he writes about trying to impress girls: 'I usually try to kid them I'm doing well as a writer but they don't fall for that one very easy' (p. 101).

Along with an apparently quite astute understanding of other minds (by autistic standards), David seems to have some degree of social awareness. So, for example, he writes about going for a job interview: 'This woman asked me why I wanted the job. I said to get some money. It was the wrong answer . . . By the end of the interview I knew I hadn't got the job' (p. 68). Later in the book he describes going along to a meeting where they started celebrating someone's birthday: 'That was one reason why I didn't like stopping, because I didn't know the person whose birthday it was' (p. 83). Although obviously socially gauche in his attempts to find a girl-friend, David does have some accurate ideas about what girls do not like, for example: 'I think I'd get more girls interested in me if I lived on my own, it seems to put girls off if they know you live with your parents, I think' (p. 85); and later, 'I find it hard to talk to girls, I never seem to know the right things to say to them. I'm in a bad set-up, so no matter what I say won't make them take much interest in me . . .' (p. 101). Again, he seems to have some idea of social dos and don'ts, as, for example, when he writes about

Jane in the passage above: 'She just turned up at our house last Sunday; perhaps if she'd have rung up it would have been an idea' (p. 90).

This last example leads us onto the question of parroting, since it sounds rather like something his mother might have said about the girl's rudeness. There is always the possibility that with autistic children and adults, who often seem to have such excellent rote memory for overheard material, some expression they use which may seem to show startling social skill is simply an echoed phrase remembered from a previous and similar context. In David's work, and in all the writings considered here, it must be borne in mind that some instances of social insight may simply be copied or taught expressions. While this seems an unlikely explanation for all David's insights, there are some instances of obvious parroting in his book which leave the reader feeling cautious. In many cases he will make a remark and then add, 'Well, that's what my mother says.' But an example from page 84 makes it clear that not all David's borrowed thoughts are so clearly accredited: 'I think the thing about the pop music industry is that everything has to be new . . . I had an old guitar teacher . . . He said the only reason for a 12-string guitar is that everything has to be new in pop music.' It is interesting, however, that David adds his own (?), contrary opinion – 'Mind you, I think you get a fuller sound with a 12-string.' The possibility of parroting must, therefore, cause doubt on the significance of apparently insightful remarks such as 'I read somewhere that certain tablets can destroy brain cells . . . Mind you, you can't believe everything you read in the papers' (p. 97).

It would be easy to overstress David's abilities, especially when reading his book in the context of other writings by autistic individuals – after which one tends to forget what a 'normal' standard of writing is. It is important not to lose sight of the many odd features of David's writing. It is clear from what he says that his behaviour has not always been as normal as it appears to be at the time of writing. He describes his delusions, obsessions and stereotypes when not on his present medication – and it is certain that if he had written his autobiography at that time we would get a very different picture of the degree of David's handicap. He says of himself, 'I think my mind is clearer taking those Haloperidol tablets. At one time I used to think I was in tune with the whole world. So if something happened on the news or something I used to think it was affecting me when I wasn't feeling very well . . . I also thought we'd got a 3-D TV at our house' (p. 87). This perhaps sheds some light on what Asperger, in his 1944 paper, referred to as the autistic child's 'long, fantastic stories, his confabulations . . . ever more strange and incoherent', it being unlikely that his patients either meant to deceive or were being overly creative in a make-believe sense.

David also writes about his obsessions at the time: 'I also had to do certain actions at certain times, I got so mixed up. Like if I didn't have a cup of coffee at 10am, something terrible would happen' (p. 87). The topic of autistic people's obsessions has been neglected in the research literature, even though the autistic child's 'obsessive insistence on sameness' (Kanner, 1943) has always been recognised as an important symptom. Baron-Cohen (1989b) has argued that autistic people cannot be said to have obsessions or compulsions since they cannot report the diagnostically vital subjective experiences of distress, ego-dystonia and resistance. Instead, he suggests that we should refer to autistic people's 'repetitive activities'. For autistic people as able as our three authors, however, this argument may not hold – since they do have some, albeit limited, insight into their own feelings and thought processes. With someone like David, then, there may be something useful to gain from the application of current theories of obsessive-compulsive disorder.

Lastly, David describes his stereotypies, saying 'it always fascinates me watching the gas man mending the stoves. It makes me very excited and I jump up and down when I see the gas flames burning. I've always jumped up and down since I've been a kid' (p. 88). This extract is indicative of the unique and puzzling blend of apparent normality and extreme oddness which characterises the able autistic person. Some of this oddness is due to a sort of delay or childishness – the acts are odd not in themselves but only in view of the person's age. For example, David – at the age of twenty-eight – writes in the passage quoted above, 'My mother . . . said girls like lads to look clean. My mother sees that I look clean' (p. 90). Later he writes: 'Sometimes when I used to go for runs in the car with my mother when I was younger I used to wave a lot to the passengers in the cars behind our car; I think I did this up to the age of 20 or so' (p. 98).

That David is so open about his past oddities, and even hospitalisations, in a text which he hopes will attract a girl-friend, demonstrates that despite some social knowledge, he still shows marked social naivety. Like Barry with his 'whiny' voice, he is not fully in tune with the cultural and social connotations of words. For example, he says, 'There was a lovely girl called Amanda . . . She had lovely long mousey coloured hair' (p. 95) – evidently not recognising the negative overtones of the phrase 'mousey coloured'. David's naivety shows itself again when he talks about making friends: 'I think I will keep writing [to the radio], it's a good way of getting to know people. I think females like men that can get their names on the radio' (p. 100). This reveals both David's odd ideas about what it is to 'get to know' someone and his rather simple and concrete ideas about what women find attractive.

David's writing also shows the characteristic flitting from subject to subject seen in the previous writer's works as, for example, in the passage above where he moves from talking about religion to talking about Jane, to his shoes, and on to the washing-machine. There is also a tendency to repetition that may in part be due to this lack of structure. David shows some perseveration in his sentence openings; for example, one paragraph contains a string of sentences beginning. 'They also . . . They also . . . I also . . . I don't get . . . I know . . . I don't know . . . I don't think . . . (p. 98). Perhaps to accommodate his swift changes of topic, David also often uses the opening, 'Well anyway, to change the subject . . .'. An explanation for these repetitions and subject changes may be given by his comment on page 101: 'I'll be repeating myself a lot if I write many more pages of A4 paper. It's a bit hard for me writing because I have great trouble sitting down for any length of time.' If Temple and Barry also wrote their works in short bouts this might explain in part their flitting from subject to subject, as well as the occasional contradictions.

To conclude, then, David seems from his writing to be in some ways the 'least autistic' of our three authors. This is interesting in view of Temple's likely superiority in terms of IQ and certainly in terms of academic achievement, and suggests that, just as autism may occur with little additional damage and hence normal IQ, so the *degree* of autistic social handicap may be independent of the child's intellectual functioning. Of course there is likely to be a minimum IQ level below which a child is unlikely to fall within the more able section of the autistic spectrum, in terms of Wing's (1981) triad of social impairments. Intelligence and social skills may interact; brighter children are more likely to develop coping strategies for their social handicap, and more sociable children may benefit more from their education and hence do better academically. It may be the case that social awareness and IQ dissociate only within the group of autistic people with near-normal or superior intelligence. However, in view of the fact that even quite severely mentally handicapped Down syndrome children may be sociable in a near-normal way, it does seem to be necessary to divide the 'able autistic' group into two subsets – those who are able in terms of IQ, and those who are relatively able socially – with only a limited degree of overlap between these sets. It may be important to recognise this distinction within the group we call 'able autistic' in formulating our definition of Asperger syndrome, as we shall see later.

David speaks out for himself and captures one's impression of his writings when he says: 'Someone says I should have written about the moods I have, but I think I have described fairly well why I think a lot that's happened to me is enough to make anybody moody. Yes, I think anyone normal would find it hard to lead the kind of existence I have' (p. 103).

Hazards of interpretation

If we hope to draw conclusions about the nature of the autistic handicap from the writings of the three authors quoted above, we must be aware of a number of factors that are potentially misleading. Analysis of these writings is obviously a subjective method of investigation and hence prey to all the problems of that type of method. Some authors, for example Wolff and

Barlow (1978), have tried to avoid these difficulties by simply counting up the number of words of different types that autistic subjects use in spontaneous descriptions of, say, their mother. It seems fair to say, however, that the more sophisticated productions presented here deserve a more sensitive, and therefore of necessity more subjective, approach.

Problems of both false negative and false positive conclusions arise, due to the nature of the writers' handicaps; for example, lack of insight and of interest in social matters may lead to a glossing over of the writer's handicaps in this area, if he simply chooses not to write about such things as family relationships, absence of friends or school teasing. On the other hand, parroting and the help of co-writers may lead us to believe the autistic writer is more socially adept than is actually the case. Again, their very naivety may make their writing (unintentionally) misleading – as, for example, when an autistic man calls any girl who has given him the time of day his girl-friend. One way around some of these problems may be to analyse *style* rather than absorb *content*. In this way, the writings of such able autistic people may have some advantages over other subjective methods such as self-rating tests, since they are amenable to an analysis of how the individual expresses himself, and what he does not express, as well as giving the person greater freedom to write as he pleases about what he pleases. The medium of the written word may also have advantages for some able (verbally advanced) autistic people, who feel more at ease writing than in a face-to-face interview.

Previous presentations of the writings of able autistic individuals have not always recognised these problems of possible false negative and false positive results. A number of researchers have included autobiographical writings in their case histories of able autistic people, but these have always been analysed in terms of content alone. So, for example, Volkmar and Cohen (1985) present 'A first-person account by Tony W.' but aim to gain from this some idea of the experience of being autistic, taking his account at face value. Similarly, White and White (1987) quote their autistic son's description of his experiences in order to find out 'what it was like when he was young,' and use what he says to support their theory of a malfunctioning of the endogenous opiate system in autism. So little has style – the way these accounts are written – been considered of importance that most researchers have simply paraphrased their subject's reminiscences (Bemporad, 1979; DesLauriers, 1978). Abstracting the content from these accounts, without considering style or possible limitations in the writer's insight, not only discards valuable data, but must lead to questionable conclusions. What are we to make for example, of an autistic person's comment that his mental processes or sensations are radically different from other people's when he is likely to have severely impaired insight into other minds? Is it not probable too, that an autistic adult will have peculiarly unreliable memories from a childhood without self-awareness? While these remain open questions, we must be careful in how we use the contents of autistic autobiographies. Therefore, in this analysis of the writings of three able autistic adults I have tried to consider both what they say and, more importantly, how they say it.

A rather different problem with drawing conclusions from the writings is the question of generalising from such an able group. Obviously, those who manage such advanced writing are not only among the highest IQ autistic adults, but also the most verbally skilled. It is possible that we would be unjustified not only in generalising from these subjects to the lower IQ end of the autistic spectrum, but also in generalising our findings to those high IQ autistic adults whose ability lies in the non-verbal domain and who are relatively disadvantaged in their language abilities. In view of the still open question of the separate status of Asperger's and Kanner's subject-types, and bearing in mind our subjects' greater resemblance to Asperger's portrait of 'autistic psychopathy' – it may be unwise to generalise from these subjects to the entire population of autistic individuals.

These problems mean that the writings of able autistic people must be viewed with caution if used as evidence for more than an appraisal of that one individual. One measure that could give us greater confidence in our analysis of the writings, however, may be the use of appropriate control works, and it is to this question that we now turn.

Making fair comparisons

It is a significant problem in our analysis of the writings of these able autistic authors that we lack an appropriate control group. We simply do not know how a 'normal' person of similar intellect and education would write. Few of us have the opportunity to read average adults' attempts at autobiography. We are all too used to reading professional writers, and even works by unknowns get into print for a reason. What we read is selected for quality. It would thus be useful to have an unselected sample of normal adults' and adolescents' writings with which to compare the works discussed here. Such control works might reveal great differences in choice of subject matter, or frequency of change of topic, which are hard to spot when reading the autistic writings in isolation. Obviously, it would be ideal to look at normal, but rather isolated, subjects' writings to control for some of the oddities of life-style contingent upon being autistic. Another factor it might be important to control for is exposure to literature, since it is a characteristic, even of the very able group, that autistic people take little pleasure in reading fiction. As a result they will have absorbed fewer of the cultural and conventional rules of story-telling.

Finding the right control group for any experiment with autistic subjects is always tricky. Experiments with autistic children have often used Down syndrome subjects as controls in whom chronological age and mental age are dissociated, and for some of the less intelligent autistic writers this comparison may be informative. On the other hand, recent work looking at Asperger syndrome subjects has taken schizophrenic subjects as controls (Bowler, 1989). This choice highlights the fact that in the very able group, some autistic people may not have seen a clinician until adolescence or later and are therefore not suitably matched with people of subnormal IQ who have been in special schools and homes all their lives. Unlike autobiographies of normal amateurs, writings by schizophrenics are relatively plentiful and accessible in published form. A good anthology of these, which takes one away from the glossier novels, is Dale Peterson's *A mad person's guide to madness*, which contains many first-hand accounts of the experience of mental illness from 1436 to 1976. A full bibliography of the accounts of mental patients, from 1960 to 1982, is also available (Sommer and Osmond, 1983). Of the single accounts published, that by Mary Barnes (Barnes and Berke, 1971) is in some ways a good comparison work for Temple's book. It is a good match because the women were of similar ages at the time of writing, and Mary Barnes – rightly or wrongly – would say that she had been 'odd' almost from birth: 'Much of me was twisted and buried, and turned in upon itself, as a tangled skein of wool to which the end has been lost . . . The big muddle started before I was born. It went on, getting worse. My mother and I battled with feelings. My father was in it, then my brother barged in. My two sisters came and the mess got bigger' (p. 13).

An interesting parallel between the two accounts is that both Mary and Temple have a machine they appeal to for relief from their problems. As we have seen, for Temple this is her squeeze machine. For Mary it is a box which her therapists have built down in the cellar: 'We try it, it's beautiful. A big wooden box. You bend down to go in the opening. There's coloured lights inside. . . . It's super. Stay in the box and you really go places. I want to try it . . . This was my biggest delight, the box. I sat still in there . . . I was "going somewhere" in the box. It was to give me experiences – out of this world. The lights went on and off. You watched them' (pp. 98, 102). Compare Temple's description of her machine: 'The squeeze chute I ultimately built was that secret, coveted cubby hole of childhood dreams. Sometimes I worried that the squeeze chute would overpower me, and I would not be able to survive without it. Then I realised that the chute was just a restrictive device made from scrap plywood. It was a product of my mind' (*Emergence*, p. 96).

Striking too is a similar, extreme reaction to tactile stimuli: 'Although I lay in a stupor for most of the time, I was very aware of what was going on. Touch seemed to mean everything. By it I moved away or inwardly moved nearer' (Barnes and Berke, p. 113). Compare this with Temple's description of her tactile experiences: 'As a child I wanted to feel the comfort of being held, but then I would shrink away from fear of losing control . . . I could barely tolerate being touched' ('My experiences', p. 151). At other times, however, Mary is clearly far more disturbed than Temple ever reports being: 'In my room, sitting on the top of a small bookcase, was a boy, with longish hair and a big bow at his neck, as worn in the past. My eyes were shut. It all seemed real, yet not a dream, nor an imagining. When it seemed so real that there were spiders and insects on the floor, I put out my hand to prove to myself they were not really there, alive, crawling all around' (p. 113), and again, 'My body did often seem apart. A leg or arm could be the other side of the room' (p. 112). Unless Mary is simply conjuring up masterfully her thought processes and expression at the time, her writing would seem to show a still very disturbed mind. The bizarreness of her writing indicates what a useful purpose comparison writings would serve – even if the writings of schizophrenics are not the ideal control works. Such writings for example, make us aware of peculiarities of expression *not* seen in autistic writing, as well as normal topics and subjects not touched on by our autistic writers.

Lastly, it would be interesting to compare our authors' works with children's writings. This may reveal which features of the autistic writer's style are found in normal development and at what ages (which might be related to other social skills and theory of mind at these ages). It seems quite likely that the flitting between subjects, repetitions and fixations, as well as the ignorance of the connotations of certain words seen in Temple's, Barry's and David's writings may also be seen in young normal children's compositions. Investigating this question may shed some light on the issue of delay versus deviance in autism.

To conclude, it seems that we must be cautious in our use of these writings, but as we shall see in the next section where we turn to a new theory of communication, this material has important implications and exciting potential if handled correctly.

Relevance theory and the breakdown of communication in autism

Sperber and Wilson's (1986) Relevance theory of cognition and communication makes explicit the role of the comprehension of intentions in human communication. This makes Relevance theory a promising framework for a deeper understanding of the autistic communication handicap.[4] It may allow us a clearer insight into the baffling variation in degree of communication problems, from the mute autistic child to those able and very verbal adults whose work is discussed above. In turn, a fuller understanding of the autistic communication handicap in its mildest (but still characteristic) form

---

[4] In this section autism and Asperger syndrome are again used interchangeably on the understanding that the underlying communication handicap is the same in both, although Asperger syndrome is a mild manifestation of this handicap.

– as seen in our authors' works – will have implications for our definitions of Asperger syndrome, since relatively good language is perhaps the only unanimously agreed distinguishing feature of this group.

In what follows, the premises and conclusions of Relevance theory are outlined, with suggestions at each stage as to the possible breakdown of normal functioning in autism.

1. Cognitive economy: the problem of optimal allocation of central processing resources

For any device with limited information processing resources, it is important that these resources be deployed as efficiently as possible. This leads to the first major premise of Relevance theory, that our attention automatically turns to what seems relevant in the environment. 'Relevant' here means capable of yielding large cognitive effects relative to small cognitive effort. New but unconnected information is seldom relevant, since it can be processed only as isolated bits and pieces and has few implications processed in the unrelated context of past information. New but related information, on the other hand, may have important contextual effects when processed in the context of old premises. As Sperber and Wilson say, 'the selection of a particular context is determined by the search for relevance', and since some contexts are more easily accessed at any one time than others, and hence are less costly in terms of processing effort, the first available context that produces sufficient contextual effects to meet the demands of relevance will be used. Since the effort to access any particular context depends on the organisation of memory, the importance of this organisation in the assessment of relevance is clear.

2. To communicate is to claim the hearer's attention

This second premise makes clear the implications of these general cognitive principles for communication. These two premises together lead to the idea that communicated information comes with a guarantee of relevance. This is Sperber and Wilson's *Principle of Relevance*; that every act of ostensive communication[5] communicates the presumption of its own optimal relevance.[6] This guarantee guides the hearer in his choice of processing context and the speaker in his choice of words – so that the first available processing

---

[5] Ostensive behaviour is behaviour which makes manifest an intention to make something manifest, for example, showing something to someone. Ostensive-inferential communication – where the communicator makes manifest to an audience his intention to make manifest a basic layer of information – is a special case of this.

[6] An utterance is optimally relevant if the set of assumptions which the speaker intends to make manifest to the hearer is relevant enough to make it worth the hearer's while to process the ostensive stimulus, and if the ostensive stimulus is the most relevant the speaker could have used to communicate those assumptions.

context yielding an adequate range of effects is usually taken as that intended by the speaker. For example, after a conversation about pet cats and dogs, the speaker who says 'Henry had a big cat' can be assumed to mean a large domestic cat – if he had meant to communicate that Henry had a lion or tiger he should have said so – while in a conversation about big game hunting the most accessible interpretation may be reversed.

In autism?

It is a common observation that autistic people seem to miss what we would regard as salient in a situation, and pay close attention to what seems to us irrelevant. This is also reflected in experimental findings, for example, Rincover and Koegel (1975) found that, in training, autistic children tended to learn responses to irrelevant details of the teaching situation such as the teacher's dress and so on, which severely limited the generalisation of learnt responses. There are at least three possible reasons why autistic children may fail to turn their attention to what we would regard as relevant. The first is suggested by Frith (1989), who argues that autistic children do not process stimuli for meaning, a tendency which is pervasive in normal human subjects. In her words, 'A good decision [about what to attend to] would be based on large amounts of pooled information. If coherence at this central decision-making point is weak, the direction of attention would be quite haphazard.' Frith suggests that it is the autistic child's inability to take account of context that both produces excellent block design performance and leads to their inability to process stimuli for meaning (as demonstrated in Frith, 1970). As we have seen, it is the processing of information in context that gives the contextual effects which are weighed against processing effort in the estimation of relevance. An individual who cannot process information as part of a larger context, therefore, would obviously be peculiar in his calculation of relevance and hence deviant in his deployment of attention.

On the other hand, just as attention would be oddly focused in a person unable to derive normal *contextual effects*, it is also possible that the autistic child's odd attention springs from peculiarities in the *costs* of processing. Throughout Relevance theory it is stressed that the interpretation of ostensive behaviours and utterances is guided by the inability to tolerate nonsense and irrelevance. For example, it is said to be a characteristic of powerful ostensive stimuli such as speech signals that they are 'stimuli which both pre-empt the attention . . . and are irrelevant unless treated as ostensive stimuli'. Thus the inability of humans to treat utterances as if irrelevant leads to a type of disambiguation of speaker's meaning – and, as we shall see, ultimately an appeal to speaker's attitudes and intentions. But what if the cognitive system did not demand meaning and did tolerate the speaker's message being interpreted as irrelevant? We began with the idea that new, unconnected information that could only be processed piecemeal would not be worth processing, since the costs would outweigh the meagre benefits and so violate the principle of Relevance. But what if such piecemeal processing was not too costly to be pursued? Is it possible that in at least some autistic people the same cognitive architecture that allows extraordinarily good rote memory, and even outstanding 'savant' abilities, could lead to an abnormally low level of processing costs? This idea is, of course, only the other face of Frith's theory of lack of central coherence leading to an inability to process for meaning. It may be that such unusual memory ability is a coping mechanism for this inability to process information in context for meaning. As usual in development the causal directions are hard to establish without experiment. It may be that the inability to process for meaning is the cause of compensatory rote memory skills. But it is also possible that someone with such good rote memory would never be driven to the cognitively economic measure of processing and storing meaning or gist. The breakdown of the usual search for relevance due to a peculiarity in either the costs or the benefits of processing are not incompatible hypotheses. It may, however, be interesting to investigate the effects of excellent rote memory on language by looking at communication as a function of 'savant' abilities, which, after all, also occur in retarded but non-autistic individuals. Certainly, it seems likely that the normal cost/benefit analysis that underlies the directing of attention towards what is relevant is deviant or defective in (many) autistic individuals.

A third and last possible breakdown in the assessment of relevance, and one that might have more subtle effects on communication than the inability to calculate normal costs or effects, also derives from the possibility that autistic people have a peculiar memory organisation. Sperber and Wilson stress 'the crucial importance of the organisation of encyclopedic memory in the pursuit of relevance'. It is only due to some assumed universality in memory organisation, and hence in the accessibility and so cost of retrieving contexts, that the speaker can estimate the relevance her remark will have for her listener. If autistic people have radically different memory organisations, this system will break down, and with it communication. It is likely that – whether due to innately different rote memory abilities, the development of superior rote memory to compensate for an inability to process information in context for meaning or just because of this last inability – autistic memory will show differences in organisation. Certainly this is a hypothesis that should be amenable to test. In its turn, this difference in memory organisation would alter the costs of processing, which, as we have seen, are a vital component in the usual calculation of relevance and hence of the normal focus for one's attention. Because of the balance of costs and benefits underlying relevance, Sperber and Wilson claim that 'At every stage in disambiguation, reference assignment, and enrichment the hearer should choose the solution involving the least effort, and should abandon this solution only if it fails to yield an interpretation consistent with the principle of relevance.' But what if those 'paths of least effort' are thoroughly idiosyncratic? The implications would obviously be tremendous. Of course, it is as well to bear in mind that whatever we postulate as the deficit underlying the autistic communication handicap, we must also defend the normal working of this particular component of the mind in those very retarded but sociable non-autistic people who communicate relatively normally.

These three possible peculiarities in memory, and hence in processing, may explain some of the features of the autistic writings discussed above. For example, it may be that the difficulty the reader has in following these writers' subject changes is in part due to the different availability of various contexts to the autistic and the normal person. Communication may break down with each party getting hold of the wrong end of the stick if the autistic speaker is intending his utterance to be processed in a context that the normal hearer does not have easily accessible at the time. It may be that autistic speakers fail to prime the right interpretation, by the usual introduction we give to new topics, which generally serves to make the intended processing context the most easily accessed.

3.   Communication versus language

Sperber and Wilson stress an important fact about communication: that language and communication are very different and logically distinct things. A language is a grammar-governed representational system and, as such tends to be a necessary prerequisite for most cognitive activities: 'Any organism with the ability to draw inferences must have a representational system where formulas stand in both syntactic and semantic relations to each other.' While it is not necessary to use a language to communicate, for example gestures can be used, communicating devices must possess internal languages. Not only this, but 'in the case of ostensive-inferential communication, this internal language must be rich enough to represent the *intentions* of other organisms, and to allow for complex inferential processes' (my emphasis).

In autism?
There is less wrong with autistic language than with its usage. Indeed, in the works above it is hard to find anything formally wrong, rather the reader is left with an overall impression of oddness. While it is true that some autistic people never develop language, it is more striking that even those who do still fail somehow to communicate fully. At its extreme, this presents as those cases of hyperlexia where language seems far in advance of communication.

While there is little work that looks directly at the inferential abilities of autistic individuals, it seems clear from the good performance found by Baron-Cohen, Leslie and Frith (1986), using mechanical and behavioural story sequencing tasks, that autistic children can reason and infer (outside the domain of mental states). It therefore seems that they do possess an internal language. However, it is doubtful that this language is rich enough to fulfil Sperber and Wilson's criteria for an internal language able to support ostensive-inferential communication. If such a language must be able to represent others' intentions, then it must include what Leslie has termed metarepresentation.[7] His hypothesis, that autistic people have a system of primary representation but lack the more sophisticated secondary or metarepresentational ability, then, makes sense of the intuition that autistic people do possess an internal language, but one too poor perhaps to allow for full ostensive-inferential *communication*.

4.   Two ways to communicate: coding versus inference

Another important distinction that Sperber and Wilson draw is between the two possible ways of communicating. First, one can communicate in the way that Morse code operators do, by a system of encoding and decoding messages. This seems to be what happens in transforming the speech stream into the linguistic meaning of the spoken sentence, occurring at a low level in specialised peripheral modules. But normal communication does not end there, as is clear from our ready comprehension of irony, metaphor and figures of speech, as well as cases of ordinary implicature.[8] Also clear from the fact that we can recognise and appreciate these modes of speaking only *in context* is the point that what goes on beyond decoding is a central, unspecialised inferential process.

In autism?

The autistic speaker, then, would seem likely to achieve only the coding method of communication, since, as we have seen, they seem to be handicapped at the level of central, global cognitive processes (Frith, 1989). We would predict, as has indeed been found (Tager-Flusberg, 1981), that phonology and grammar, which are products of the specialised coding modules, would be normal in autism. What autistic speakers will lack is just that which lies beyond coded communication. Here it is significant that it is exactly those modes of communication that go to prove that we use more

---

[7] For a full discussion of metarepresentation see Leslie (1987). A metarepresentation is a representation of a representation, for example, a thought about a thought or a belief about a desire.

[8] Implicatures are contextual assumptions or implications intended by the speaker but not explicitly communicated. The following indirect answers are relevant because of implicatures following from them – the propositional form of the replies does not directly answer the question. For example, Q: What do you want to do tonight? A: I have an awful headache. Or, if you come in with a heavy and hot dish of food, I may simply say 'Put it on the table.'

than coding in normal intercourse (that is, irony, metaphor and less special cases of indirectness), which seem incomprehensible to even the more able autistic person (recall Temple and her 'door').

5. Inferential communication and the recognition of intent

The other way to communicate, apart from using codes, is by providing evidence for an intended inference about your informative intention – that is, by inferential communication.[9] Such inference is thought to fill the gap left after the decoding process of comprehension. Inferential processes operate on the output of the specialised decoding modules to derive from the linguistic meaning of the sentence the speaker's intention in uttering it. A communicator intentionally engaging in inferential communication produces an ostensive stimulus with two intentions; first, the *informative intention* to inform the hearer of X, and second, the *communicative intention* to inform the hearer of his intention to inform him of X. Thus the communicative intention is itself a second-order informative intention. The normal process of ostensive-inferential communication relies upon the capacity to recognise both these intentions. (This is because it is knowing that X was deliberately and intentionally communicated that allows the listener to use the guarantee of relevance to disambiguate the speaker's intention in using the utterance.)

In autism?

Research into the autistic child's theory of mind (Baron-Cohen, Leslie and Frith, 1985) has found a severe impairment in most autistic subjects' ability to comprehend another person's false belief. Leslie (1987), in his metarepresentational conjecture, has shown how representing such mental states, along with pretence, requires a more advanced form of representation (the representation of representations). This level of secondary representation or metarepresentation seems to be lacking in the autistic person's processing of social situations. Thus most autistic people are handicapped in the understanding of others' mental states. For such people, inferential communication – which requires the recognition of *intentions* – may be an unattainable goal. This would leave them, perhaps, with only coded communication, which may be what underlies the repetitious echolalic or single word instrumental speech of many less able autistic individuals. Without the ability to recognise the intention to inform, many autistic people may be unable to recognise ostensive behaviour, or to distinguish it from non-ostensive behaviour. This might explain the apparent 'deafness' and delay in

---

9 Inferential in the sense that the audience infers the communicator's intentions from evidence provided for this purpose. For example, in reply to the question 'How are you feeling?' I may do a cartwheel and three back-flips. There is no code to tell you this means I am pretty well, but I have made clear my intention to show you just that.

language learning seen in many autistic children who do not orientate to speech, but seem to treat it as part of the background noise. Normal children, by contrast, pay attention to speech sounds as specially salient stimuli produced with intention towards the hearer.

However, it is a consistent finding of those experiments that suggest a deficit in theory of mind underlying the autistic handicap, that around 20 per cent of those autistic children tested *do* pass first-order false belief tasks (understanding that someone can have a false belief about the world). While it is an as yet untested possibility that these subjects are using some heuristic but do not have a theory of mind, it is likely that at least some autistic people do develop metarepresentational ability sufficient to comprehend others' first-order mental states (including intentions). These individuals still show peculiarities of expression, as we can see from the works quoted above, and these require explanation.

It may be that some of this able 20 per cent do understand first-order intentions, but not second-order intentions (Baron-Cohen, 1989a) – that is, intentions about others' mental states rather than about the world. This would make them capable of recognising the speaker's informative intention, but not their communicative intention, which, as we have seen, is itself a second-order intention. This inability would have surprisingly far-reaching consequences. This is because the guarantee of relevance which our communication carries and which allows us to take a short-cut in grasping the speaker's meaning, depends upon our capacity for recognising the communicative intention. Without this capacity, true ostensive-inferential communication cannot take place. An autistic person without second-order metarepresentations, then, will be communicating intentionally, but the transparency of intentions that normal communicators enjoy, will be gone. This will leave the able autistic person in very much the same position as the rest of us find ourselves when we try to figure out someone's intentions from their ordinary, non-ostensive behaviour. In such situations we have to puzzle out intentions from the evidence – the immediate ease of reading intentions, as in communication, is gone. The able autistic person may have to do this hard detective work even in understanding communication. This is not to say that they will not become proficient in working out meanings, but they will rely heavily on typical schemata and familiar situations in which the intentions are predictable. Unusual reactions, new figures of speech and other situations that call for flexible interpretation may leave them baffled.

6.   Recognising intentions allows the same sentence to convey different meanings

There are many situations in which the speaker aiming at optimal relevance should not give a literal interpretation of her thoughts. This is the case, for example, where pedantry is avoided. If someone asks you how much you earn, you will in most cases *not* give the precise figure but a rounded estimate that is less costly for the hearer to process (in the absence, that is, of any indication of need for greater precision that would justify the greater processing costs). Sperber and Wilson claim that there is no discontinuity between such loose uses and figurative speech. Both occur simply as a result of the speaker's search for relevance, which leads her to adopt a more or less literal interpretation of her thought.

It is because in communication we are concerned with the speaker's *intentions*, that, as Sperber and Wilson put it, 'the same piece of evidence can be used, on different occasions, to make manifest different assumptions, even mutually inconsistent assumptions, as long as it makes manifest the intention behind the ostention'. The initial message we derive from the speaker saying 'The weather is lovely', for example, is not <The weather is lovely> but rather <The speaker is saying that 'The weather is lovely'>. Thus the speaker's attitude to what she is saying, her intention in saying it, becomes of vital importance. Why is the speaker saying this? If the weather is obviously horrible then the search for relevance may lead the hearer to understand the speaker as being sarcastic. Thus the same surface form may make manifest different assumptions, according to the different communicative intent underlying its utterance. And, as before, it is the criterion of consistency with the principle of Relevance that allows us to decide which assumptions are warranted.

Metaphorical expression then, is just another way of striving for relevance in one's communication. Therefore, 'whatever abilities and procedures are needed to understand it [metaphorical expression] are independently needed for the interpretation of quite ordinary, nonfigurative utterances'. As above, in metaphors the logical form of the utterance is not an explicature (that is, not part of the intended interpretation). So, as with the weather example, the explicature the hearer derives from the utterance, 'This room is a pig-sty' is not <This room is a pig-sty>, but rather <The speaker is saying that 'This room is a pig-sty'>. (Note the similarity between this form and Leslie's form for metarepresentations, Agent-informational relation-"expression", for example, I PRETEND "this empty cup contains water".)

In autism

If, as I have suggested above, even able autistic people are communicating without the guarantee of relevance (due to an inability to represent second-order intentions), then communication should be most likely to break down for them where the speaker's attitude must be taken into account in modifying the literal meaning of the sentence used. Those autistic people who lack even first-order theory of mind may be operating with the propositional form of the utterance as the explicature they derive in communication, that is, they will be doing precisely what we have just said normal communicators using ostention do not do.

It is widely reported that even the most verbally able autistic people (that is, people with Asperger syndrome) fail to understand non-literal speech such as sarcasm, joking and metaphorical expressions. From Sperber and Wilson's theory it follows that these autistic people must also be handicapped in their understanding of literal, non-figurative utterances. This is likely in view of the common finding that able autistic speakers are inappropriately pedantic in their communication (for example, Szatmari *et al.* (1989) found that 60 per cent of their sample of able autistic adults showed 'overly formal speech'). Similarly they seem to fail to recognise the connotations behind words – the attitude people have to the words they use or the intentions behind their choice of word (recall David's 'mousey coloured hair'). Without the principle of Relevance to guide them the autistic person may fall back on a literal interpretation of all utterances. So when someone says 'The weather is lovely' the autistic person derives the explicature <The weather is lovely>. This may serve well enough to get by when the speaker is speaking literally, but the autistic person must be baffled by ironic or figurative usage – and also, perhaps, where the speaker is simply mistaken, or is lying. A highly intelligent person with autism/ Asperger syndrome, such as Temple, may learn to recognise situations where people 'do not mean what they say' – working on simple rules such as:

> literally false or puzzling speech + smile = joke
> literally false or puzzling speech + frown = sarcasm

But without the principle of Relevance to guide them, the transparency of intentions that allows us to use language in a truly flexible way is not open to autistic communicators. In the face of the puzzle that our ostensive communication must pose them, they may have no choice but to adopt a rigid interpretation – a default value of the propositional form of the utterance – in place of our shifting and mercurial intentions.

7.   Interpretive and descriptive representations

Sperber and Wilson claim that any representation with a propositional form (for example, an utterance) can represent things in two ways: 'It can represent some state of affairs in virtue of its propositional form being true of that state of affairs; in this case . . . the representation is a *description* . . . Or it can represent some other representation which also has a propositional form – a thought for instance – in virtue of the resemblance between the two propositional forms . . . here the first representation is an *interpretation* of the second one' (my emphasis). On a fundamental level, then, every spontaneous utterance is an interpretive expression of a thought of

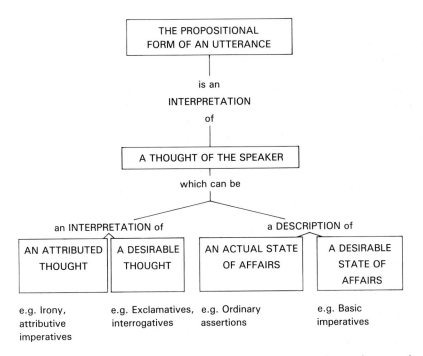

Fig. 7.1 The possible interpretive and descriptive relations between the propositional form of an utterance, the speaker's thought and what that thought represents (from Sperber and Wilson, 1986)

the speaker. Figure 7.1 adapted from Sperber and Wilson, shows the two sorts of representative relations at play in various types of speech act, plus some examples of the types of utterance that might fall into each category. According to the figure, some types of utterance are interpretive representations of interpretive representations of states of affairs. It is tempting to equate Sperber and Wilson's two types of representation with Leslie's (1987) representation/metarepresentation distinction. This leads to some interesting predictions. If 'interpretations' are metarepresentations, and 'descriptions' are primary representations, then every utterance is understood as a metarepresentation, since an utterance is 'an interpretive expression of a thought of the speaker and the hearer makes 'an interpretive assumption about the speaker's informative intention'. As such, the implication is that without a theory of mind, autistic communication never works like normal communication, and perhaps succeeds only by keeping to a strictly literal expression of the meaning, where the explicature they derive is simply the propositional form of the utterance. So, in the figure, the propositional form of the utterance will always be taken as a *literal* interpretation of the speaker's thought. In other words this parameter will be fixed in autistic communication, whereas in normal communication this interpretation can be more or less literal (allowing for loose usage, where the speaker is not committing herself to all the implicatures of her expression).

Figure 7.1 also leads us to more specific predictions. If interpretation is metarepresentation, then anything on the right-hand branch of the diagram requires first-order metarepresentations and anything on the left-hand branch of the diagram requires second-order metarepresentations (since it involves interpretations of interpretations of the world). So the prediction would follow that an autistic person who proves unable to process second-order metarepresentations (for example, second-order false beliefs), would also be incapable of using properly or understanding normally such speech acts as attributive imperatives, irony, interrogatives and exclamatives[10] – since all these lie under the left-hand branch of the diagram. On the other hand, anyone who has first-order theory of mind should be able to operate with ordinary assertions and imperatives. These are very specific predictions and would be worth testing, since they suggest some non-intuitive communication handicaps that might follow from impairment in metarepresentational capacity. An encouraging start is the finding by Winner and Leekam (in press) that in normal children recognition of irony relies upon the ability to process second-order metarepresentations.

Summing up – the possible points of breakdown in autistic relevance

It may seen from what has been said that Relevance theory leads one rather to over-determine the cause of the autistic communication handicap. I have suggested three distinct places in the working of relevance in communication, where autistic people might fail. However, it is plausible that this gradation of possible deficits may represent a way of understanding the great variation in the severity of communication handicaps seen within the autistic continuum.

The possible points for the breakdown of relevance in autism can be summarised as follows:

(a)   Autistic individuals are unable to calculate what is relevant in the normal way, hence the observation that the focus of their attention seems peculiar. This failure would probably result from differences in memory organisation (which might follow from a lack of theory of mind?). They may fail to calculate relevance as normal speakers do because:

  1. they lack central coherence and cannot process information in context to derive normal *contextual effects*; 2. their different

[10] Note, however, that interrogatives and exclamatives are generally marked grammatically, at least in English. Where there is an invariant linguistic form to show an intention, one would expect able autistic people to manage deceptively well.

cognitive system leads to a tolerable *cost* to processing unrelated and irrelevant information; 3. a radically different memory organisation means that the most accessible *context* is idiosyncratic and not that which the speaker intended, even if the autistic person is attempting to interpret the message in the way a normal listener would.

(b)   Inferential communication requires comprehension of *intentions*, so autistic subjects lacking a theory of mind would be barred from proper use of this mode of communication – perhaps leaving them with coded communication alone.

(c)   Using the guarantee of relevance in ostensive-inferential communication to allow the reading of intentions requires the capacity for recognising the speaker's *communicative intention*. So any individual who has only enough theory of mind to process first-order intentions but lacks second-order metarepresentations will be barred from full ostensive-inferential communication. He will be unable to read the speaker's intention and will be left having to puzzle out their meaning from situational cues and learnt rules. In addition, lack of second-order metarepresentations may lead to a distinct set of impairments involving utterances which are 'interpretations of interpretations' (see figure 7.1).

These possible sites of breakdown are listed in descending order of the severity of their imagined outcomes, and although they deal explicitly with understanding, parallel impairments would be expected in production. Many of the features found in the autobiographical works quoted above are explicable as due to a lack of theory of mind and failure of normal relevance principles. For example, the writings of all three subjects were said to be hard to follow in places, often flitting between topics. This can be understood, perhaps, as due to a failure of relevance calculation – the autistic person does not go through the process of introducing new topics in order to make most accessible the intended processing context. This may be due to idiosyncratic memory associations – where the autistic speaker has accessible at certain moments in the conversation contexts which the normal listener does not have 'at the forefront of their mind'. At other times the writings may be hard to follow because the autistic author does not take account of the reader's lack of knowledge concerning things about which he himself knows.

Another interesting feature of the writings upon which Relevance theory sheds some light is our authors' use of metaphor, simile and irony. According to Relevance theory, similes can be understood at a purely literal level – saying 'He was like a lion' is no different from saying 'He was like his father'. In both cases the hearer is set the task of deciding in what respect there is a similarity. We would therefore predict that even autistic speakers who lack a theory of mind should be capable of using and understanding similes. And indeed we find many examples of simile in the works of our three autistic writers. For example, Temple writes: 'relations between people are like a glass sliding door. The door must be opened gently, if it is kicked it may shatter' ('My experiences', p. 145). Barry too uses similes, for example, he says about having a new girl-friend: 'I think it wouldn't be wise behaviour to both spend money on her and practice behaviour with her at the same time. It's just like you cannot build the roof of a house first then the foundation later.'

Metaphor, on the other hand, requires some understanding of intentions. In a metaphor the propositional form of the utterance is a more or less *loose interpretation* of the speaker's thought. Therefore metaphors cannot be fully understood or properly used without a first-order theory of mind – using a default value of literalness will not work. Not surprisingly, then, examples of metaphors are much harder to find in the writings. Temple, for example, seems to have a tendency to take metaphors literally – as in the 'I am the door' example. Rather like examples of humour, metaphors are conspicuous by their absence. Barry does use some metaphors, in passages of the letters which appear to be parroted, but in a strange way: 'I read an article on the trouble of our transportation. They are finding cures for the illness of our transportation. Transportation has been getting sick before I was born, and is getting sicker every year.' Interestingly, Mary Barnes, the schizophrenic writer quoted above, often uses rich and evocative metaphors in her book, for example, she writes: 'Slowly I worked free from the past, from the web . . . A whole lifetime could be spent making, outside oneself, webs to match how one is inside. To go into madness, to start to come out, to leave the web, is to fight to get free, to live . . .' (p. 162).

Lastly, irony is more demanding still, requiring as it does an understanding of second-order metarepresentations – since it is an interpretation of an interpretation (an attributed thought). There is not, to my knowledge, a single example of irony in any of the writings by our autistic authors. Here again control works would be useful to tell us the usual incidence of irony, metaphors, similes, exclamatives and so on – and a more direct test of the comprehension of such forms may circumvent the problems of parroting or rote learning.

Relevance theory can lead us to make some non-trivial and non-intuitive predictions about autistic language use – and, with theory of mind explanations of autism, may help us to understand many of the features of our autistic authors' writings. In addition, Relevance theory may shed light on other elements of autistic behaviour not explained by a lack of theory of mind. For example, I have mentioned the poor understanding we have of obsessive behaviours and interests in Asperger syndrome. One explanation may be that these behaviours are a consequence of the failure to calculate relevance normally, and part of the autistic person's odd focus of attention. Imagine, for example, if the driver of a car paid as much attention to the position of his seat-belt as to what was going on in the road in front of him. Or if someone placed as much importance on the fact that their lunch was late as most people would on the very late return of a loved one who is usually prompt. Such odd focusing of attention would appear obsessional. It may be, then, that it is not the degree of attention or anxiety, but its odd focus and subject – the peculiar attachment of importance to apparently irrelevant things – that makes the autistic person seem obsessive. Much the same point could be made about the incidence of fixations in autistic people – it may be the oddness and incompleteness of their interests that earns this label rather than any great difference in passion between them and the normal train-spotter. A child who talks about electricity pylons all the time is more likely to be thought oddly fixated than one who talks about horses or football teams. Such phenomena as obsessions and fixations may be seen as in part a result of the breakdown of normal relevance.

Conclusions

Current interest in Asperger syndrome may be seen as a response to the puzzle which autistic people as able as our three authors present to researchers in this field. These writers represent the most optimistic answer to the question 'How far can autistic children go in matters of social adaptation?' (Kanner, 1973). We asked at the start of this chapter just what it could be that makes us say these impressively able people are still autistic. Here we have looked at their writings, which are a testament to their success, and picked out some elements of style and content that seem to be characteristic of the autistic handicap.[11] To do this I have applied the most stringent analysis – judging these writers by normal rather than handicapped standards. As can be seen, they come off very well, but I would suggest that what flaws their writings do show are significant. My suggestion is that even these very able autistic adults show some characteristic handicap in communication.

Having suggested that there is a communication handicap, Relevance theory was presented as a framework for understanding this deficit. This theory helps us to understand the autistic communication handicap by showing how a theory of mind, and specifically the ability to handle metarepresentations such as intentions, may be vital to the full ostensive-inferential communication that we as human beings enjoy. In Sperber and Wilson's words, 'Communication exploits the well-known ability of humans to attribute intentions to each other.' Relevance theory, therefore, allows us to reason from the now well-known work showing a deficit in autistic subjects' theory of mind (Baron-Cohen, Leslie and Frith, 1986) to the well-documented autistic communication handicap. It goes further than

---

[11] I would like to thank Temple Grandin and David Miedzianik for their kind permission to quote from their writings.

this too in relating degree of metarepresentational capacity to degree of communication ability in a quite specific way. The application of Relevance theory to autism, therefore, both generates testable predictions about the nature of the autistic communication handicap and leads to a possible method of testing Relevance theory itself. Sperber and Wilson have regretted that 'the view developed in "Relevance" is very speculative and, as it stands, too general to determine . . . specific experimental tests'. Autistic communication may serve as a valuable test case for Relevance theory.

Lastly, relating the autistic person's social and communication problems more directly, via theory of mind and relevance, may have important implications for our definitions of Asperger syndrome as a diagnostic entity. Good expressive language is one of the few universally agreed criteria for saying that an autistic person has Asperger syndrome. If this proves to be more than a good vocabulary and a fully developed grammar – that is, if these people have better *communication* than most autistic people – it may be that we can begin to be more specific about what we mean by 'able autistic' in this context. In other words, it appears from what has been argued above that communication will be good when, and only when, theory of mind is relatively good. So the group of able autistic people defined by good communication may also be those who are able *socially*. We may want to distinguish *this* 'able' group from another 'able' group whose skills are shown in non-verbal intelligence tests, and who, I would predict, do not show comparably good social adjustment. The label Asperger syndrome may be useful, then, to cover those autistic people who are able in terms of communication and social skills, as opposed to those who have special skills or simply a high performance IQ. If communication and social skills co-vary due to a common reliance on social metarepresentational capacity, labelling this group separately on the basis of these features may have more validity.

As a last thought, it is interesting to note that this analysis sheds new light on two of the features of development that have been pin-pointed as being indicators of a good prognosis. Researchers since Kanner have found that acquisition of communicative language by the age of five years bodes well for the autistic child's future development. In addition, Kanner (1973) writes of his most successful autistic patients that 'unlike most other autistic children, they became uneasily aware of their peculiarities and began to make a conscious effort to do something about them'. This suggests that these children, who became relatively high-functioning adults, were distinguished by a sense of self-awareness, which can be seen as the emergence of some degree of theory of mind (since metarepresentations are needed to think about one's own mental states, just as they are to reflect upon someone else's thoughts). Good communication and the emergence of theory of mind, then, appear to be indicators of a good prognosis, and their co-occurrence may be far from coincidental.

References

Asperger, H. (1944). Die 'Autistischen Psychopathen' im Kindesalter. *Archiv für Psychiatrie und Nervenkrankheiten*, 117, 76–136.

Barnes, M. & Berke, J. (1971). *Mary Barnes – two accounts of a journey through madness*. New York: Penguin.

Baron-Cohen, S. (1989a). The autistic child's theory of mind: a case of specific developmental delay. *Journal of Child Psychology and Psychiatry*, 30, 285–98.

Baron-Cohen, S. (1989b). Do autistic children have obsessions and compulsions? *British Journal of Clinical Psychology*, 28, 193–200.

Baron-Cohen, S., Leslie, A. M. & Frith, U. (1985). Does the autistic child have a 'theory of mind'? *Cognition*, 21, 37–46.

Baron-Cohen, S., Leslie, A. M. & Frith, U. (1986). Mechanical, behavioural and intentional understanding of picture stories in autistic children. *British Journal of Developmental Psychology*, 4, 113–25.

Bemporad, J. R. (1979). Adult recollections of a formerly autistic child. *Journal of Autism and Developmental Disorders*, 9, 179–97.

Bowler, D. (1989). Theory of mind in Asperger's syndrome. Paper presented at the conference of the British Psychological Society, London.

DesLauriers, A. M. (1978). The cognitive-affective dilemma in early infantile autism: the case of Clarence. *Journal of Autism and Childhood Schizophrenia*, 8, 219–28.

Frith, U. (1970). Studies in pattern detection in normal and autistic children: I. Immediate recall of auditory sequences. *Journal of Abnormal Psychology*, 76, 413–20.

Frith, U. (1989). *Autism: explaining the enigma*. Oxford: Blackwell.

Grandin, T. (1984). My experiences as an autistic child and review of selected literature. *Journal of Orthomolecular Psychiatry*, 13, 144–75.

Grandin, T. (in press). An inside view of autism. In E. Schopler and G. B. Mesibov (eds.), *High-functioning autism*. New York: Plenum.

Grandin, T. & Scariano, M. (1986). *Emergence labelled autistic*. Tunbridge Wells: Costello.

Kanner, L. (1943). Autistic disturbances of affective contact. *Nervous Child*, 2, 217–50.

Kanner, L. (1946). Irrelevant and metaphorical language in early infantile autism. *American Journal of Psychiatry*, 103, 242–6.

Kanner, L. (1973). How far can autistic children go in matters of social adaptation? In L. Kanner, *Childhood Psychosis: initial studies and new insights*. Washington: Winston.

Leslie, A. M. (1987). Pretence and representation: the origins of 'theory of mind'. *Psychological Review*, 94, 412–26.

Miedzianik, D. C. (1986). *My autobiography*. Intro. by Elizabeth Newson. Nottingham: Child Development Research Unit, University of Nottingham. (Available from publisher, £2.50 incl. inland postage. All proceeds go to author.)

Peterson, D. (1982). *A mad person's guide to madness*. Pittsburgh: University of Pittsburgh Press.

Rincover, A. & Koegel, R. L. (1975), Setting generality and stimulus control in autistic children. *Journal of Applied Behaviour Analysis*, 8, 235–46.

Sommer, R. & Osmond, H. (1983). A bibliography of mental patients' autobiographies, 1960–1982. *American Journal of Psychiatry*, 140, 1051–4.

Sperber, D. & Wilson, D. (1986). *Relevance: communication and cognition.* Oxford: Blackwell.

Szatmari, P., Bartolucci, G., Bremner, R., Bond, S., & Rich, S. (1989). A follow-up study of high-functioning autistic children. *Journal of Autism and Developmental Disorders*, 19, 213–25.

Tager-Flusberg, H. (1981). On the nature of linguistic functioning in early infantile autism. *Journal of Autism and Developmental Disorders*, 11, 45–56.

Volkmar, F. R. & Cohen, D. J. (1985). The experience of infantile autism: a first-person account by Tony W. *Journal of Autism and Developmental Disorders*, 15, 47–54.

White, B. B. & White, M. S. (1987). Autism from the inside. *Medical Hypotheses*, 24, 223–9.

Wing, L. (1981). Language, social and cognitive impairments in autism and severe mental retardation. *Journal of Autism and Developmental Disorders*, 11, 31–33.

Winner, E. & Leekam, S. (in press). Distinguishing irony from deception: understanding the speaker's second-order intention. *British Journal of Developmental Psychology*.

Wolff, S. & Barlow, A. (1978). Schizoid personality in childhood: a comparative study of schizoid, autistic and normal children. *British Journal of Psychology and Psychiatry*, 20, 29–46.

Name index

Subject index